D1360854

Desperately Seeking Solutions

Solutions

The Macintosh Troubleshooting Guide
Erica Kerwien

HAYDEN

Desperately Seeking Solutions

Copyright ©1993 Hayden Books, a division of Prentice Hall Computer Publishing

All rights reserved. Printed in the United States of America. No part of this book may be used or reproduced in any form or by any means, or stored in a database or retrieval system, without prior written permission of the publisher except in the case of brief quotations embodied in critical articles and reviews. Making copies of any part of this book for any purpose other than your own personal use is a violation of United States copyright laws. For information, address Hayden, 11711 N. College Ave., Carmel, IN 46032.

Library of Congress Catalog No.: 93-077555

ISBN: 1-56830-009-3

This book is sold as is, without warranty of any kind, either express or implied. While every precaution has been taken in the preparation of this book, the publisher and author assume no responsibility for errors or omissions. Neither is any liability assumed for damages resulting from the use of the information or instructions contained herein. It is further stated that the publisher and author are not responsible for any damage or loss to your data or your equipment that results directly or indirectly from your use of this book.

95   94   93   4   3

Interpretation of the printing code: the rightmost double-digit number is the year of the book's printing; the rightmost single-digit number the number of the book's printing. For example, a printing code of 93-1 shows that the first printing of the book occurred in 1993.

Trademark Acknowledgments:

All products mentioned in this book are either trademarks of the companies referenced in this book, registered trademarks of the companies referenced in this book, or neither. We strongly advise that you investigate a particular product's name thoroughly before you use the name as your own.

Dedication

*To Mom and Dad, and Matthew, who understand what
I do for a living.*

*To Craig, for reminding me that there is life before, during,
and after a book.*

To Jupiter, for fulfilling his fur quotient on my keyboard.

*To the many people I have worked with and continue to work
with to make computers a fun tool for the task at hand.*

*And to all technical support people, the unsung heroes
of the industry.*

Credits

Publisher
David Rogelberg

Development Editor
Karen Whitehouse

Production Editor
Dave Ciskowski

Technical Reviewer
Craig O'Donnell

Cover Designers
Tim Amhein and Kathy Hanley

Illustrator
Mario Noche

Designer
Scott Cook

Production Team
Diana Bigham, Katy Bodenmiller, Tim Cox, Mark Enochs,
Lisa Daugherty, Mitzi F. Gianakos, Linda Koopman, Tom Loveman,
Roger Morgan, Linda Quigley, Joe Ramon, Carrie Roth, Greg Simsic,
Marcella Thompson, Alyssa Yesh

About the Author

Erica Kerwien

Erica Kerwien is the author of MacUser's *1001 Hints & Tips* and a senior support analyst at Lotus Development Corporation in the Notes Group. Erica was a Macintosh manager at Ziff-Davis Publishing Company and is an Apple Certified Consultant. Besides being a Macintosh trouble-shooter since 1986, she has taught chemistry, physics, and geometry, and restored paintings. Erica graduated with a B.A. in chemistry from Binghamton and an M.A. in Math & Science Education from Columbia University Teachers College.

We Want to Hear from You

What our readers think of Hayden is crucial to our sense of well-being. If you have any comments, no matter how great or how small, we'd appreciate your taking the time to send us a note.

We can be reached at the following address:

David Rogelberg
Hayden Books
11711 North College Avenue
Carmel, IN 46032

(800) 428-5331 voice
(800) 448-3804 fax

E-mail addresses:

America Online	HaydenBks
AppleLink	hayden.books
CompuServe	76350,3014

If this book has changed your life, please write and describe the euphoria you've experienced. Do you have a cool book idea? Please contact us at the above address with any proposals.

Acknowledgments

Thanks to all the software vendors who graciously sent me information and software, including Kim Agricola and Sue Jenson of ON Technology, Stuart Saraquse at Ceres, Rebecca Smith at MicroMat Computer Systems, Brett Tosel at Vision Software, Ken Abott at Abott Systems, Michael Micheletti at FWB, Inc., Terry Morse and Elissa Murphy at Fifth Generation Systems, Jonathan Kahn at Aladdin System, Mike Mihalik at La Cie, Theresa Polacek at Central Point Software, Judith Fry at Casady & Greene, and Paul Gidelis at Ziff-Davis Publishing.

Thanks to Claudette Moore, Trudy Neuhaus, David DeJean, Dale Lewallen, and Philip Goodman for sharing their insight on the book-writing process.

Thanks to Noreen Shillue at Lotus Development Corporation for being flexible with me as I tackled Notes by day and this book by night and weekend.

Thanks to Michelle Flaum at Ziff-Davis Publishing, who asked me a while ago if I would be interested in putting together a few tips.

Thanks to the software authors, Robert Polic, Bill Steinberg, John Norstad, John Mancino, and Kevin Aitken, for contributing great and free software.

Special thanks to Karen Whitehouse, who approached me with a great idea for a book, and made this all so much easier.

This book was made with the help of Vision Software's CameraMan for screen shots, Ceres' Inspiration for brainstorming the troubleshooting map, and ON Technology's ON Location for searching for files scattered across two hard disks and three Bernoulli disks.

Erica Kerwien
Lexington, MA
April, 1993

Table of Contents
at a Glance

Table of Contents

5 Fonts and Sounds

9 CPU Attachments   179

10 Storage Devices 213

What's On The Disk   487

Preventive
Medicine

I Need To Know!

Chapter 1

How to Use This Book

This book is, foremost, a resource for getting you through that tense moment when a Macintosh computing problem arises.

What's in the Book

Even if you picked up this book to solve a problem immediately, you will notice there are tips, advice, and topics of interest here beyond the Macintosh arrghs, darns, zaps, and crashes. For example, Part I includes hardware and software maintenance routines to save you from the problems described in the rest of the book!

TIP: Part I also has a section on data backup. If you do only one thing to secure your data, invest in, devise and follow a backup scheme. You can spend several thousand dollars on hardware, but the time and energy taken to create all those files is immeasurable, and data recovery tools are not always successful.

Chapter 3, "Troubleshooting Tactics," tells you how to build a first aid kit for your Mac. No mention of aspirin and Band-Aids here—just some essential tools to have around in case of Macintosh emergencies.

Part II covers software problems in detail, and Part III does the same for hardware problems. Issues such as how to reinstall damaged system software and how to resolve software conflicts are covered in depth in Part II, which includes Chapter 4, "System Software;" Chapter 5, "Fonts and Sounds;" Chapter 6, "Applications and Files;" and Chapter 7, "Viruses." Hardware topics such as SCSI configuration and hard disk recovery are covered in depth in Part III which includes Chapter 8, "The Macintosh CPU;" Chapter 9, "CPU Attachments;" Chapter 10, "Storage Devices;" Chapter 11, "Printers and Scanners;" and Chapter 12, "Networks and Modems."

Part IV includes Chapter 13, "Symptoms and Solutions," which is a categorized collection of common symptoms and solutions, and Chapter 14, "Technical Resources," which covers other Macintosh resources such as user groups, Apple Computer, trade journals, and online services that specialize in the Mac.

Appendix A is a glossary of Macintosh and other computer technical terms that are used in this book and/or that you may have heard or read elsewhere.

Appendix B is a list of Macintosh System error codes and some help with the more common system errors.

Finally, Appendix C, "Product Information," contains categorized hardware and software product information for troubleshooting tools, software and hardware vendors, and their phone numbers and addresses.

And finally, there is a fold-out Macintosh troubleshooting map in the back of the book that begins with turning on the Mac and carries you all the way to problems with a document in an open application. Use this map to help you follow a route to isolating your problem.

One important note: many features, functions, and system messages have been added and/or changed in System 7. Whenever possible, the differences between System 6 and 7 are highlighted in the context of the problem.

Urgent! How to Solve a Problem Now

The best way to resolve a problem is by minimizing data loss and hardware damage. Back up your data, if possible, and power off all hardware before disconnecting cables and diving into troubleshooting mode.

It doesn't pay to panic, so give yourself time to determine what could be going wrong. Most of the time the problem is resolvable with your ingenuity, and without an expensive repair bill or reformatting your hard disk!

Here's how to use this book to solve your problem:

* Figure out whether your problem is a software or hardware problem. This may not be obvious. If it's not clear what the problem is, jump start yourself by following the troubleshooting map, to pinpoint when the problem begins, and look at the symptoms in Chapter 13, "Symptoms and Solutions."

* If the Mac displays a system bomb or error code, check Appendix B, "System Errors." If the error looks like a program error code generated by a problem within the program, look at the program's manual and contact their technical support.

* If you know the problem is in a specific area, check all the topics that relate to that problem. For example, if you have a hard disk problem, check Chapter 10, "Storage Devices."

* If you cannot find symptoms or topics for your problem, scan the index for words or terms that might be used to describe the problem.

How to Use the Disk

The software on the disk with this book can be used to solve many problems.

If you suspect or know for sure your Macintosh is infected by a virus, Disinfectant can detect and remove the infection. Make sure the disk is locked (the write-protect tab is exposing a hole in the corner of the floppy disk), and then insert the disk into the floppy drive and double-click on the Disinfectant icon (application).

Once in the Disinfectant application, use the Disinfect menu to select a disk to disinfect (see figure 1.1).

Figure 1.1 Disinfectant's Disinfect menu for choosing a disk to disinfect.

SCSIProbe is another tool on the disk; it can be used to troubleshoot a hard disk (or other SCSI device) that is not showing up on the Desktop. To use SCSIProbe to troubleshoot this problem, install the SCSIProbe control panel file in the System Folder, and then launch SCSIProbe through the Control Panels folder (or from the Control Panel in System 6).

For more information on how to install and use the software on the disk with this book, see "About The Disk" at the end of the book.

I Still Can't Solve My Problem!

If all else fails, turn to Chapter 14, "Technical Resources," and Appendix C, "Product Information," for an alternative resource to solve your problem.

Conclusion

Most Macintosh hardware and software problems are easy enough to solve on your own with this book and a few utilities; however, the best way to solve problems is to prevent them from happening. Performing a few maintenance tasks will keep your Macintosh in good working condition and safeguard your files. The next chapter, "Macintosh Maintenance," details what steps to take to maintain your Macintosh.

I Need To Know!

Chapter 2

Macintosh Maintenance

Macintosh maintenance is like preventive medicine: If you do these things now, your Macintosh will live a longer and more enjoyable life. Some of the maintenance tasks are mundane and can be automated, and there a few that will pay off handsomely, saving you from tackling some of the problems in the rest of this book.

Startup and Shutdown

The Macintosh startup and shutdown routines are the important beginning and end to Macintosh computing sessions.

Startup lasts from the moment the Mac power is turned on until you see the Finder's desktop (see figure 2.1). The startup process tests the Macintosh hardware and loads system and initialization software into memory (RAM). The startup sequence is explained in greater detail in Chapter 9, "The Macintosh CPU."

Figure 2.1 The friendly Welcome dialog box that appears during startup.

Powering on the Macintosh

What is the best way to turn on a Macintosh? There are many ways to do this, depending on your Macintosh model and your hardware setup.

If you have a modular Macintosh (a CPU with separate monitor), then you switch on your Mac from the keyboard by pressing the Power On key. The Power On key is on the top of Apple keyboards, either the top center or the top right corner. If the Power On key doesn't work with your Macintosh, turn it on by pressing the power switch found on the back panel.

Compact Macs, like the Classic II and the PowerBook, are powered on with the power switch on the back panel. The Macintosh Portable and PowerBook 100 don't have power switches, but instead are turned on by pressing any key on the keyboard. (Pressing the Caps Lock key or the trackball button, or moving the trackball, will not turn on the computer.)

TIP: The PowerBook 100 has a storage switch, which is used when it will be turned off for a long period of time. When you are turning on the PowerBook 100, make sure the storage switch is in the "on" position.

What about all the other hardware that needs to be switched on? Besides your Macintosh, you may have a hard disk, scanner, tape backup unit, and other peripherals. You can use a power strip or a similar power unit to plug all your power cables into one unit. This way, you just turn on the power strip, and then tap the Power On key (or power switch) to turn on all the peripherals and start the Macintosh.

CAUTION: Your hardware setup may require that you turn on the Macintosh after you have powered-on connected devices that contain the System folder (such as an external hard disk). In some cases, a device is not recognized by the Macintosh unless it has had time to start up. An external hard disk that is the startup disk (it has the "blessed" System folder) should be powered on before the Macintosh is turned on.

Shutdown

Don't just flick the switch! Shut down by choosing Shut Down from the Special menu in the Finder (see figure 2.2). Do this before powering off the Mac.

Figure 2.2   To turn off the Mac, choose Shut Down under the Special menu in the Finder.

Most Macs power down automatically after you choose Shut Down. If you have a Mac that does not power down automatically when shutting down, a dialog box appears on the screen telling you that the Macintosh is ready to be turned off—your cue to cut the juice.

The shutdown routine is very important for saving information that the Macintosh uses the next time it is turned on. It updates Finder and disk information, and writes disk information to the startup disk.

Before you shut down, close all open documents and applications. If a document has been changed, the application usually asks the user to save it before it quits, but don't rely on this message alone. Even though the Shut Down command (under System 7) closes open files and quits all open applications, make sure you have saved work in progress. Under System 6 you might only get a warning that applications are open, so make sure to close all open applications.

Connecting and Disconnecting Peripherals

Always power down the Macintosh before connecting or disconnecting devices. By connecting or disconnecting ADB, SCSI, or serial devices that are powered on, you risk damaging the devices, the software, and the Macintosh.

Power Protection

The Mac is grounded to prevent electrical damage by the three-pronged plug at the end of the power cord. Always plug the Macintosh into a grounded 3-prong outlet.

To further protect your Macintosh against a power failure, plug the Macintosh power cord into a surge protector (power strip with surge protection) or UPS (uninterruptable power supply).

Place the surge protector between your computer and the power outlet. Figure 2.3 shows a Macintosh power cord plugged into a surge-protected power strip. A surge protector is sufficient for occasional brownouts, power spikes, and sags (electrical current fluctuation). For most individual users, a surge protector or power unit with surge protection is enough protection for hardware and software.

 TIP: Some offices have special power outlets with built-in surge protectors. Power strips with a fuse offer better protection.

A more expensive solution, recommended for file servers and other network devices containing valuable data, is a UPS (uninterruptable power supply). A UPS maintains a steady current and usually has a rechargeable battery that takes over in the event of a power failure. This gives you time to perform a safe backup and shut down.

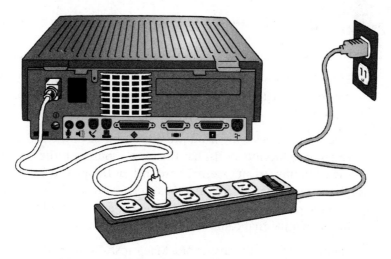

Figure 2.3 A Macintosh plugged into a power strip.

A UPS is substantially more expensive than a surge protector, and there are two kinds: an online and offline UPS. The price of an online UPS is greater than an offline UPS. An online UPS always monitors the current in the background, whereas an offline UPS switches on the battery only when the UPS detects a current fluctuation.

WARNING: If you do have a power problem, turn off the Macintosh and do not turn the Mac on again until you know the power is back to a normal state.

Floppy and Hard Disk Care

Floppy and hard disk care can save you great pains from file loss and performance problems. Understanding how the disk works and what you are doing when you write to a disk is the key to managing data on disks.

Preventing Disk Damage

Here are some measures to prevent floppy and hard disk damage.

* Keep disks away from magnets and devices that contain magnets or create a magnetic field, such as telephones and electrical power sources.

* Place disks drives away from the power source in the computer. For example, a Macintosh IIsi has the power source on the right side of the computer, so an external hard disk or floppy drive should be placed on the left side of the Macintosh. You can figure out which side the power source is on by looking at a diagram of your computer in the manual that came with your Mac, or by opening up the case.

Figure 2.4 shows the inside of a Macintosh IIsi from the front of the Macintosh. Notice that the power supply is on the right side of the Mac.

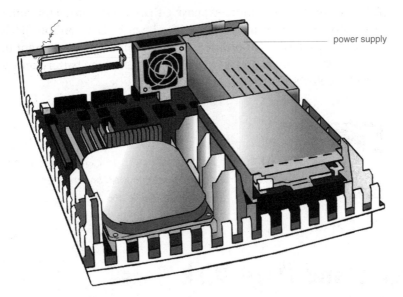

power supply

Figure 2.4 The inside of a Mac IIsi.

* Avoid storing disks in extreme heat because they may melt or warp. Just like audio tape cassettes that are destroyed in overheated cars, floppy disks can become unreadable.

CAUTION: Extreme temperatures, in general, are not good for hardware. Check your hardware manual to find the temperature range at which it is safe to store your hardware.

* Keep the metal shutter on a floppy disk closed to protect the magnetic media from dirt, dust, liquids, and fingerprints.

* Transport disks in a protective casing such as a padded disk wallet, bubble wrap, or insulated envelope.

* Lock floppy disks to protect them from virus infection or accidental file deletion. If you are not saving files to the disk, shift the write-protect tab on the disk to lock the disk. Locking the floppy disk reveals a small hole in the top right corner of the disk. You can read from the disk, but cannot write to it—hence the term "write-protected."

In the Finder, a tiny padlock icon in the upper left corner of the disk window indicates that the disk is read-only, or write-protected (see figure 2.5). The padlock is on all CD-ROM drive windows as well, because CD-ROM disks are read-only.

Figure 2.5 A locked disk has a padlock on the top left of the disk window.

Rebuilding the Desktop

Macintosh disks have an invisible Desktop file that the Finder uses to keep track of applications and documents, their icons, and the Get Info comments.

The Desktop file can become large over time. If you add and remove many applications and documents during the course of a year, rebuild your desktop frequently to improve Finder performance. Otherwise, once every few months, rebuild your desktop by holding down the ⌘ and Option keys while restarting your Macintosh (for hard disks) or while inserting a disk (for floppies). There is one side effect of rebuilding the desktop—you lose any comments placed in the Get Info box.

Defragmenting Hard Disks

Hard disks become fragmented over time as you continually create, change, and delete files. When you save a file to disk, if enough contiguous space cannot be found to store the file, it is divided up and stored in pieces on the disk. As a result, the disk access time slows down because the disk has to hop around to read all the fragmented file segments.

The simplest way to defragment a hard disk is to copy the entire contents onto another drive. This copies the files to contiguous sectors on the drive.

A more effective method is to use a utility that optimizes your hard disk by defragmenting the files and clearing up all the free space between files. Disk utilities such as Norton Utilities, DiskExpress II, and MacTools include a disk defragmentation feature—also referred to as an optimization feature.

Figure 2.6 shows Norton's Speed Disk looking at the hard disk media before it has defragmented files; in figure 2.7 the hard disk files have been defragmented. Figure 2.8 shows MacTools window reporting all the fragmented files on a hard disk.

CAUTION: Back up your hard disk before you perform maintenance tasks such as defragmenting your hard disk. If something were to go wrong during the defragmentation procedure, your data might be lost!

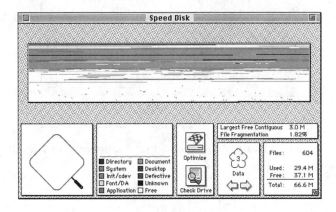

Figure 2.6 Norton's Speed disk showing fragmented files on a hard disk.

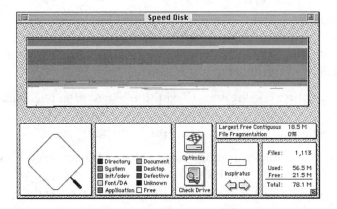

Figure 2.7 Norton's Speed disk showing the hard disk after defragmenting files.

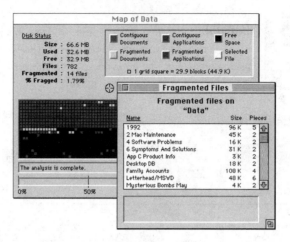

Figure 2.8 MacTools also defragments files and reports the files that are fragmented across the disk.

Partitioning a Hard Disk

Partitioning creates two or more individual Macintosh volumes out of a single hard disk. Each is logically independent of the other, just like attaching two or more hard disks to your Mac. Both disks show up separately on the desktop.

There are three good reasons to partition a hard disk: file management, disk space management, and performance. Hard disks larger than 80M are more manageable when segmented into partitions.

A large single volume is tough for the Finder to manage. With so many files and applications to keep track of, the Desktop file grows huge and the disk performance suffers. By partitioning a disk, the disk partitions have smaller desktop files and fewer files to be managed.

For example, you can partition a 100M hard disk into a 40M partition to store the System folder and utilities, and a second 60M partition for applications and documents.

There are some drawbacks to partitioning your hard disk. Partitioning software quite often requires that you reinitialize your hard disk to create a partition or to change the size of a partition.

Another partitioning issue to be aware of is the two types of partitions: *soft* and *hard* partitions. Hard partitions treat each partition as an independent volume; however, soft partitions are managed with a system extension (INIT).

Partitioning software comes with most hard drives, or you can purchase a hard drive formatting utility that formats drives into partitions. FWB's Hard Disk ToolKit is a disk utility for creating and customizing hard partitions.

Figure 2.9 shows the window for creating partitions, changing the size, password protecting, making a partition a startup disk, and setting other partition attributes.

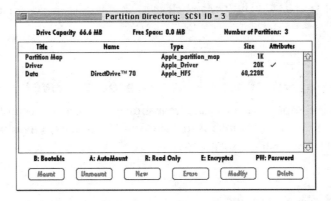

Figure 2.9   FWB features hard disk partitioning.

Disk Drive Care

Over time, dust settles in floppy disk drives. Dust can clog the mechanism and causes problems reading and initializing disks. Specialized drives, like CD-ROM and removable-media drives, may also suffer from dust accumulation. Some Macs (like the PowerBooks) have a flap over the disk drive opening to prevent dust entry from the outside environment.

Cleaning the Disk Drive

One solution is to buy a cleaning disk from your local computer store. Apple recommends the 3M Cleaning Kit for Macintosh floppy disk drives.

Another cleaning option is to use a can of compressed air or other non-electrical source of compressed air. Be careful not to bring these instruments close to the drive parts or exert too much pressure on the drive. Take the computer cover off first to allow the dust to escape.

CAUTION: Before cleaning the Macintosh, power off the Macintosh completely.

How often should I clean a disk drive?

If your computer is in a clean environment, once a year is probably enough. If your computer is in a smoke-filled or dusty environment, clean the drive more frequently.

WARNING: If you find you are cleaning the drive often, you may have a more serious problem than just dirt accumulation. Bring your floppy disk or the Macintosh to an Apple authorized repair center.

How can I protect the floppy drive when I am moving the computer?

Unless you are traveling a long distance over a rocky road, it is not necessary.

Inserting a regular floppy disk will not protect the drive heads because this leaves the heads exposed and in contact with the disk media, without providing cushioning. Insert the plastic or cardboard "disk" that came with your Mac.

Logic Board Care

Dust accumulation adversely affects any computer's logic board components. Most Macs have slits in the case to circulate air. This keeps the logic board components cool but allows dust to enter. As a result, dust accumulates on the logic board. The dust retains heat, causing component overheating and failure.

Ground Yourself Before You Clean Anything

You can damage the components on your logic board by touching the logic board (or any computer circuitry for that matter) without grounding yourself first. Ground yourself by touching the power supply first or another metal object to transfer excess static electricity. Computer vendors sell anti-static wrist-straps with which to ground yourself.

CAUTION: Power off the Macintosh and all other devices before you do anything else.

Cleaning Your Logic Board

Clean your logic board using a can of compressed air, or by blowing through a straw. Be careful not to touch components. Before cleaning, power off the Macintosh, unplug it from the outlet, ground yourself and then open the Macintosh. You may want to place the Macintosh on a grounded or non-conductive platform.

Data Backup and File Management

Take it from countless numbers of Macintosh users who learned the hard way: "save frequently and back up, back up, back up."

Spend the extra time to duplicate and secure your data because when something happens you will never regret a minute of time spent. All it takes is one bad incident to convince you that a backup procedure is worth it, but don't learn the hard way if you haven't already.

TIP: Back up important files twice, on two separate backup disks.

In addition to your data files, create backups of all your applications—apart from the floppy disks they come on—and store them in a safe place. Archive old files on the most reliable media possible; consider a safety deposit box or a fire-proof vault at an offsite location.

Here are routine backup steps to follow:

* Establish a routine.

* Label everything.

* Store the backup in a safe place—store a set of archives at a remote location if possible.

Backup Media

Choose backup media according to the size of the data source you are backing up. If your hard disk is 300M, then look for a system that will support at least 300M. If possible, choose a backup drive to support twice as much storage capacity as you have now. This will allow for future growth. Keep in mind some backup applications can also compress data while archiving your files, leaving you with more storage space.

Floppy Disks

Floppy disks may be sufficient if you don't have very large files or many files to back up. The most simple backup procedure is to drag the icon from the original disk to the floppy disk in the Finder. The Finder duplicates the file on the floppy disk.

Most floppy disk backup programs automate the floppy backup process for you by formatting, labeling, numbering, and cataloging the disks so you have a record of what is on each disk.

Hard Disks

Using a hard disk for backup is of limited value. Once you run out of hard disk space you will have to buy another hard disk or erase files to free up space for new files.

It is not a good idea to write backup files to your working hard disk. For example, do not setup a backup partition on your working hard drive. The hard disk could fail, leaving you without access to either partition.

Disk Mirroring

Hard disk mirroring or duplexing schemes use two hard disks and write the data to two disks at the same time. This technique prevents interruption due to sudden hard disk failure. If one hard disk fails, you immediately switch to the second hard disk and continue working.

Disk mirroring is not a fool-proof backup scheme because you do not have a history of files. If a file is corrupted while writing to disk, you now have a bad copy of the file on both disks. If you use a disk mirroring scheme, use a backup scheme along with it. Disk mirroring is also expensive; however, it does provide you with a substitute hard disk if one disk fails.

Removable Media Drives

Removable media drives allow the storage media to be removed from the drive—like removing a huge floppy disk. Removable drives differ in speed, capacity, and price. Removable drives are comparable in performance to hard drives, so they can be used as both storage devices for backup and archiving as well as mountable hard drives.

Removable disks have substantially larger storage capacity than floppy disks. Iomega's Transportable Bernoulli drive can have as much as a 150M capacity, and drives based on the Syquest mechanism have up to a 90M capacity. Costs are relatively the same for magnetic removable drives like the Bernoulli and Syquest; 90M Bernoulli drives are about $600 and the removable disks are about $160. Syquest drives and removable disks are slightly lower in cost.

 TIP: Keep removable drives clean from dust and dirt, and change the drive filter at a prescribed interval or when build-up is evident. Use a drive cleaning kit if available.

Optical Drives

An alternative removable-type drive is the optical drive. Optical media uses laser light to write the data to the disk, as opposed to writing data onto magnetic media.

Optical drives are slow to write files because the head makes three passes over the disk. Reading takes only one pass. This means the backup procedure is slow while file retrieval is fast.

Optical drives are the most expensive backup solution; however, the media will last the longest. Capacities range from 128M to over 10 gigabytes (10,000M). There are two types of optical media: Magneto-Optical (MO) and WORM (Write Once Read Many) drives. MO drives are erasable, and WORM drives are not. A 3.5-inch MO disk holding 128M of data costs about $1,000 for the drive and $50 per disk. WORM drives cost about $5,000 and the disks hold around 600M of data for $60 per disk.

Tape Drives

Tape drives are economical for backing up large amounts of data. There are several types of tape drives, including DAT (digital audio tape), 8mm videotape, DC 6000, and DC 2000 tape cartridges, and data cassettes (like audio cassettes). Tape drives vary in capacity, from 60M to over a gigabyte (1,000M).

There are some drawbacks to tape. You cannot boot from a tape or mount the tape volume on the desktop like you can with removable drives and other media. Tape drives require special software for file backup and retrieval. Also be aware that all magnetic media, including tapes, lose data after a lot of use and long shelf time.

Table 2.1 compares the overall advantages and disadvantages of each backup media type. These are general pros and cons; however, some technologies may vary in their optimal performance and cost. Consult the industry trade journals for the latest access times and costs for optical and removable drives—they are improving all the time.

Table 2.1   Backup Media Comparison Table

Type	Advantages	Disadvantages
floppy drives	inexpensive	not efficient for full backups or large amounts of data; low capacity; cannot perform unattended backups; slow; high cost per M
hard disks	fast retrieval of files	high cost per M; easily damaged; low security (files can be deleted easily); inflexible
removable media drives	flexible, fast file retrieval	high cost per M; lower capacity than most others
data cassettes	moderate cost per M; good performance	slow access times; special software required
DC2000	affordable drives; good performance	high cost per M; special software required
DAT	low cost per M; high storage capacity	high initial cost for hardware; special software required
8mm tape	can be used with UNIX and VAX systems; low cost per M; high storage capacity	high initial cost for hardware; slow file retrieval; special software required

continues

Table 2.1 Continued

Type	Advantages	Disadvantages
DC6000	can be used with DOS, Windows, UNIX, VMS, and VAX systems	high cost per M; special software required
Magneto-Optical	fast file retrieval; high capacity	high cost per M; slow; expensive hardware
WORM	long shelf life; high capacity	cost per M varies; expensive hardware; not erasable

Individual Backup Strategy

Base your backup strategy on how much data you back up and how often. Two basic schemes are an incremental backup and a full backup. The incremental backup copies only files that have changed since the last backup. The first backup takes time to create, but after that the incremental backup is faster than creating a full backup every time.

A full backup copies every file, every time. This can take too much time. To safeguard yourself against your full backup disk going bad, employ two or more full backups and alternate them every scheduled backup.

Backup Software

Figure out how often you want to back up your files. You may not need to back up all your files every time; back up some on a daily basis, others on a weekly or monthly basis. Devising a backup scheme will also help you determine which backup software will work best for you.

Use the following criteria to help you decide what you need from a backup program.

* Does the program support my backup media? Some backup programs support almost all existing media, and others only support floppy disks or tape drives. Check support of the following media types and

check by brand name as well: floppy disks, hard disks, removable drives, DAT drives, optical drives, 8mm drives, and tape drives.

For example, DiskFit Pro do not support tape drives, but Retrospect supports virtually all existing media and is constantly adding to their list.

✳ Is the backup software capable of backing up multiple volumes in a single backup? This is important if you have more than one disk or volume that you want to back up. The software keeps track of all the volumes in one backup sequence.

✳ Can the backup software catalog files, keep a record of each backup completed, and log backup errors?

✳ Can I create scripts to perform routine backups? Can I automate backup procedures by combining two or more volumes into one backup sequence?

✳ Can I restore a single file, or must I restore the entire backup to retrieve just one file?

✳ Can I schedule unattended backups?

✳ How easy is file retrieval?

✳ How fast is the software at performing backups? The less time it takes to backup files, the more frequently you can perform them.

✳ What happens when I run out of backup media space? How does it handle interruptions?

✳ Is the software easy to use?

✳ Can I eliminate redundancy in my backup using this software? The software should be able to distinguish between files you have already backed up and new files.

✳ Can the software perform backups in the background? The software needs to support SCSI data transfer while the Macintosh goes on to another task (while using System 7, or MultiFinder under System 6).

✳ Can I restore from the backup if I lose the backup catalog or directory file?

* Can the software utilize file compression? This can significantly reduce the size of your backup files. Less storage space means less cost.

* Can I password-protect and/or encrypt archives?

* When is technical support available (in your time zone), what does it cost, and how extensive is it?

 TIP: If you are buying a backup drive note any software bundled with the drive. Drive vendors often bundle Retrospect or other programs.

Network Backup

On a network, use high capacity media and software that supports network backup. Retrospect Remote and NetStream are two programs that back up Macs across a network. Network administrators can back up local workstation hard disks to server volumes and backup drives.

Look for the same features as with individual backup software, including cataloging of access privileges, volume origination, and password protection and encryption.

Along with the criteria for individual backups in the previous section, here are additional criteria for network backup software.

* Can I schedule unattended backups?

* Can I create backup scripts?

* Can the software back up file server volumes across a network?

* Is there backup support across AppleTalk zones?

* Is there support for remote users or backup for individual Macs on the network?

* What is the cost per user?

File Compression Software

File compression software reduces file size. Depending on the type of file, a file can be reduced to at least half its original size. Text files compress to smaller sizes than graphics or audio files.

Once the file is compressed, it can be decompressed either by double-clicking on it (if it is a self-extracting file), or using a utility to decompress the file.

Three popular file compression utilities are Compact Pro, DiskDoubler, and StuffIt Lite. StuffIt Deluxe is the commercial version of StuffIt Lite.

Online services, such as CompuServe and America Online, compress files into StuffIt and Compact Pro archives to reduce the cost of transferring (downloading) files over phone lines.

You can compress files to reduce transfer time by modems or across networks. Before you compress a file, back up the file. If the file is being transferred to another user, the other user may need to have a program to decompress the archive.

Figure 2.10 shows information about a Compact Pro compressed file. Notice that the total file compression is 50 percent. Compact Pro was able to compress this file to half its normal size, from 4K to 2K.

Release Notes

| File Type: TEHT | Created: | Tue, Oct 22, 1991, 1:32 AM |
| Creator: ttxt | Modified: | Tue, Oct 22, 1991, 1:32 AM |

	Expanded	Compacted	Saved
Data Fork Size	3083	1477	52%
Resource Fork Size	0	0	0%
Archive Overhead		59	
Total File Size	3083	1536	50%
	(4K)	(2K)	

☐ Delete original after save
☐ Encrypted   [Cancel] [OK]

Figure 2.10   Information for a file compressed with Compactor Pro.

Compression software can also create self-extracting archives. When double-clicked they automatically expand, without any additional software. Files can also be split so they can fit on more than one disk. Compressed files usually have an extension added to the file name. Table 2.2 shows some common file extensions for compacted files:

Table 2.2   Common Filename Extensions for Compressed Files

Extension	Type of file	What can decompress it?
.cpt	Compact Pro	Compact Pro, Extractor, StuffIt Expander
.sit	StuffIt	StuffIt, StuffIt Expander
.sea	all	self-extracting archive
.PKG	AppleLink	AppleLink, StuffIt Expander

Automatic Compression

AutoDoubler and More Disk Space are examples of file compression utilities that save disk space by compressing files when they are not in use. Files decompress when you need to work with them.

Compression/decompression is fairly transparent; however, there may be a noticeable performance decrease when launching applications.

TIP: Back up your entire hard disk before using an on-the-fly compression utility. Also make sure your backup software can work with your compression software.

Floppy Disk Duplication

You can easily duplicate a floppy disk in the Finder. Drag the original floppy disk to another disk image. If you drag the floppy disk over another floppy disk, the Finder will replace the contents of the second floppy disk with the contents of the first floppy. If you drag the floppy disk to another kind of disk, such as a hard disk, the floppy disk contents will be copied to a folder on the second disk. This works for floppy disks as well as other mounted volumes.

Copying the contents of one floppy disk to another floppy disk—with only one disk drive—means there may be a lot of disk swapping (ejecting and inserting different floppy disks). To avoid disk swapping, there are programs that copy the entire floppy disk contents into memory and then copy the contents to another disk, without asking for the original disk again and again. DiskCopy or Norton Floppier are two examples of floppy copying programs that read the master floppy to memory and then copy the disk contents to another floppy disk.

Figure 2.11 shows Norton's Floppier program window for duplicating floppy disks. Norton Floppier comes with Norton Utilities.

Figure 2.11 Norton Floppier window for duplicating disks.

Data Security

If you want to secure your Macintosh data or hardware, there are utilities that do everything from password-protecting a folder to physically locking and bolting your disk drive. Below are security features to consider:

* Password protection of disks at startup and during screen-saving activity

* Prevention of file deletion

* File Encryption (encoding data)

* Hardware and power locking

* File, folder, and disk locking

* File "shredding"

* Prevention of file viewing, modification, and copying

Password Protection

If you work at home or in a controllable environment, you may not worry about others accessing your data. However, if you want to prevent access to your computer, you can password-protect your computer, individual volumes, or individual folders.

Two utilities that offer disk, folder, and file locking, along with password protection, are DiskLock and FolderBolt. PassPort prevents users from copying files on to an inserted floppy disk.

Some screen savers have a password protection feature. After Dark can be set to request a password while in screen-saving mode; however, someone determined to get past this can restart the Macintosh with a different startup disk to get around the password protection.

More sophisticated password schemes prevent easy work-arounds, and may require a floppy disk and/or a software key to start up the Macintosh.

Finder-Level Protection

To allow access to your computer and at the same time safeguard against accidental trashing of files, Apple's At Ease may work for you. At Ease is a Finder desktop substitute for System 7. All accessible applications and documents are placed as buttons on the desktop. A user cannot move, delete, or rename files while At Ease is running. At Ease can easily be disabled by restarting with a floppy disk.

A utility called FolderBolt allows a user to run applications but not copy them. FileGuard allows you to copy protect software so that copies will not work or will cease to work after a set time.

One simple solution to prevent accidental deletion of files is to lock the file while in the Finder. To do this, go to the desktop (the Finder) and highlight the application or file you want to lock. Next, choose Get Info from the File menu (or press ⌘).

Figure 2.12 shows the Get Info window for the application TeachText. The Get Info window appears with information about the file, including the Lock checkbox in the bottom left corner. Click on this box to lock the file, then close the box.

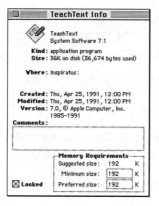

Figure 2.12   TeachText's Get Info window showing the application is locked.

TIP: Locking a file will prevent it from being changed or deleted. If changes need to be made to a file it will have to be unlocked again in the Get Info box.

Encryption

Encryption scrambles the data in a file using a mathematical algorithm, so the file is unintelligible until decrypted. When someone does have access to your files, they cannot read encrypted data without having a means to decrypt the file.

There are many types of encryption schemes, the most popular being DES and RSA. You can find encryption options in many applications such as StuffIt Deluxe, Empower II, Hard Disk ToolKit, and Norton Encrypt (which comes with Norton Utilities).

Hardware Locking

There are also hardware solutions to prevent computer access. The simplest technique is to remove the keyboard and mouse (or even the power cords) when leaving a Mac unattended.

A commercial product called MaccessCard Reader is a magnetic-identity card reader that prevents access to the Mac without the card. It requires FileGuard software on the Macintosh.

Apple and third-party vendors sell steel cables that fit into the lock port in the back of most Macintosh computers.

File Shredding

When you empty a file from the Trash in the Finder, the information about the file's location is removed, but the data is still on the disk until it is overwritten by a new file.

Most of the time, deleted files can be recovered with a file recovery utility. To prevent a file recovery utility from recovering deleted files, use an electronic file shredding program.

Two commercial programs that will shred files for you are Shredder and Norton Utilities' Wipe Info.

Hiding Files

Some disk utilities and file utilities have a hide file feature. By setting the invisible flag for a file, the file is invisible to the Finder and does not appear on the desktop.

DiskTop, a file management utility, shows all files, including invisible files. You can change the hide file setting on a file by choosing Get Info... from the DiskTop menu while in DiskTop. Figure 2.13 shows the information window for the invisible System 7 Desktop DB file.

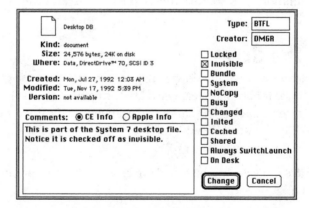

Figure 2.13   DiskTop's Get Info feature allows the user to change the invisible file setting.

Monitors

Whether you have built-in monitor support in your Mac or a video card in a slot in your Mac attached to the monitor, you will want to get the most out of the display system you are using. Caring for the monitor hardware and display screen will make Macintosh computing a lot easier on you and the monitor.

Saving Your Tube

Whether you have a color, grayscale, or black-and-white monitor, turn the screen intensity down when you're not using the Macintosh. This prevents images from burning into the video tube. If an image is burned into the tube you will see ghost or shadow images on the screen.

PowerBook screens react differently when not turned down. Images left on the LCD screen for a long time leave a ghost image. The ghost image eventually fades away if the PowerBook is turned off or placed in sleep mode.

Alternatively, there are a number of screen savers available, with some nifty animations and sounds. A very popular screen saver is After Dark.

Cleaning The Screen

When cleaning or wiping down the glass screen, don't use glass cleaner on the screen or touch the screen with anything but a very soft anti-lint cloth. Use a commercial cleaning product designed specifically for use on computer monitors. Alcohol and a cotton cloth or tissue can substitute for commercial screen wipes.

If you have a special mesh screen, check with the vendor on how to clean the screen.

Your Viewing Comfort

There are several factors that can make your life in front of a monitor either pleasant or hellish. Check a monitor for flicker, jitter (image instability), screen shrinkage, and noise. Image distortions can usually be adjusted by you or a qualified service technician.

Room lighting affects glare and flicker as well. Soft-color light, indirect light, and lighting that does not flicker will reduce the stress on your eyes. Image refresh rates above 65 hertz are sufficient to eliminate visible flicker. Fluorescent lighting typically flickers at a different rate than your monitor and causes further interference and eye strain.

A monitor with good glare protection reduces brightness and preserves focus. Most monitors are now made with anti-glare coating on the screen, and vendors offer anti-glare screens to place on the front of your monitor. Use an adjustable monitor stand to customize your viewing angle.

Some Tips for a Healthy Working Environment

There are so many things that can affect the your workspace environment. Here are some suggestions on making your computing space a more comfortable, healthier place to work.

* Adjust your chair so your feet are flat on the floor.
* Place your keyboard at the same height as your elbows so your wrists do not bend or tilt.
* Clean your screen regularly to keep it free of dust and dirt.
* Place your mouse at the same height as your keyboard.
* Position your monitor so you view the screen at eye level or slightly below eye level.
* Adjust your monitor's brightness and control settings for your comfort.
* Place your laser printer in a well ventilated area.
* Take frequent breaks away from the computer to rest your eyes and stretch your muscles.

Conclusion

Maintaining a backup of all software, rebuilding the Desktop file, and properly shutting down the Macintosh are three ways to preserve your files and avoid catastrophes.

When something does happen though, you can be prepared and trouble-shoot your problem logically. Chapter 3, "Troubleshooting Tactics", tells you how to prepare and tackle Macintosh problems.

I Need To Know!

Troubleshooting Tactics

Troubleshooting requires patience, logical thinking, and sometimes some black magic and luck. But to help you bring your Macintosh out of the dark, gather some troubleshooting utilities together.

Building a Troubleshooting Kit

Just a few tools are all you really need to get out of most simple Macintosh jams. Here are the top five items to assemble for a Macintosh troubleshooting kit.

* Emergency startup disk with a disk repair utility on it

* Startup disk with a virus program on it

* Spare, formatted, empty floppy disk

* Startup disk with your backup software on it

* Emergency hardware tools

* The Macintosh manual

Emergency Startup Disk

Surprise! You may already have one. Your Macintosh system software install disks come with a disk called "Disk Tools" (with System 7 disks). With System 6 disks, the disk is called "Utilities 1."

Figure 3.1 Disk Tools disk which comes with the Macintosh system software disks.

Figure 3.2 Disk Tools disk contents, including Apple's Disk First Aid utility.

This disk has a slimmed-down System folder, Disk First Aid, and the Apple HD SC Setup programs on it. Disk First Aid is for repairing floppy and hard disks. Apple HD SC Setup is for formatting and updating Apple hard disks. Disk First Aid will work with a disk whether it is an Apple disk or not, so it's a good tool to have around. The System folder allows the disk to be a startup disk as well. So you can use a copy of this disk as a startup and repair disk.

TIP: Make a backup of the "Disk Tools" disk for use as an emergency disk, and keep your original disk with the installation disks. It is a good idea to make a backup of all your System installation disks as well, in case a disk or file goes bad.

You may have yet another emergency disk if you purchased a disk repair utility such as Norton Utilities, Public Utilities, or MacTools. These packages include two emergency disks: one 800K disk for Macs running System 6 and a high-density disk for Macs running System 7. The System 7 disk is a high-density disk because (as you will see if you try to make your own disk) there is very little disk space left when you create even a minimum System folder on a high-density floppy disk (and you can forget about using an 800K disk).

These repair utility disks are good to have because they include the disk repair and optimization tools as on the emergency disk, so you can use these disks for startup, repair, file recovery, and optimization. Make a backup of the startup disk as well as all the included application disks with these utilities.

Making Your Own Startup Emergency Disk

You can copy the System folder from one of the System installer disks, or you can use the system installer to create a "minimum startup disk for your computer." Figure 3.3 shows the Macintosh minimum system install.

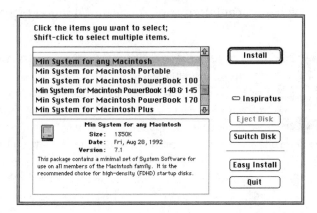

Figure 3.3 Minimum install window is reached by clicking on the Customize button in the Installer program.

You can get there by double-clicking on the Installer program on the first install disk ("Install 1") to open it, and then click on the Customize button in the installer window.

System folders under System 6 don't completely fill a high-density (1.4M) or an 800K disk, however System 7 is different. The minimum install for System 7 takes up 1.1M of disk space, which means that it cannot fit on an 800K disk and barely fits on a 1.4M disk. This leaves you less than 300K of disk space for your utilities—not a lot! Disk First Aid and some other small utilities can fit on it, but it's going to be tight.

Other Utilities to Consider Putting on The Emergency Disk

If you have the space, here are some other utilities to load on the emergency disk. If you don't have the space, consider making two or more emergency disks and labeling them so you know what to use.

* Essential system extensions (INITs) and control panels needed to mount attached drives such as Bernoulli or Syquest drives

* A printer driver if you want to print from the Mac in an emergency

* SCSI disk tools, like the SCSIProbe (included with this book) to mount stubborn disks

* Virus protection extension (INIT)

* A reporting utility, such as TattleTale (included with this book), for gathering system information for technical support representatives

TIP: You can create a system startup disk to start up any Macintosh by using the Macintosh system software install disks. Use the custom installer script called System Software For Any Macintosh. If you are using System 7.1, it has an installer script for all Macintosh models that have shipped before the release of System 7.1 (from the Macintosh Plus to the Macintosh Quadra 950 and PowerBook 145). To make a custom disk for Macintoshes released after System 7.1, add the appropriate System

enabler which comes on a disk with the Macintosh and with System 7.1 system install disks. System Enablers are located at the top level of the System Folder.

Startup Disk with a Virus Program on It

Follow the directions for creating a startup disk and then copy the virus program to your startup disk.

If you have a System 7 startup disk, you may not have enough space to fit the virus program on it, but at least install a protection extension (INIT) in the System folder.

Alternatively, you can use a disk which has just the virus software on it. Just lock the disk by pushing the write-protect tab on the disk upwards so the hole is exposed. Then you can insert the disk into a floppy drive. Since the disk is locked, changes cannot be made to the disk, including changes a virus would make. You can also lock the file on the disk, by highlighting the virus program icon, selecting Get Info from the File menu, and clicking on the "Locked" checkbox in the bottom left corner.

Spare, Formatted, Empty Floppy Disk

This always is handy for the obvious reasons; however, when you cannot save a file to disk for some reason (out of disk space or memory), you can try saving the file to this empty floppy disk. You can do this by choosing the Save As… option in many Macintosh applications. If you need to eject one disk before you insert this one, press the Eject button in the Save As… dialog box to eject a disk, or press ⌘ -Shift-1 (⌘ -Shift-2 if the disk is in a second floppy drive).

TIP: Don't forget to format your spare floppy disk beforehand!

Startup Disk with Backup Software On It and a Spare Backup Disk

Having a copy of your backup software on a floppy disk will help if you can only start up your Macintosh from a startup floppy disk. This way you can try to back up your files to the floppy disk or your backup media. Make sure you also install the software driver on the startup disk if the backup media requires one.

Keeping spare backup media, like removable cartridges or tapes, is never a bad idea. It can be used as a substitute work disk (with most removable drives, but not tape drives) when you cannot mount your hard disk, or if you need to back up your entire hard drive for transfer, file recovery, or disk recovery.

Emergency Hardware Tools and The Manual for Your Macintosh

Depending on the type of Macintosh you have, you may need a special torx screwdriver to open the case. Most modular Macs (like the Mac II series) are easy enough to open with a small Philips screwdriver.

Also keep the Macintosh manual for your Macintosh handy. It often has directions on how to install add-in cards and diagrams of where things are on the inside.

You can pick up a computer hardware tool kit with the necessary screwdrivers from many computer hardware and software dealers, mail order companies and distributors. See Appendix C, "Product Information," for more information on where to obtain computer tools.

Is It A Software or Hardware Problem?

When you are first faced with a problem it may be difficult to tell whether the problem is hardware or software related. Mysterious system bombs and sudden mouse freezes don't help the situation. A quick way to determine whether your problem is software or hardware related is to restart the

Macintosh with a startup floppy disk (like the one you created in the beginning of this chapter). If the problem goes away after restarting with another startup disk, the problem is probably with the software or hardware on your original startup disk.

If you have determined that the problem is hardware-related, you also need to decide whether you want to venture into the hardware repair business. Most Macintosh models are easily approachable when it comes to upgrading RAM and installing various add-in cards. The difficulty comes when diagnosing and fixing hardware problems that cannot be simply solved by changing the cabling, a fuse, or the configuration. In most cases, hardware repairs are best left to a qualified Apple-certified technician. To find a technician, refer to Chapter 14, "Technical Resources."

Troubleshooting Map

In the back of the book is a fold-out troubleshooting map for solving some common Macintosh problems. If you follow one path on the map and it does not solve the problem, be sure to back-track over your path to make sure you haven't missed a slightly different solution route.

Conclusion

Troubleshooting requires persistence and patience. If you keep plugging away, you will almost always come to a solution. This section has covered the basics of troubleshooting; the next two sections deal with specific problems that can occur, in both software and hardware. The next chapter covers the Macintosh System—the software that you use more than everything else put together.

Part II

Software

I Need To Know!

Chapter 4

System Software

The System folder is at the heart of software operations for the Macintosh. System software loads into memory (RAM) at startup along with other files installed in the System folder, such as control panels and extensions.

If a System software problem crops up, you can isolate it in a number of ways. Restart the Mac with a floppy startup disk; then test your problem again. If the problem doesn't appear when starting up with an alternate startup disk, then you know there is a software conflict (or other problem) on the original startup disk—quite possibly with the System software.

If you recently upgraded your System software and are now experiencing problems, your problems may be related to the upgrade.

Upgrading System Software

Apple Computer releases new System versions when they release new Macintosh models, fix software bugs and limitations in the previous version, or enhance the System software.

The latest large scale change to the Mac's System software was going from the System 6 series to System 7. System 6 included versions 6.0, 6.01, 6.02, 6.03, 6.04, 6.05, 6.07, and 6.08. (These are often referred to as "point releases.") After System version 6.08, there was a major release—System 7. The System 7 series includes System 7.0, 7.01, and 7.1 (as of this printing).

Upgrading to System 7

With most System software upgrades you can reinstall directly over the previous System folder. Upgrading from System 6.0x to System 7 requires preparation. You will probably need more RAM, hard disk space, and you also may need to upgrade your applications, hardware drivers, and network devices for System 7 compatibility.

System 7 Upgrade Checklist

If you are upgrading your Mac's System software, here is a checklist of things to do so the upgrade goes smoothly. If you are upgrading a group of Macs on a network, Apple has an upgrade kit, The System 7 Group Upgrade Kit. The kit provides a great way to organize your task. You can order System 7 software from Apple, by mail order, or from dealers. For more information see Appendix C, "Product Information."

✳ You must have at least a Mac Plus, 4M of RAM, and a hard disk for System 7. Even if you create a minimum System install on a high-density floppy disk, you would not have any space left on the floppy disk for applications and files.

Also, if you plan to use System 7 features (such as virtual memory and 32-bit addressing), you will need one of the latest Mac models and/or some additional files. For more information on whether your Mac has these capabilities, see appropriate sections in this chapter, and in Chapter 8, "The Macintosh CPU," that address these features.

✴ Obtain Apple's System 7 Upgrade Kit. Apple offers phone support, manuals, advice, and disks. See Chapter 14, "Technical Resources," for more information on System 7 support.

✴ Make sure that all your software (including applications, utilities, and INITs) are System 7-compatible. Obtain upgrades to software that require an upgrade. Use Apple's Compatibility Checker (included with the System 7 upgrade kit), to determine what software will need to be upgraded.

You may not need to upgrade all your software. Most software is either compatible or takes advantage of System 7 features. To be sure, however, contact the software manufacturer for further information.

✴ Determine your memory (RAM) needs. The amount of memory you will need depends on the type or model of Macintosh you have; what kinds of applications, fonts, and INITs you use; and what hardware you attach to your Macintosh.

Realistically, you will need a minimum of 4M of RAM to use System 7 and one application. To calculate how much more you will need, check the amount of RAM your applications require by highlighting each application's icon in the Finder and choosing Get Info from the File menu (see figure 4.1). Don't forget to add up all the fonts, desk accessories, and extensions you load in the System folder.

Figure 4.1 The Get Info window for Microsoft Word shows how much memory (RAM) it will consume in the Memory Requirements box.

On average, the System 7 System files take up at least 1.5M of RAM, and if you start adding fonts and INITs it can hit the 2M mark easily.

System 7 also allows you to have more than one application open at the same time—if you have enough RAM. So the more RAM you have the better.

✳ Make a backup of all your files before you install System 7.

✳ Find out if your hard disk and other hardware peripherals will need hardware driver upgrades. Hard disk drivers may need to be upgraded. If you have an Apple Hard Disk, you can update your hard disk driver with the System 7 Apple HD SC Setup utility (found on the "Disk Tools" disk). There are also other commercial utilities that can update your driver. Contact your hardware vendor for information on how to upgrade your hard disk for System 7, and see Chapter 10, "Storage Devices," for more information on hard disk drivers.

After you check all of the above items, you are ready to upgrade to System 7.

Usually, installing a system upgrade over a current System folder will work. However, if you are having difficulty performing this type of install, try disabling all System file additions such as extensions (INITs), control panels, and startup files. Under System 7, restart the Macintosh and hold down the Shift key as the Macintosh starts up to disable the extensions. Then run the install again.

Under System 6, create a folder called something like "Disabled," and drag all the System file additions into this folder. Restart the Macintosh and try the installation again.

Installing an Older System Version

To install an older System version, you can install over the newer folder. When you install over the newer System folder you will be asked to confirm that you want an older version installed over newer files.

Why a System Upgrade May Not Be Working and What to Try

If you are having difficulty starting the Mac or keeping it running after an upgrade or install, check the following:

✳ There may be an extension or control panel conflict. Hold down the Shift key (under System 7) while restarting the Mac. This disables all extensions. Under System 6, drag INITs and control panel devices out of the System folder and restart the Macintosh.

✳ Prior to System 7, the installer could not install on the active startup disk. Restart the Macintosh with the first install disk as the startup disk and then double-click on the Installer program again.

✳ You may not have enough disk space. If you press the Custom button in the Installer program, you can select the System install for your Mac and the installer will tell you how much disk space you will need for the selected files.

✳ You may not have enough contiguous RAM for the Installer program. Quit all applications and restart the Mac. Now try the Installer program again.

✳ Make sure you are installing from the correct install disk and you are double-clicking on the correct program. Click on the Installer program (as opposed to other files on the disk).

Custom Versus Easy Install

You have the option of pressing the Easy Install button (or the Install button from the main window) and letting the installer do its thing. Alternatively, you can press the Customize button to select what type of install you actually want.

Easy Install installs the files you need for the particular Macintosh on which you currently are installing. You can use the Custom Install to install a broader or narrower set of files; click Customize to open the Custom Install dialog box. Hold down the Shift key and click on the specific files you want to install (see figure 4.2).

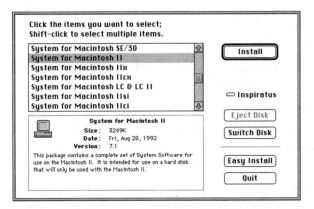

Figure 4.2 Access the Custom installation list by clicking on the Customize button in the main installer window.

To remove System files, go back into the Custom Install dialog box (press the Customize button), hold down the Option and Shift keys, and click on the items you want to remove from the System folder.

TIP: Because of the differences in Macintosh system ROMs and video architecture, each Macintosh configuration has a slightly different system memory usage and System size. This depends on a number of factors, including the amount of RAM installed in the Macintosh, the microprocessor present, and if the RAM cache is on and what it is set to.

Updating and Adding Files to the System Folder

Use the System Installer to update files, add files, and remove files from the System folder. For example, suppose you just attached a LaserWriter to your Mac and you need to install all the necessary files to the System folder. Go to the Installer program and click on the Custom button (see figure 4.3). You will find LaserWriter files and other printer files that you can install separately—without running through the entire System install again.

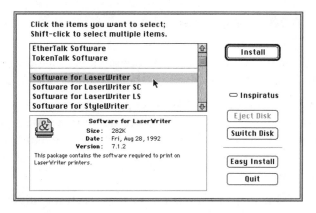

Figure 4.3 Custom install option for the LaserWriter.

Reinstalling Damaged System Software

When you suspect your problems are the result of damaged System software, the best way to reinstall the software is with Apple's System installer program.

If you know or suspect which file(s) are damaged in the System folder, it is a good idea to delete the file(s) that are damaged and run the installer program again.

If you need to delete the System or Finder file, you will not be able to delete those files while they are in the active System folder (the folder the Mac started up from). To delete the System and Finder file, restart the Mac with a startup floppy disk and then drag the Finder and System file into the trash.

CAUTION: Don't trash the System file until you have a copy of all fonts, sounds, and other files that you installed in the System file! Make sure you have a copy of all items added to the System file—such as fonts and sounds. Under System 6, all desk accessories (DAs) and fonts are installed directly into the System file with the Font/DA Mover utility. Use the Font/DA Mover to make a backup copy of your fonts and DAs. Under System 7, simply drag the fonts, sounds, and other files out of the System folder.

System 6 and 7 on the Same Network

Macintosh computers using Systems 6 and 7 can coexist on the same network and continue to share network services—including the printers—by upgrading the printer drivers on the System 6 Macs.

The printer drivers of System 7 users upgrade automatically when you install the new system software. If there are System 6 Macs printing to the same printer as System 7 Macs, the printer(s) will be reinitialized constantly. To settle the printer initialization wars, install System 7 printer drivers on System 6 Macs.

There is a Printer Update folder on the Printing Install disk with System 7 that contains all the software you will need to upgrade a System 6 Mac's printer software. The Printer update installs the new version of PrintMonitor, a new Background file for background printing, and new LaserWriter drivers based on the previously installed printer drivers.

Make sure other devices on the network, such as bridges and routers, are System 7-compatible. In System 7, Apple upgraded the network portion of the system software to *AppleTalk Phase 2*. AppleTalk Phase 2 enhances the capabilities of AppleTalk networks; however, you will need to upgrade your network devices to support Phase 2.

AppleTalk Phase 2 networks can coexist with AppleTalk Phase 1 networks if you have a "transition router" between the Phase 1 and Phase 2 networks. The transition router transfers data between Phase 1 and Phase 2 networks.

For more complete information, obtain the System 7 Group Upgrade Kit from Apple and contact the network vendors of your devices. To obtain the kit, see Appendix C, "Product Information."

One System Folder or Two?

Normally you should not have more than one System folder installed on a startup disk. To make sure you have only one System folder, use a search utility—such as the Find File desk accessory in System 6, or the Find feature in System 7 (located in the File menu in the Finder)—to find all the System folders or files on one disk.

If you need to switch between System 6 and System 7, or between two or more System folders, you can use a utility such as System Picker (included on the disk with this book) or The Blesser.

Figure 4.4 shows System Picker finding all the System folders available from which to choose. One System folder is selected and used as the startup folder the next time the Mac is started.

Figure 4.4 System Picker enables you to have more than one System folder, and to switch between them in order to restart with a different System folder.

Preventing Crashes and Data Loss

The best defense against crashes is to back up your applications, utilities, and files and save documents frequently while working on them. Some applications have an auto-save feature that will save your document automatically at specified intervals. You also can obtain shareware and commercial utilities that will add the auto-save function while you are working.

To aid in Macintosh crash recovery there is a utility called Crash Barrier. This is a control panel device (cdev) that has auto-save features, and that tries to fix or recover from crashes when they occur. Crash Barrier gives warnings for low System memory and it enables you to save your work before bringing the Mac down from the crash (see figure 4.5). See Appendix C, "Product Information," for where to obtain Crash Barrier.

Figure 4.5 Crash Barrier's control panel for setting System crash recovery settings.

Recovering From System Crashes, Bombs, and Freezes

When your Mac crashes or freezes, it is unlikely that you will recover without restarting the Mac. Most likely, you will have the data that was saved before the crash; however, you probably lost unsaved data and possibly have damaged files.

If your Mac has crashed, is frozen (also referred to as a "hang"), or is displaying a System error, here are a few ways to recover:

The Cursor or the Screen Is Frozen

❊ You may not be permanently frozen. Some application tasks take a long time—especially if you are working over a network. You may be able to judge how long a specific task takes normally, but give the Mac a fair amount of time before you decide you are frozen. If you think the application is stuck in an infinite loop, try pressing ⌘-Period, which will stop some application processes (like printing).

❊ Check the mouse and keyboard cables. They may be loose or disconnected. Also check network cable connections and any other cable connections that may be loose or damaged.

✳ Try quitting the active application by pressing the following key combination: ⌘-Option-Escape (under System 7). If this works, it will close the program that was frozen and enable you to save documents in other open applications. Restart the Macintosh and check the document and application for any file repair or recovery.

✳ Press the reset switch to restart the Macintosh. For more information on the reset switch, see Chapter 8, "The Macintosh CPU." If the reset switch doesn't work, or isn't installed, then turn the power switch off. Wait a few seconds and then start the Mac again with an emergency startup disk to repair or recover any lost files.

✳ As a *last* resort, if the power switch is not working, pull the power cord.

There Is a System Bomb with a Message and/or Error Code

✳ Write down all the information in the dialog box. At this point, you probably won't have much choice except to either restart the Mac by clicking the button in the error dialog box, or to restart following the suggestions below.

✳ Press the Reset switch (part of the programmer's switch) to restart the Macintosh. For more information on the reset switch, see Chapter 8, "The Macintosh CPU." If the reset switch doesn't work or isn't installed, then turn the power switch off. Wait a few seconds and start the Mac again with an emergency startup disk to repair and recover files.

To find out more about troubleshooting System errors, see Appendix B, "System Errors."

Troubleshooting System Software Problems

Below are some common questions and troubleshooting tips related to system software:

How do I know where to copy a file in the System 7 folder?

If you are not sure where to place a file, you can drag the file over the closed System folder icon; the Finder will place it in the appropriate folder. You can determine where a file belongs if you highlight the file in the Finder and choose "Get Info" from the File menu. The Get Info window will tell you where the Finder placed your file.

For example, figure 4.6 shows the dialog box that appears when you drag font files over the System folder icon in System 7.1.

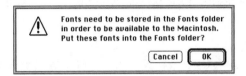

Figure 4.6 Dragging fonts over the System folder in System 7.1 brings up a dialog box that will tell you where the Finder will place the fonts.

Where are my Finder settings stored in System 7?

The Finder settings are stored in the Finder Preferences file, in the Preferences folder, within the System Folder. If you throw away the Finder Preferences file, the Finder creates a new one at the next startup with default settings. Here are Finder preference settings and defaults values:

* Font used for Finder views can be changed from the Views control panel. The default is Geneva 9.

* Icon alignment settings for the Finder can be changed from the Views control panel. The default is a straight grid. "Always snap to grid" is deselected by default.

* Icon List View Settings for Finder can be changed from the Views control panel. The default is smallest icon; display sizes, kinds, labels, and dates. "Calculate folder sizes" and "Show disk info in header" are deselected.

✳ Trash warning dialog box (which can be changed from the Get Info dialog box for the Trash can) is selected to "Warn before emptying."

TIP: The settings for Virtual Memory, File Sharing, and Window color settings are stored within their respective control panel files. Virtual Memory and File Sharing can be disabled temporarily by holding down the Shift key while starting the Macintosh. Hold down the key until "Extensions Off" appears in the "Welcome to Macintosh" screen.

How can I tell which files are System files?

One way to determine a number of things about a file is to click on the file to select it (while in the Finder) and choose Get Info from the File menu (see figure 4.7).

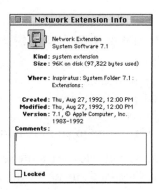

Figure 4.7 The Get Info dialog reveals information about the file, including the kind of file.

Another way to view information about a file is to view a folder "by Kind." This is achieved by activating the window that contains the folder with the files and selecting By Kind from the View menu in the Finder.

How can I tell what System version I have?

Under the Apple () menu in the Finder, the first menu choice reads "About This Macintosh" (or "About The Finder" in System 6). Choose this command and a window appears with information, including the System software version currently running (see figure 4.8).

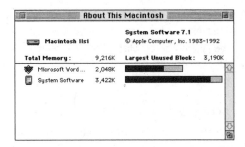

Figure 4.8 "About this Macintosh" under the Apple menu in the Finder.

My Mac is freezing and/or behaving strangely.

* Make sure you have only one System folder. If you have duplicate System folders or individual files, or more than one Finder or System file, you will have problems working in the Finder. You may have inadvertently slipped a System-related file into the wrong folder or duplicated the System files in another folder.

   To find duplicate System files, use a file search utility or the Find utility in System 7 (or Find File under the Apple menu in System 6).

* Make sure you are not mixing different versions of system files in one System folder.

* Make sure that you are using applications and System extensions that are compatible with your System software version.

* You may have an extension or application conflict. See the section below on how to resolve application and System extension conflicts.

Resolving Extension (INIT) and Control Panel Conflicts

Erratic behavior, system freezes, and crashes are often the result of software conflicts between system extensions (INITs) or control panel devices (cdevs).

System extensions are programs that load into RAM at startup and remain active and in memory until the Macintosh is shut down. System extensions are in the Extensions folder, within the System folder. Under System 6, extensions are called "INITs" or startup documents, and can be found in the System folder.

Apple includes several extensions with the system software, and many third-party products also add extensions. Figure 4.9 shows some of the extensions in the Extensions folder.

Figure 4.9　A view of the Extensions folder in the System 7 folder.

Control panels can be combination files; they usually load into RAM upon startup, like extensions, but they also enable the user to change certain settings. Some control panel devices only control settings. The combination control panel/extensions load into memory at startup and remain active. They can conflict with other extensions and applications just like normal extensions.

WARNING: Apple menu Items (desk accessories) also can conflict with open applications, extensions, and control panels.

Sometimes extensions cannot coexist without causing problems. This may be because an extension has not been well developed by the software manufacturer. (That is, there is a software "bug" in the extension.) Other times an extension may require a different version of System software than what you installed, or it may be conflicting with an open application.

Steps to Resolve an Extension Conflict

There are a number of ways you can approach a conflict—depending on the problems you are confronting. If you are continually crashing, you will need to restart the Mac with another startup disk before you can isolate the conflict.

Here are the steps to resolve a system extension conflict:

1. Recover from the conflict.

   Hold down the Shift key while restarting the Macintosh, or restart the Macintosh with a startup floppy disk. Holding down the Shift key while you restart the Mac disables all extensions under System 7. Hold down the key until "Extensions Off" appears in the "Welcome to Macintosh" screen.

2. Create a folder inside your System folder (or outside it—it doesn't matter where the folder is) and call it something like "Disabled Extensions." Remove all extensions and control panels from the System folder and place them in the "Disabled Extensions" folder.

3. Begin testing two extensions at a time. Drag two extensions back into the Extensions folder and restart the Mac to see if the two can coexist peacefully. If they do, then this combination is not the problem. Continue this until you have found which two extensions cause a conflict.

Alternatively, you can load them one at a time until a problem unfolds. By loading them one at a time, you still may have to isolate which two files are in conflict.

4. Sometimes you can resolve the conflict by loading the extensions in a different order. To change the loading order of extensions, place a different character in front of the extension name (see figure 4.10).

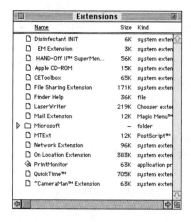

Extensions		
Name	Size	Kind
Disinfectant INIT	6K	system exten
EM Extension	3K	system exten
HAND-Off II™ SuperMen...	56K	system exten
Apple CD-ROM	15K	system exten
CEToolbox	65K	system exten
File Sharing Extension	171K	system exten
Finder Help	36K	file
LaserWriter	219K	Chooser exte
Mail Extension	12K	Magic Menu™
Microsoft	–	folder
MTExt	12K	PostScript™
Network Extension	96K	system exten
On Location Extension	383K	system exten
PrintMonitor	63K	application pr
QuickTime™	705K	system exten
~CameraMan™ Extension	63K	system exten

Figure 4.10 A view of the Extensions folder with some files renamed to alter the loading order.

For example, in figure 4.10, the CameraMan extension will load after all the other extensions because a ~ character was placed in front of the name. On the other hand, the EM Extension will load first because there are three spaces in front of the name.

5. You may have a damaged extension or it may have been written to a damaged part of the disk. Replace the extension with a good copy. You also can run a disk repair utility to determine if there are any problems with the area of the disk where the file is located.

6. If you have not been able to isolate an extension conflict, you may have other problems indirectly affecting your extensions. Try the fixes listed below:

   ✳ Disable all your extensions and then run a disk repair utility on your disk to make sure the disk is okay. You may have a damaged extension or the disk may be damaged.

* Rebuild the Desktop file. To do so, hold down the Option and
  ⌘ keys when you start your Mac. Hold them down until the
  Finder launches; a dialog box will appear asking you if you want
  to rebuild the desktop on your hard disk. Click Yes.

* Run a virus detection program to check for a virus infection.

TIP: Work on your Macintosh for a while without the file(s)
you think may be conflicting. If you don't experience more
problems you know the problem was caused by the files you
removed.

Using an Extension Manager

As an alternative to the conflict resolution steps mentioned above, you can
obtain an extension manager or conflict resolution utility to resolve file
conflicts and manage your extensions.

Extensions Manager is an extension that is free and is available from
online services and user groups. With Extensions Manager (see figure
4.11), you can enable and disable the extensions and create sets of loading
files. After enabling or disabling a file, or set of files, restart the Mac; your
new selections take effect.

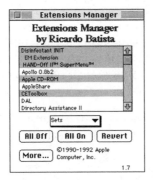

Figure 4.11 Extensions Manager control panel for selecting and deselecting
extensions and control panels at startup time.

Other utilities that work like Extensions Manager are Conflict Catcher and INITPicker. HELP!, a troubleshooting utility, runs and examines every file on your System. HELP! will then create a report detailing what may be causing the conflict and whether you need to upgrade applications, extensions, or other software on your Mac. For more information on these products, see Appendix C, "Product Information."

NOW Utilities is a collection of utilities that contains a Startup Manager utility that enables you to turn extensions and control panels on and off, compose sets of startup items, and contains a linking feature that enables you to define connections between a group of startup items.

CAUTION: There is no way around having to Restart your Mac for extensions to load or unload, with or without an extension manager.

System Memory

To see how much RAM all your System files take up, go to the Finder and select About This Macintosh from the Apple menu (figure 4.12).

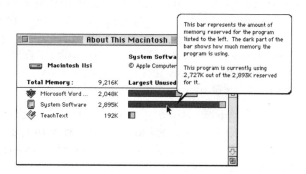

Figure 4.12   About This Macintosh shows the amount of memory used by the System.

The "About" feature will provide information about fonts, Apple Menu items (desk accessories), extensions, and control panel devices that you have in your System folder—along with the System and Finder.

The System Heap

During the Macintosh startup, a portion of your memory (RAM) is designated for System files for your Mac and other applications to use at all times.

This memory space that the system files take up in RAM is often referred to as the System heap. Under System 7, the System memory space is dynamically managed; however, under System 6 the System heap is not managed as well.

 TIP: If you are running System 7 you do not need to worry about the System heap because it is dynamically managed. When running MultiFinder under System 6, the heap is also dynamically managed; however, it is not as well managed as in System 7, so you might still want to adjust the heap size as discussed below.

Normally, it is recommended that the System heap have about 20 percent of its memory free. So if the System heap is 2M, then it should have about 400K of free space. Under System 6, the System heap space can become tight and cause your Mac to slow down, run out of memory when performing operations, or cause the system to crash. The space gets tight due to loading too many INITs (extensions), or loading INITs that do not manage memory well. You may receive a System Error ID = -108 if the System heap runs out of memory.

To adjust the heap size in System 6, remove some INITs from the System folder. To remove INITs, use a tool such as BootMan or HeapTool—both of which are available from user groups and online services—that will enable you to adjust the size of your System heap.

The Finder

The Finder, along with the System file, is the most important file in the System folder. The Finder loads into memory when the Mac starts up and is always available. The Finder manages the Desktop, the Trash, keeps track of files, and manages document and application information.

Disappearing Files

If you find that your files are disappearing, here are a few possible solutions to this problem.

✳ You may have misplaced or accidentally moved the file(s). Use the Find feature in System 7 to find the file (figure 4.13), or the Find File desk accessory under the Apple menu.

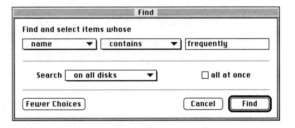

Figure 4.13 The Find dialog box in System 7.

✳ Disappearing files is a problem with System 7.0 and 7.01; however, System 7.1 no longer has this problem. You can locate the files with the Find feature. Apple released a System software improvement upgrade called "System 7 Tune-Up" to fix this problem before System 7.1 was released. Tune-Up solves the problem of disappearing files and folders, as well as improving printing speed and memory management (fewer "out of memory messages").

To determine if Tune-Up is installed on a Mac, go to the About This Macintosh under the Apple menu. If there is a • (dot) next to the System software version, then Tune-Up was installed. Otherwise, install Tune-Up or upgrade to System 7.1. System 7.1 does not require Tune-Up.

If you installed Tune-Up on your Macintosh but still have the disappearing folder and file problems, use Disk First Aid (the latest version or version 7.1) to fix any remaining problems you may have with your disk directory. Disk First Aid (with System 7), as well as other disk repair utilities, will fix any remaining problems.

✳ Use a disk repair utility such as Disk First Aid, Public Utilities, or Norton Utilities to fix the disk information and disk directory. The disk directory keeps track of files and folders and may be damaged.

The Desktop File

The Desktop file is a hidden file that the Finder creates and uses to keep track of information about applications, documents, the Get Info comments, and the icons associated with all files.

Every disk formatted by the Macintosh operating system has a Desktop file on it. Disks over 2M in size and formatted by System 7 have two files that make up the Desktop file—the Desktop DF and Desktop DB files. The System 6 Desktop file and floppy disk Desktop files are one Desktop file.

Viewing the Desktop File

You can view the Desktop file, and other invisible files, with a utility such as DiskTop, Apple File Exchange (it comes with Macintosh System software), or another file utility that can view invisible files. Figure 4.14 shows a view of the Desktop files on a hard disk using DiskTop.

There are three files on the disk in figure 4.14: Desktop, Desktop DB, and Desktop DF. The file "Desktop" is from System 6. If you are running System 7, the Desktop files consist of two files: Desktop DB and Desktop DF. This particular hard disk has both a System 6 and a System 7 folder installed—so both types of Desktop files are on the disk. (See the section, "One System Folder or Two?," earlier in this chapter for more information on installing more than one System folder on a disk.)

Another place you may see two Desktop files (DB and DF) is if you have an AppleShare File Server. The file server includes a utility called the "Desktop Manager," that helps the Finder manage a large number of files and creates two Desktop files: the "Desktop DB" and "Desktop."

| DiskTop | | | | | | |

DiskTop

HFS
71127K Used 91%
7610K Free 9%
27 items

Copy   Move
Delete Rename
Find   Sizes

Inspiratus
Drive(s)

Inspiratus   Eject   Unmount

Name	Type	Creator	Data	Resource	Modified
Move&Rename	0 files/folders		---	---	12/12/92
AppleShare PDS	BTFL	pds	9K	1K	12/12/92
Applications	16 files/folders		---	---	11/14/92
Assorted Tools	30 files/folders		---	---	11/28/92
Communications	5 files/folders		---	---	11/5/92
Desktop	FNDR	ERIK		134K	1/1/4
Desktop DB	BTFL	DMGR	102K		12/19/92
Desktop DF	DTFL	DMGR	529K		12/19/92
Desktop Folder	3 files/folders		---	---	12/19/92
EKERWIEN.ID	TEXT	????	4K		11/14/92
Fonts	3 files/folders		---	---	9/22/91

Erica Litsky   #25121

Figure 4.14   Viewing invisible files with DiskTop.

The Desktop file (the single invisible file in System 6) slows down when there are more than 800 files in one folder, so don't store all your files in one folder level. The Desktop Manager utility is not needed with System 7 or for only 1 to 2,000 files in System 6; however, it may help if you have more than 2,000 files and are running System 6. You can obtain the Desktop Manager utility with the purchase of the AppleShare File Server.

TIP: The Desktop Manager only works with System 6 (it goes in the System folder), and is not needed with System 7 because its features were incorporated into System 7.

Rebuilding the Desktop File

The Desktop file is updated when you add new applications or documents to a disk, or add Get Info comments to a file. A new application icon is added to the Desktop file to display the application and document icons. All this information is stored in the file and never deleted, so the Desktop file only grows larger over time, and eventually slows down the Finder and the startup time.

To update the Desktop and bring its size down, you can rebuild the Desktop. Do this by holding down the Option and ⌘ keys while restarting the Macintosh. You also can rebuild the Desktop of a floppy, or removable disk, by holding down the same keys while you insert the disk in the disk drive. You will see a dialog box like the one in figure 4.15, which gives you a chance to cancel the operation.

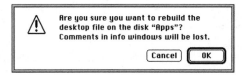

Figure 4.15   The dialog box that appears when you rebuild the Desktop file.

CAUTION: When you rebuild the Desktop, all comments that have been saved in the Get Info windows are lost. For this reason, it isn't a good idea to use the Comments section of the Get Info window.

TIP: If you try to rebuild the Desktop of a floppy disk but nothing happens, the disk may be locked. Eject the disk and make sure that the disk lock slider covers the hole.

The Desktop rebuilds every time I start the Mac.

If you have canceled this process in the past, don't cancel it now because chances are the Mac hasn't been able to complete the rebuilding process. Here are some other possibilities:

✳ If you switch between System 6 and System 7, the System rebuilds the Desktop so it is compatible with the new startup System folder or the newly installed system version.

✳ You may have a damaged Desktop, or it may have written to a damaged area on the disk. Use a disk repair utility to check the disk media and the disk information, and to repair the disk.

✳ Check the Option and ⌘ keys on the keyboard. They may be stuck or dirt may be interfering with the key contacts.

The Desktop file cannot be created on a disk.

The Desktop file is damaged, it may be written to a damaged area of the disk, or the disk is locked. Use a disk repair utility to check the disk media and the disk information, and to repair the disk.

Why does my Desktop file get so big?

The Desktop file is an invisible file that the Finder uses to keep track of icons and creator names—so that when you double-click on a Word document, for example, Word actually opens. The file can get very large because it doesn't delete information when it is no longer needed.

Icons take up a fairly large amount of space. When the Desktop file grows too large it can slow things down noticeably; however, rebuilding the Desktop will solve this problem.

Apple Menu Items

Files that are placed in the Apple Menu Items folder in the System folder (using System 7) appear in the Apple menu in the Finder (see figure 4.16).

You can add desk accessories, programs, documents, or aliases of files or folders to the Apple Menu Items folder. You can then launch them directly from the Apple menu, from any application.

To create an alias and then place it in the Apple Menu Items folder:

1. Highlight the file in the Finder.

2. Choose Make Alias from the File menu (see figure 4.17).

Figure 4.16 The Apple menu is available from all applications and the Finder.

Figure 4.17 Making an alias of a file in the Finder.

3. Place the alias in the Apple Menu Items folder, and the file will appear in the Apple menu the next time you open the menu.

The Font/DA Mover and the Apple (🍎) Menu

You can add desk accessories to the Apple (🍎) menu under System 6 using the Font/DA Mover. The Font/DA Mover comes with System 6. Figure 4.18 shows the Font/DA Mover dialog box used to copy files into and out of the System file.

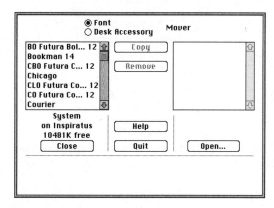

Figure 4.18 The Font/DA Mover dialog box.

Under System 6, you use the Font/DA Mover to add or remove fonts and desk accessories from the System file. You also can create suitcases with the Font/DA Mover to store fonts and desk accessories.

 TIP: Even though you no longer need the Font/DA Mover to move files into and out of the System file with System 7, you still can use Version 4.1 of the Font/DA Mover to create and combine fonts and desk accessories (DAs) into suit-cases to transfer and copy fonts and DAs. To create a suitcase, click on the Open button on the bottom right or left side and in the other side of the dialog box click on the New button.

Where can I find fonts and desk accessories under System 6?

The easiest way to find the standard desk accessories and fonts that come with System 6 is on the System software disks. You can open the Font/DA Mover and copy the DAs and fonts directly from the System file on the System software disks onto another System disk; or copy them from a suitcase on the Utilities 2 disk in System 6 (see figure 4.19). The Utilities 2 disk has the Font/DA Mover and the Fonts and Desk Accessories suitcases.

Figure 4.19   The Utilities Disk in System 6 has the Font/DA Mover and fonts and desk accessories.

Chooser

The Chooser is where you assign output via the modem and printer ports, select printers, and locate network file servers and file sharing volumes. The Chooser is also quite handy for troubleshooting printing and network problems.

If you are experiencing trouble printing, confirm that the printer was selected and is shown in the Chooser. If you are losing access to a network volume, check to see that the volume is not "ghosting" or fading in and out of the Chooser. There may be a problem with the network connection on the Macintosh, elsewhere along the network, or at the server end of the network.

The Chooser isn't listed in the Apple Menu.

The Chooser is a desk accessory—so confirm it is in the Apple Menu Items folder. If not, place it there and it will show up under the Apple menu.

If you are running System 6, the Chooser needs to be installed with the Font/DA Mover. See the section "The Font/DA Mover and the Apple Menu" earlier in this chapter. The Chooser is normally installed by default with the Apple System installer.

A printer or server is not showing in the Chooser.

If network services and devices are not showing or fading in and out of the Chooser, check the following:

* You may have too many devices connected to a single LocalTalk network segment. There is a recommended limit of 32 devices on one LocalTalk network segment, which includes all Macs, printer, servers, and anything else connected to that individual network.

* You may not have terminated the network adequately. When daisy-chaining network devices there should be a terminator at each end of the network.

* There may be a loose connector somewhere along the network cabling.

* A cable may be damaged or blocked by heavy equipment, or there may be electromagnetic interference along the network cabling. Keep heavy machinery, power transformers, fluorescent lights, and other sources of electromagnetic radiation away from cabling.

* You may have exceeded the maximum network cable length. Check the limitations for your network.

* The device not showing in the Chooser may be turned off or not receiving enough power, warming up (initializing), or offline. Also check the network cables and connectors to the device.

* A network router or other device connecting network segments may not be working properly. Check the network configuration and make sure the zone in which the device should be appearing is selected in the Chooser.

Printing

Printers are selected in the Chooser (which is launched from the Apple menu). Apple's System software includes printer drivers for printers, including LaserWriters and ImageWriters.

Under System 7, the printer drivers are Chooser extensions and are installed in the Extensions folder within the System folder. All the print drivers are on the "Printing" disk that comes with the System 7 software disks.

Under System 6, the printer drivers go directly in the System folder and they are found on the "Printing Tools" disk that comes with the System 6 software disks.

Background Printing and the PrintMonitor

Background printing is a feature in the Mac's system software that enables you to continue working while your documents are printed. Background printing is a background process; you must have either MultiFinder or System 7 to use background processes.

To turn on background printing, go to the Chooser (under the Apple menu) and select the LaserWriter printer driver (see figure 4.20).

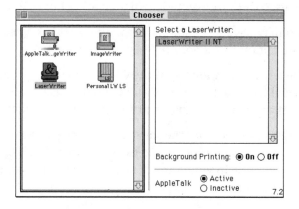

Figure 4.20   Background printing is turned on in the Chooser.

You might notice that your Mac slows down while a document is being processed to be sent to the printer. This is normal; the extent to which your computer is slowed depends on the size and complexity of the document being printed.

TIP: To enable background printing you must be running System 7 and have the PrintMonitor file installed in your System folder. Under System 6 you need the MultiFinder, Backgrounder, and PrintMonitor files installed in the System folder.

The PrintMonitor

The PrintMonitor is an application that comes with the System software and is installed in the Extensions folder within the System folder. (Under System 6 it goes directly in the System folder.)

The PrintMonitor manages background printing and other document printing features. When you print a document, PrintMonitor is available from the Application menu on top right corner of the menu bar under the application menu (see figure 4.21).

Figure 4.21 The PrintMonitor under the application menu while printing in the background.

Here are some other things you can do with PrintMonitor:

* While you are printing you can see the name of the document that is currently being printed, its status in the print queue, and the name of the printer (see figure 4.22).

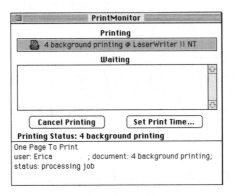

Figure 4.22 The PrintMonitor status window.

❋ You can cancel a print job before or while it is being processed by pressing the "Cancel Printing" button in the PrintMonitor status window.

❋ You can specify a date and time for a document to be printed (see figure 4.23).

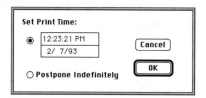

```
Set Print Time:

◉ | 12:23:21 PM |        ┌─────────┐
  | 2/ 7/93    |        │ Cancel  │
                         └─────────┘
○ Postpone Indefinitely  ┌─────────┐
                         │   OK    │
                         └─────────┘
```

Figure 4.23   Setting the print date and time in the PrintMonitor.

❋ The PrintMonitor alerts you if the printer is out of paper and when it starts a manual feed job (such as labels and envelopes).

❋ You can adjust PrintMonitor settings by choosing Preferences under the File menu while the PrintMonitor is open.

❋ When the printer or the Macintosh is having difficulty printing a document, the PrintMonitor will flash an icon in the top right corner of the menu bar. Pull down this menu and choose the PrintMonitor. It will have a diamond next to it if it is trying to notify you of a problem.

TIP: If you are not printing a document and want to open the PrintMonitor to change settings, go to the Extensions folder in the System folder and double-click on the PrintMonitor—as you would with any other application.

I don't have enough memory to print.

If you are receiving a message that says you do not have enough memory to print the document, troubleshoot this message with these suggestions:

* Increase the suggested memory partition for the PrintMonitor. To do this, go into the System folder and highlight the PrintMonitor application. Then choose Get Info from the File menu. Increase the memory in increments of about 25K to 50K until you are able to print the document.

* The printer driver or the PrintMonitor file may be damaged. Drag the current printer driver or PrintMonitor into the Trash and then reinstall a new one with the system installer.

* Immediately after you select the Print command in an application, quit the application. This may work if you have background printing on because you will free up memory for the PrintMonitor to print the document.

* Simplify or break the document up into parts. The document may be too complex and require too much memory for your Macintosh to process it all at one time.

* Make sure your print drivers and system printing files are the correct version for your printer and the system software version you are using.

My Mac crashes when I print a document.

If you freeze, crash, or receive an error when you try to print, try the suggestions below:

* Quit the application and increase the suggested memory partition for the application. To do this, quit the application, go to the Finder and highlight the application. Now choose Get Info from the File menu and increase the suggested memory size to 10 to 20 percent more than the suggested memory size.

* The document may be damaged. Try printing just one page of the document or try printing another document to determine if it is the document that is causing the problem.

* Simplify or break the document up into parts. The documents may be too complex and require too much memory for your Macintosh to process all at once.

* The printer driver or the PrintMonitor file may be damaged. Drag the current printer driver or PrintMonitor into the Trash and then reinstall a new one with the System installer.

* You may have an extension (INIT) conflict. Remove or disable extensions and try printing the document again. Try printing from another application to determine if the problem is with just this application.

* The application may be damaged. Reinstall the application from a good copy and try printing again.

Color Settings

You can change the color settings for a monitor through the Monitor control panel in the Control Panels folder. Under System 6, go to the Control Panel under the Apple menu. Figure 4.24 shows the Monitor control panel settings under System 7.

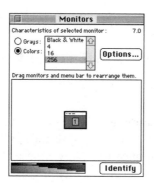

Figure 4.24   The Monitor control panel.

Table 4.1 shows how many colors each mode represents on a Macintosh.

Table 4.1   Monitor color levels

Colors	Mode
2	1-bit black & white
4	2-bit color or grayscale
16	4-bit color or grayscale
256	8-bit color or grayscale
32,768	16-bit color or grayscale
16.7 million	24-bit color or grayscale

Built-In Monitor Support

If you are using the built-in video feature in your Macintosh, you can adjust some color settings by pressing the Option button in the Monitor control panel (see figure 4.25):

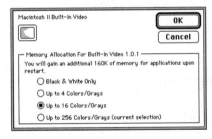

Figure 4.25   Controlling settings for the built-in monitor support.

32-Bit QuickDraw

QuickDraw is how the Macintosh draws and displays images on the screen. The highest quality of color image is when you are in 24-bit color mode—which is not to be confused with 32-bit QuickDraw.

32-bit QuickDraw means a Macintosh can use up to 16.7 million colors in images at one time. Twenty-four of those 32 bits are used for color information (so 32-bit and 24-bit color really handle the same amount of color). 32-bit QuickDraw also improves support for grayscale images.

To use up to 16.7 million colors (24-bit color) your Macintosh must have the following:

* Support for 32-bit QuickDraw (in the ROM).

* Have a 16-, 24- or 32-bit video card installed (or built-in video and video RAM in some newer Macs).

If you have a Mac II or SE/30, you will need to install the 32-bit QuickDraw file which comes with System 6 software on the "Printing Tools" disk. The System 6 32-bit QuickDraw file allows a Macintosh II and SE/30 to display images that have more than 256 colors.

If you are running System 7, you do not need the 32-bit QuickDraw file in your System folder. 32-bit QuickDraw has been integrated into System 7 and the System 7 Installer will delete the old 32-bit QuickDraw file during System installation.

The only benefit to installing 32-bit QuickDraw for an 8-bit video card is enhanced dithering on 8-bit images.

32-Bit Addressing

System software Version 6 (6.0 through 6.08) is a 24-bit operating system. When a Macintosh is running System 6, the Macintosh is in 24-bit mode, which means the Macintosh can only address up to 8M of RAM. System 7 is a 32-bit operating system, so it can address more than 8M of RAM if: a) 32-bit addressing is turned on; and b) your Macintosh can support 32-bit addressing. For more information on 32-bit addressing see Chapter 8, "The Macintosh CPU."

My Mac has more than 8M of RAM installed, but can only use 8M.

You need to be running System 7 and turn 32-bit addressing on to recognize more than 8M of RAM.

If you are not running in 32-bit mode, when you look at the memory configuration in About This Macintosh (or About the Finder in System 6) under the Apple menu it will report over 8M of RAM is installed, but only 8M is usable with the remainder being assigned to the System Software. This extra memory assigned to the System is unusable. For more information on 32-bit addressing see Chapter 8, "The Macintosh CPU."

WARNING: Make sure your applications are 32-bit clean also! If they aren't, they can crash when 32-bit addressing is turned on.

QuickTime

QuickTime enables you to work with and integrate sound, text, images, video, and animated graphics into documents called movies. QuickTime is made by Apple (see Appendix C for product information). To enable QuickTime support, you need to install the QuickTime extension in the Extensions folder in the System folder and then restart the Macintosh.

With QuickTime installed, you can play back a QuickTime movie on any 68020-based Macintosh that supports color QuickDraw—like the Mac II and Mac LC models—at least 4M of RAM, and System 6.07 or higher installed.

Figure 4.26 shows the QuickTime extension; figure 4.27 shows what a QuickTime movie looks like when selected in an application that supports QuickTime.

To view QuickTime movies you can use an application by Apple called MoviePlayer that comes with the QuickTime kit from Apple, or you can use another application that can play QuickTime movies.

Figure 4.26   The QuickTime extension file.

Figure 4.27   A QuickTime movie with playing controls.

TIP: The QuickTime extension adds support for movies; you also need an application that can play QuickTime movies. The extension cannot play movies by itself.

File Sharing

File Sharing is a System 7 feature that enables users on a network to share all or some of their disk files with other users on their network. System 6 users can see File Sharing volumes from System 7 computers, but they cannot share their own files without upgrading to System 7.

If you are sharing your own files using the File Sharing feature, it will take up more of your RAM (about 300K of RAM) and slow your Mac down while others are using your files.

Listed below are common questions and problems you may encounter when using File Sharing.

How do I share a folder or disk?

You can share folders and disks by first going to the Control Panels folder under the Apple menu and double-clicking on the Sharing Setup control panel. Click the Start button; sharing will take a moment to start. Then go to the Finder and highlight the folder or disk that you want to share and choose Sharing from the File menu. You will see a dialog box that allows you to enable sharing, as well as assign various levels of access to this shared volume.

How can I see what privileges I have assigned to a folder?

Select the folder and choose Sharing from the File menu (in the Finder).

How do I add Users to my Mac for file sharing purposes?

In the Control Panel folder is a control panel called Users & Groups. Double-click on this file and a window will open with two users: you and a Guest. Use the File menu to add new Users and Groups.

How do I add Users to Groups?

In the Users & Groups control panel, drag a user to a group name; the user becomes a member of that group. You can see who is a member of a group by double-clicking on the group icon.

How do I change User privileges?

In the Users & Groups control panel, double-click on the user icon to change a user's individual privileges.

How can I see who is using my shared files?

The File Sharing Monitor control panel shows you who is signed on to your Macintosh. The File Sharing Monitor is in the Control Panels folder in the System folder.

How can I disconnect a user?

Open the File Sharing Monitor, select the user, and click the Disconnect button.

How can I sign off a shared volume?

Drag the volume over the Trash until the Trash is highlighted and let go, or highlight the volume and press ⌘-Y. (Either way, the procedure is the same procedure you would use to eject a floppy disk.)

How do I log on to a File Sharing Mac ?

The way to log on to a network file server is identical to the way you log on to another Mac's File Sharing volumes: go to the Chooser and highlight the AppleShare icon. If you don't have the AppleShare file installed, you can install File Sharing software by using the System 7 system software installer. The AppleShare file is installed in the Extensions folder.

Logging on to a File Sharing Macintosh is the same as logging on to an AppleShare File Server, although File Sharing supports a maximum of 10 users logged on at one time.

How do I remove a User from a Group?

Double-click on the group icon; drag the user name into the Trash. You can delete both users and groups this way.

How do I delete a User or a Group?

Drag the User or Group name from the Users & Groups control panel into the Trash.

How do I turn File Sharing off?

Open the Sharing Setup control panel and click the Stop button. (This button says Start when File Sharing is turned off.)

If it is a folder or hard disk that is being shared, you do not need to turn File Sharing off to stop sharing the specific folder (or disk); just highlight the folder or disk and choose Sharing from the File menu to turn the specific folder's (or disk's) sharing off.

My disk cannot be ejected because it is being shared.

You cannot unmount (remove the disk image from the desktop) a removable drive (like a Bernoulli disk) while File Sharing is turned on if the disk was on the desktop when sharing started. You need to turn File Sharing off, eject the disk, and turn File Sharing back on again.

One or more volumes cannot be shared.

Removable drives cannot be shared after File Sharing has started. You must turn Sharing off in the Sharing Setup control panel; insert the disk; and then turn sharing back on.

The file server has closed down (or is closing down in X minutes).

The network file server has been shut down, or a Mac with a shared volume has turned off File Sharing.

If you see a warning that the file server or file sharing on a volume will be turned off in X number of minutes, your connection to a remote volume is about to be shut down. Make sure to finish up what you are doing.

Conclusion

Many of the problems Macintosh users face ultimately can be traced to problems with the System software; after all, the System software controls everything done on the computer!

A common source of trouble and confusion are fonts and sounds. The next chapter covers common problems (and their solutions) that fonts and sounds can cause.

I Need To Know!

Chapter 5

Fonts and Sounds

Fonts and sounds are similar in that they both generally must be installed in the System to work. Fonts deal with the display of alphanumeric characters, while System sounds are used primarily for the system beep sound.

A Macintosh font is a file stored in the System folder. Each font controls the display and printing of characters in a specific style. Fonts installed in the System show up in the Font menu in applications.

Three Types of Fonts

There are three types of fonts: bitmap or screen fonts, outline or printer fonts, and TrueType fonts (see figure 5.1).

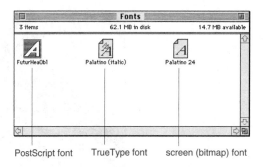

Figure 5.1 Three types of fonts: TrueType (outline font), screen, and Adobe PostScript outline font.

A *bitmap* (screen) font is used to represent the font on the screen; it will look jagged when printed.

An *outline* font is a description of the font which maps the character's outline. With an outline description of the font, printers can print the font in varying resolutions while keeping the shape of the font the same. Outline fonts (PostScript fonts are the most common example) are scalable fonts—they can display and print at different point sizes with equally good resolution. PostScript printers rely on the outline font when it comes time to actually print the font displayed on the screen. Adobe and other companies sell fonts that have a screen font and a matching outline font. Both must be installed to print the font as it appears on the screen.

Adobe Type Manager (ATM) is a System extension created by Adobe that governs the display of PostScript font onscreen (and on non-PostScript printers, like the StyleWriter). ATM is discussed in greater detail later in this chapter.

TrueType fonts are scalable fonts (like PostScript outline fonts) and is used for both screen display and printing. You only need the TrueType font installed in the System file and it can be used with any application that supports the use of TrueType fonts. You may see both the bitmapped font and the TrueType font installed in the System file; this enables documents created with earlier System versions to be viewed and printed.

Installing Fonts

How you install fonts depends on the System version you are using.

Installing Fonts under System 7.1

Under System 7.1, there is a Fonts folder in the System folder. It is a special folder, like the Apple Menu Items, Extensions, Control Panels, and Preferences folders. The Fonts folder stores all bitmapped, Adobe Type1, and TrueType fonts. Font suitcases also can be placed in this folder; up to 128 fonts or font suitcases can be opened by the System from this folder.

You can merge font suitcases by dropping one onto another. You can remove fonts from a suitcase by double-clicking on a suitcase to open it and dragging the fonts out. As fonts are added to the Fonts folder, if one font has the same font ID as a font already in the folder, the font ID conflict is resolved by the Finder. For more information on font ID conflicts, see "Symptoms of a Font ID Conflict" later in this chapter.

If you install fonts while an application is open, you must quit that application and open it again to use the newly installed fonts. You copy a font by dragging it over the System folder—the Finder knows if it needs to go in the Fonts folder—or you can place the font directly in the Fonts folder.

Installing Fonts under System 7.0 And 7.01

In System 7.0 and 7.01, fonts are stored in the System file. Double-click on the System file in the System folder to display the fonts that are currently installed (see figure 5.2).

You install fonts by either dragging the font(s) over the System folder, or dragging them over the System file. If you drag PostScript fonts (bitmap and outline) over the System folder, the Finder places the bitmap fonts in the System file and the outline fonts in the Extensions folder. (Outline fonts don't go in the System file). TrueType fonts are placed in the System file along with bitmap fonts.

Figure 5.2 The inside of the System file with fonts installed (System 7.0 and 7.01).

Font Management Utilities

You may want to install your fonts with a font management utility (such as MasterJuggler from ALSoft or Suitcase II from Fifth Generation Systems) that adds fonts to your system using font suitcases.

This is an alternative to installing your bitmap fonts in the System file or Fonts folder. Either of these utilities can open up font suitcases anywhere on your disk or on multiple disks.

These management utilities can control when fonts are loaded for use, as opposed to having all the fonts loaded at all times. They also can create sets of fonts for use at different times. Another advantage is that the utilities are faster at opening and closing fonts than the Finder is at adding and removing fonts from the System folder. Both utilities compress fonts so they take up less disk space.

Using Fonts with Printers

Choose the font type you will use based on the printer you are using. For non-PostScript printers like the StyleWriter and HP DeskWriter, you can use bitmap, TrueType, or ATM (Adobe Type Manager) with PostScript outline fonts. These printers do not use a special language to print documents (unlike PostScript printers) and will print a bitmapped representation of whatever font you choose.

PostScript printers can take advantage of the extensive collection of PostScript fonts that Adobe and other font makers have created. PostScript printers can also print out documents with TrueType fonts, since TrueType (like PostScript outline fonts) creates the font based on an outline description. PostScript and TrueType fonts must be downloaded to the printer when a document uses their fonts; this can make the print job longer. Most printers come with some standard fonts (like Helvetica and Times), stored in the printer's ROM; in these cases the font does not need to be downloaded to the printer.

How Fonts Are Accessed for Display and Printing

It helps to know how the system looks for the fonts assigned in an application—especially if you are not getting from the printer what you see onscreen, or if you are not seeing onscreen what you are selecting from the Font menu.

When the system needs to display a font onscreen, it begins by looking for a bitmap version of the font; then for a TrueType version of the font; and finally (if ATM is installed) for the PostScript Type 1 version of the font, which will be scaled by ATM.

If you are printing to a non-PostScript printer, the system looks for TrueType fonts in the System folder; then for a Type 1 font (if ATM is installed); and finally for a bitmap font that can be scaled (which may distort its appearance).

If you are printing to a PostScript printer, the system looks for a PostScript font in the printer's ROM (all Laser printers come with some built-in fonts in their ROM chip); then for a PostScript font already downloaded in the printer's memory (RAM); then for a PostScript font on the printer's hard disk (if one is attached); then for a PostScript font in the System Folder; then for a TrueType font in the System Folder; and finally for a screen font that can be scaled (which will distort its appearance).

Downloading Fonts to the Printer

When you print a document to the printer, any fonts not built into the printer's ROM that are used in the document are downloaded with the document to the printer and then discarded when the printer

DESPERATELY SEEKING SOLUTIONS

completes the job. To save time printing documents, download fonts to the printer beforehand.

You can download fonts to the printer using a font downloading utility such as Apple's LaserWriter Font Utility (which comes with the system software). Fonts you download before the print job are stored in the printer's memory (RAM) to be used when printing documents with those particular fonts. The fonts are lost when the printer is turned off.

If a hard disk is attached to the printer, fonts can be downloaded and stored on the hard disk. Those fonts are now available to the printer; they will not need to be downloaded again. You can use Apple's LaserWriter Font Utility to set up a hard disk that is attached to a printer, and to download fonts to the disk. The LaserWriter Font Utility tells you what printer fonts are available in the printer's ROM, hard disk, and RAM.

Adobe Type Manager (ATM)

Adobe Type Manager is a system extension that enables you to install only one bitmap font size for each font plus the PostScript font that matches it. It then draws all the other font sizes on the screen based on the one size you have installed. For example, you only need to install Garamond 12 (point size) and the Garamond PostScript fonts in order to display and print Garamond italic, bold, italic-bold, and regular Garamond, in any size.

ATM works with both PostScript and non-PostScript printers. ATM saves disk space because only one screen font is required to scale fonts to almost any size. It also improves the quality of printouts for non-PostScript printers and allows you to use PostScript fonts on non-PostScript printers. ATM works with all Type 1 PostScript fonts.

What Is a Type 1 Font?

Type 1 fonts are those fonts created according to Adobe's font "hinting" technology to optimize printing on low-resolution (low dots-per-inch) printers. At one time the technology was proprietary and used only by Adobe. Today, however, many font makers use the Type 1 technology for PostScript fonts.

How to Create a Font Suitcase

You can use the Font/DA Mover (version 4.1 if you are using System 7) to create a font suitcase; you can also use an existing suitcase to create a font suitcase. To create a font suitcase using the Font/DA Mover:

1. Open the Font/DA Mover, and click on the Open button on the right side of the dialog box (see figure 5.3).

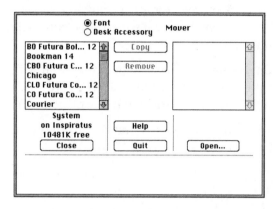

Figure 5.3 The Font/DA Mover with the System file open.

2. Click on the New button and name the new font suitcase, then click the Create button. Add at least one font to the suitcase before quitting the Font/DA Mover.

To make a font suitcase using System 7:

1. Make a copy of an existing font suitcase from the Fonts folder or the System file; rename it and the double-click on it to open it.

2. Drag the unneeded fonts from the suitcase to the Trash and then copy the ones you want to include by dragging them over the suitcase. You can also combine font suitcases by dragging one suitcase over another.

A Printout with the Jaggies

If your document is printing with fonts that have jagged or "staircased" edges, it could mean one of the following:

* You do not have the printer fonts installed properly or they are not available on your workstation or the printer. Check the printer's hard disk if there is one.

* The LaserWriter driver (or other printer driver) in your System folder may be damaged. Replace it with a good copy—throw the current one in the trash first.

* The font is damaged. Replace the printer font with a good copy. If the printer font resides on the printer's hard disk, replace the one on the hard disk by removing it and downloading the font again.

* There is a font ID conflict. To resolve it, see the next section in this chapter, "Symptoms of a Font ID Conflict."

CAUTION: Don't rename the font files, because the computer will not be able to recognize the fonts in order to send them to the printer.

Symptoms of a Font ID Conflict

Every font has an identifying ID number; however, you occasionally might have two different fonts with the same ID. In most cases, when you install the font with the Font/DA Mover or System 7, the font ID conflict is resolved on the fly. You also can resolve font conflicts with a utility such as Font Harmony, which comes with Suitcase II.

You may have a font ID conflict if you have one of the following problems:

* A document prints out fine on one Macintosh, but prints with the wrong typefaces on another Macintosh.

Possible solutions: bring the System folder with you when you print the document elsewhere, or make a custom suitcase with all the fonts needed to print the document (using the Font/DA Mover or System 7). Yet another option is to print a document as a PostScript file from the original computer with the System 7 Print dialog box.

✳ A font added to the System folder or a suitcase doesn't show up under the font menu. Does it show up after quitting and reopening the application?

✳ You select a font from the menu, but the screen representation of the font is not the font you selected.

System 6 Laser Prep File

Under System 6 use LaserPrep along with the LaserWriter driver to process print jobs. Under System 7, the Laser Prep file has been incorporated into the LaserWriter driver. If you use older software with System 7 and need the Laser Prep file, you can still find it on the Printing disk that comes with System 7 software install disks.

Sounds

Every Macintosh has a speaker to play sounds from the system software and applications that support sound. You can control the sound with the Sound control panel in the Control Panels folder in the System folder (see figure 5.4).

If you have an Apple microphone (or another sound digitizer) you can record sounds using the Sound control panel (System 7 only). Just click on the Add button and a dialog box will appear, ready to record your sound. When you are finished recording, you can save the sound as a sound resource and use it as a system alert sound (the "beep" sound).

If you double-click on the System file in System 7, you will see all sounds stored in there, such as the sound you choose for your system alert.

Figure 5.4   The Sound control panel.

TIP: You can mute all sounds coming from a Macintosh by plugging a "Walkman"-type stereo plug or a set of head-phones into the audio out port.

TIP: Suitcase II lets you open two or more sounds, from one or more disks.

TIP: Drag a sound out of a System 7 window (or the System file in the System folder) and it becomes a stand-alone sound file. Just double-click on the file to play the sound.

Conclusion

Problems with both fonts and sounds are usually resolved fairly simply; however, problems with applications and files are often much more complex. The next chapter deals with the headaches that applications and files can give users.

I Need To Know!

Chapter 6

Applications and Files

A wide range of problems occurs within specific applications. While these problems can be of almost any sort, there are some general techniques that can be applied to most application problems. Problems with files often can be traced to problems with the application that created the file; this chapter will provide techniques for solving problems with both files and applications.

Applications

There are many types of Macintosh applications, in categories ranging from word processors to video editing software, and all applications interact with the Macintosh hardware and system software. Application problems can be a result of a conflict with other software, the hardware, or faulty software development (often referred to as "bugs").

Application Memory Management

All applications use memory (RAM) while open. When you open an application, it takes up a designated portion of memory to run the program and to load information and documents for use. The RAM not used by the application is then available to other applications.

Under System 7, you can see and change the amount of RAM an application uses by highlighting the application in the Finder and choosing Get Info (⌘-I) from the File menu.

Figure 6.1 shows that Aldus PageMaker has a suggested memory partition of 1,500K; in figure 6.2 that memory partition is adjusted to 2,000K (2M). This is handy for troubleshooting yourself out of memory errors, opening a large number of documents, or working on a very large, complex document. You simply need to make sure that you have that much RAM available for the application.

Figure 6.1   PageMaker with 1,500K of allocated memory.

Figure 6.2   PageMaker with 2,000K of allocated memory.

You can see how much RAM an application is using and how much of that RAM is free by choosing "About This Macintosh…" under the Apple menu while in the Finder (when in MultiFinder and System 7). You also can turn Balloon help on under System 7 to see exactly how much of the application's memory is being used out of the total RAM allocated to the application.

Troubleshooting Application Problems

There might be a number of reasons why an open application is having problems. You may need to eliminate many possibilities before identifying the source of the problem. Before you do any testing, back up all your valuable data. Here are some troubleshooting suggestions for solving application problems.

I Can't Install the Application

* Disable virus-checking programs and other extensions (INITs) and control panels. Under System 7, hold down the Shift key while restarting the Macintosh to disable extensions. If you are running System 6, drag Control Panels and INITs out of the System folder and restart. See "Resolving Extension (INIT) and Control Panel Conflicts" in Chapter 4, "System Software."

* You may need to upgrade your system software or you may not have enough memory (RAM or disk space) to run the installation. Check the application manual for its system and memory requirements.

* Close all applications and try installing again. There may be a conflict with another open application.

* Use a disk repair utility to ensure the disk you are installing on is in good condition. The application or document may be residing on a damaged area of the disk. Make a backup of your data immediately!

* Try installing the application on another Macintosh. The application may not support the Macintosh you are using, or the installation disks may be damaged.

An Application Is Crashing or Freezing

* The application may be damaged; the disk the application is on may be damaged; or the application may be damaged from a previous problem. Delete the application and reinstall from a good copy. Also run a disk repair utility on the disk to ensure the disk is in good working order.

* The application may be missing files it needs to operate successfully. Reinstall the application.

* There is an extension (INIT) conflict. You will need to test and resolve the conflict. See "Resolving Extension (INIT) and Control Panel Conflicts," in Chapter 4, "System Software."

* There is an application conflict, and another application, while open, interferes with this application. It also may be a combination of several conflicts including desk accessories, extensions, or control panels. This is due to the way one or more of these applications were programmed, resulting in a software bug. See "Resolving Extension (INIT) and Control Panel Conflicts," in Chapter 4, "System Software."

* Many applications create Preferences files that are stored in the System folder. In System 7, they are stored in the Preferences folder within the System folder. An application's Preferences file may be damaged. Make a backup copy of the Preferences file and then delete the Preferences file for the application. The application will create a new file the next time it is opened.

✳ If there is a System bomb with an error ID (number) on the dialog, check the System Errors appendix to troubleshoot the error.

✳ Contact the application's customer service to find out if there are any known bugs or application limitations with your particular system setup.

✳ The application runs out of memory and cannot process the document; or your document may be damaged. See the file recovery section in Chapter 6, "Applications and Files," if your document is damaged.

✳ You may have more than one System folder installed. To check, use the Find File desk accessory or the Find option in System 7 in the Finder (press ⌘-F). Reduce multiple System and Finder files to one System folder and make sure the system software is running the correct version of critical system files.

✳ The system software is damaged. To test this theory, place a copy of the application on a startup floppy disk and restart the Macintosh with the startup disk. If the application does not crash again, the problem is with the system software. Reinstall the damaged system software.

✳ If you are running MultiFinder under System 6, turn off MultiFinder (Set Startup under the Special menu in the Finder) and restart the Macintosh. Open the application and see if the behavior goes away.

✳ Your document may be damaged. Open a different document and carry out the same steps to see if it is the document or the application. The catch here is if the application is damaged, it may corrupt other documents. Back up all your data before you do any testing.

Files

Applications save documents in their own proprietary file format; however, there are some universal file formats. These enable you to open a file with applications different from the one in which it was created, as well as to transfer files to other operating systems such as DOS, OS/2, and Unix operating systems.

Graphical File Formats

The file formats listed below are used by many Macintosh graphics, design, and layout packages.

MacPaint

The MacPaint format is a simple bitmap file format. Bitmap graphics are formed with dots. The file is limited in size to 8 by 10 inches, and images larger than this are cropped (and lost) when the file is saved in this format. The resolution is 72 dots per inch.

PICT

The PICT format supports a combination of a bitmap and object-oriented graphics (scalable graphics such as geometric shapes and text). The resolution can go higher than 72 dots per inch; the PICT format supports only eight colors.

PICT2

The PICT2 format is similar to the PICT format; however, it supports 256 colors as an 8-bit graphic, or 16.7 million colors as a 24-bit graphic. Save grayscale images in this format for best resolution.

PICS

The PICS format is an animation file format. This file format saves a series of PICT or PICT2 images that can be played as an animated sequence by applications that support this format.

TIFF

TIFF (Tagged Image File Format) supports black-and-white, grayscale, and color images. TIFF files offer high-resolution images, but the files can take up a lot of disk space. High-end graphics, scanner, and layout software support this format.

EPS or EPSF

EPSF (Encapsulated PostScript File) is a combination of the PostScript code description of a graphics file, together with a PICT or bitmap representation of the file as it will look when printed. This format is used by layout and PostScript-based software and is smaller than a TIFF file.

MooV

MooV is a movie file format for use with QuickTime; it supports video, sound, and animation in a file.

Text-based File Formats

Text files are files that have alphanumeric characters, line breaks, and paragraph breaks. They do not retain formatting, styles, or paragraph settings. A text file is essentially an ASCII file (see the next format). Other formats that save text information also save some of the formatting.

ASCII

ASCII (American Standard Code For Information Interchange) is a 7-bit character code providing 128 possible character combinations. The first 32 of the 128 are used for printing and data transfer.

Since the common character unit is one byte (for 256 possible combinations) and ASCII uses only 128 characters, the extra bit is used as a file transfer parity bit, or for special symbols. On the PC the extra bit is used for graphic and foreign language symbols. On the Macintosh the extra bit is used for added font characters such as the ¢, ©, and ™.

TIP: Macintosh and PC files have the first 127 characters in common. Characters 128 through 255 are different—which leads to some strange character representation when a Mac file is opened on a PC file. In order to see a Mac file clearly on a PC, and vice versa, save files in ASCII format. You lose all style and paragraph formatting when a file is saved in ASCII format, but you will be sure that the text will translate correctly.

TeachText

TeachText is a simple word processor that creates text files that support ASCII text and PICT files. TeachText files can be read by most Macintosh word processors.

MacWrite

MacWrite files once were very common because the first word processor for the Mac was Apple's MacWrite. MacWrite II is available today and many applications can save to and open this file format. MacWrite II files have a different format than the original MacWrite file format.

RTF

RTF (which stands for Rich Text Format) is a common text file format on both the PC and Macintosh. RTF supports both graphics and text formatting, and many word processing applications can open and save files in the RTF format.

Cross-Platform Application Files

Many applications are now available on both the PC and the Macintosh. Applications such as Lotus 1-2-3, Microsoft Excel, and Aldus PageMaker can open their respective files whether they were created on the PC or the Macintosh.

MacBinary Files

MacBinary is a file format used for transferring Macintosh files between computer operating systems and networks. The MacBinary format retains the integrity of the Mac file during transport. This format is used for transferring applications and other Macintosh files that have both data and resource information. Normally, a Mac user never actually sees a MacBinary file—it is used only to transfer files.

PostScript Files

You can save a file entirely in PostScript code (text) for downloading to a PostScript printer. Graphics applications can save in this format and the Macintosh Print dialog box can also save a file as a PostScript file by checking the "PostScript®File" radio button (see figure 6.3).

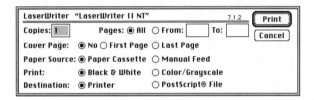

Figure 6.3 The System 7 Printer dialog box enables you to save a file in PostScript format; do so by checking the "PostScript®File" radio button.

Unlike the EPS file, this file has the PostScript text without the PICT representation of the image.

Mac and PC File Transfer

There are a variety of options for transferring files between Macintosh and PC computers (DOS, OS/2, or Windows). An easy way to transfer files between Macintosh and PC computers are floppy disks. Transfers work in both directions: from PC to Mac and from Mac to PC. Described below are a couple of options to accomplish a transfer of data between platforms:

Apple File Exchange (AFE)

You can use Apple File Exchange, an application that comes with the Macintosh system software, to both read and write to PC disks. You will need a SuperDrive (the high-density floppy disk drive) or another external floppy disk drive that can read PC-formatted disks. Current Macintosh models come with a SuperDrive. For more information see Chapter 11, "Storage Devices."

Here is a step-by-step way to transfer files between Mac and PC disks.

1. Double-click on Apple File Exchange (AFE) to open it. Your hard disk or floppy disk shows up on the left side of the dialog box. (You can change the drive showing on the left side by clicking on the Drive button.)

2. After you insert the PC disk, it shows up on the right side of the dialog box.

3. Highlight the file(s) that you want to copy from the PC disk to the Mac disk (see figure 6.4).

   Alternatively, you can highlight a Mac file that you want to copy to the PC disk.

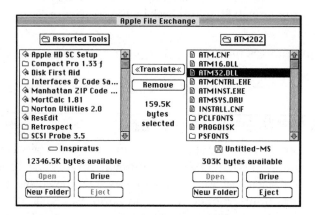

Figure 6.4   Using Apple File Exchange to copy files to and from PC disks.

4. You can choose a translation format (under the Mac to DOS or DOS to Mac menu) to use, or you can simply copy the file onto the Macintosh disk. Click on the Translate button and the file copies to the folder and disk you selected on the Macintosh disk.

5. When you quit AFE, the PC disk is automatically ejected from the disk drive.

You also can add other third-party translators to the AFE folder on your disk to have more translation options. For more information on where to buy third-party translators, see Appendix C, "Product Information."

Automatically Mounting PC Disks

Instead of using AFE every time you transfer a file, you can purchase a commercial product that automatically mounts your PC on the Macintosh desktop. AccessPC and DOS Mounter are two products that will mount PC disks under both Systems 6 and 7. Apple's PC Exchange also transfers files between Mac and PC disks. Apple's PC Exchange requires System 7.

Once the disk appears on the desktop, you can copy, save, and delete files from the disk like any Macintosh disk on the desktop.

Transferring Mac and PC Graphics Files

TIFF and EPS files produced on the PC and Mac differ somewhat because of the way the digital information is stored on the PC and Macintosh. As a result, transferring TIFF and EPS files between the Macintosh and PC is not seamless.

To ease this transfer, it is recommended that you use Mac-PC translation software, or save the graphic files in a format specifically intended for the destination platform. Adobe Photoshop is a Macintosh application that both accepts and saves graphics files in both Mac and PC graphic file formats.

Hidden Files

There are some files that are meant to be hidden from view on the Finder's desktop. For example, the Desktop file is not visible. You can view hidden files with some applications and utilities such as Apple File Exchange and DiskTop from CE Software Inc. Figure 6.5 shows a view of file information using DiskTop.

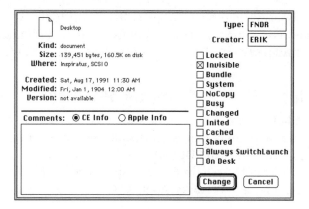

Figure 6.5 DiskTop view of file information.

 WARNING: If your files are disappearing (do not appear on the desktop) and you are running System 7.0 or 7.01, you need to either install Apple's Tune-Up or upgrade to System 7.1. You can find files using the Find option under the File menu in the Finder. Check your disk with a disk repair utility such as Disk First Aid and then restart with Tune-Up or the new system version installed. The Tune-Up will not restore your "lost" files, but it will prevent more files from becoming lost.

Another tool that Macintosh programmers use, called ResEdit, can be used (with caution!) to view invisible files. ResEdit enables you to view the file's information, including whether the file is invisible or not (the checkbox named "invisible" controls this attribute).

Figure 6.6 shows the ResEdit file information for the invisible Desktop file. This is accessible by choosing "Get File/Folder Info..." from the File menu.

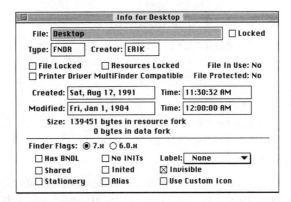

Figure 6.6 ResEdit's file information dialog with settings like the invisible checkbox for a file.

File First Aid

Here are some troubleshooting tips for situations that require file rescue and recovery. Although file recovery can be successful, your best defense is to back up your data frequently!

I Can't Delete a File

✳ The disk the file is on may be locked. If it is a network volume or a shared volume (File Sharing) you may not have enough privileges to delete the file.

✳ The file is locked. Select the file in the Finder and choose Get Info from the File menu (or press ⌘-I). If the Lock checkbox in the bottom left corner is checked, uncheck it and close the window.

✳ The file may be damaged or locked by the Finder. Use a file management utility such as DiskTop to unlock and delete the file.

✳ The file may be open in an application. Quit all applications and then try deleting the file again.

✳ Restart the Mac with a floppy startup disk and try deleting the file.

I Can't Open a Document

* If you are double-clicking the document in the Finder, try opening the application first and then opening the document from within the application.

* The application may be missing, or the disk that has the application may not be mounted. Use the Find command (found under the File menu in the Finder), or the Find File desk accessory, to find the application.

* Rebuild the Desktop file. Each document contains information that identifies it as being created by an application. If this information does not match information in the Desktop file where the information is stored, the Finder cannot open the document using the matching application.

* The application or the document may be damaged. Reinstall the application or recover a good copy of the file from a backup copy. If the file is damaged, try recovering the file with help from the next section, "Recovering Damaged Files."

* The document has been created with a different version of the application. Open the application first and then open the document from inside the application. If this doesn't open the document, contact the vendor technical support for this application—you may require a software upgrade.

Recovering Damaged Files

If a file is damaged and you cannot access it using the application the file was created with, here are some file recovery steps to take to recover all or part of the file data.

* Use a backup copy of the file. If you do not have a recent backup, or the backup file is damaged as well, try the following alternatives.

* Try opening the document with another application that may be able to import the document. Many applications can import graphics or text files from other applications.

✳ Use a utility that can view any file. One utility that can open most files and extract the parts of a damaged file is CanOpener 2 (see figure 6.7).

Figure 6.7 shows an Adobe Illustrator file, with both text and graphics. With CanOpener, even if you can't open the file, you can still recover the individual parts of each file and save them as either a PICT or a text file.

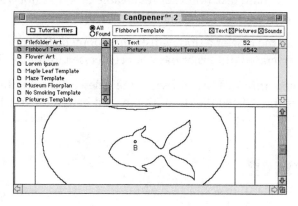

Figure 6.7 CanOpener can view the entire contents of a file and recover all or part of a file.

Recovering Deleted Files

You can recover a file that has been deleted in the trash. An erased or deleted file is one that has been placed in the Trash and the Trash has been emptied. Recovery utilities recover files that have been accidentally or mistakenly deleted.

TIP: You can recover a file placed in the Trash (if the Trash has not yet been emptied) by double-clicking on the Trash and dragging the file back to a disk or to the desktop.

The following utilities can assist you in recovering deleted files: Norton Utilities, Public Utilities, MacTools, Complete Undelete, and 911 Utilities.

File recovery and undelete utilities can recover files when:

* The space occupied by the deleted file has not been used (written over) by a new file.

* The hard disk (or other removable disk) has not been reformatted with a low-level formatting program.

* In the case of a floppy disk, the floppy disk has not been initialized or erased (that is, it has not been erased in the Finder).

For more information on recovering deleted files, see the sections on recovering deleted files from floppy and hard disks in Chapter 5.

Conclusion

Problems with files and applications can take on many different forms. This chapter has given you techniques that should be applicable to many general kinds of problems. Viruses pose a special breed of problem; the next chapter discusses techniques for preventing, recognizing, and eradicating virus infections.

I Need To Know!

Chapter 7

Viruses

A computer virus is a small program that attaches itself to files by way of software distribution, infected floppy disks, infected network file servers, and file sharing. Some viruses on the Macintosh do nothing more than create a nuisance, while others can cause erratic freezing and crashing, and destroy valuable data and applications.

Luckily, it is easy to protect your software against virus invasions with a virus program. There are a number of freeware, shareware, and commercial anti-virus programs to choose from, and there is one included with the disk in this book, called Disinfectant (see "About the Disk"). For more information on virus programs see Appendix C, "Product Information."

Protecting Your Macintosh from Viruses

There are two types of protection, and you should have both. One is a program that can seek out, find, and kill viruses in files already infected (eradication). The other is a system extension that is always watching for potential infection from inserted floppy disks and downloaded files (from file servers and modem lines).

Most virus programs offer both an eradication and a protection extension, including popular virus programs such as SAM (Symantec AntiVirus Utilities for Macintosh), Virex, GateKeeper, and Disinfectant.

TIP: Files that are locked in the Finder will not be infected by viruses because no changes can be made to a locked file. To lock a file, highlight the file in the Finder and choose "Get Info" (⌘ -I) from the File menu. Check the checkbox in the lower left corner and close the window.

TIP: Store a locked floppy disk that contains your virus eradication program so you can kill a virus if it has already infected your disks. Keep a clean, untouched copy of your virus program available to make copies from.

Diagnosing a Macintosh Virus Infection

Here are some Macintosh virus symptoms. For a more complete listing of actual viruses, see the Disinfectant Help Manual that comes as an electronic file with Disinfectant (on the disk with this book).

* The size of a file is growing wildly or is much larger than its normal size.
* Files are losing their icons, appearing as generic files.
* Several different applications are suffering system crashes and printing problems.
* Strange messages are appearing in dialog boxes.
* The mouse pointer behaves strangely and moves erratically.

✳ The system slows down, applications react slowly, and folders and files take much longer than usual to open.

 TIP: One common virus, called WDEF, infects the invisible Desktop file on any disk. It is spread by the sharing of disks and causes Macs running System 6 to crash. Macs running System 7 are immune to this virus. You can remove the WDEF virus from the Desktop file by rebuilding the Desktop, as well as by running a virus program.

Disinfecting Your Macintosh

If you know or think you have a virus on your Mac, here are tactics to eradicate the infection and protect your Mac from future viruses.

An Infected Floppy Disk

Install a virus protection extension on your Macintosh and a virus eradication program. Then insert the infected disk into the floppy drive and disinfect the disk with the eradication program.

An Infected Hard Disk

Lock a floppy disk with the virus eradication program on it. Also lock the anti-virus program (lock it in the Finder using "Get Info" from the File menu) on the locked floppy disk. Then insert the floppy in the infected Mac's disk drive and run the eradication program.

An Infected File Server

Bring the file server down and disinfect all the files on the server volumes. Then install a virus protection extension. You also can store a locked copy of the virus eradication program on a file server volume.

Conclusion

Viruses are usually easy to avoid; this is certainly a case where an ounce of prevention is worth a pound of cure. Make sure to update your virus protection software regularly, because new versions of the programs are released to counter new viruses.

This section has covered the problems you might have with your software. The next section will look at the problems that can be caused by hardware; specifically, the next chapter looks at the Macintosh CPU itself.

Part III

Hardware

I Need To Know!

Chapter 8

The Macintosh CPU

This chapter covers the Macintosh CPU itself—the basic unit. The back of the Mac, the inside of the Mac, memory, the startup procedure, and upgrading your CPU are all covered in this chapter. (Topics such as monitors, keyboards, power, and cables are covered in Chapter 9, "CPU Attachments.")

The Back Of The Macintosh

The back of the Macintosh (see figure 8.1) has multiple ports, each with an icon above it. Not all Macs have all the ports—the kinds of ports your Mac has depends on the Macintosh model. Almost all Macs have Modem, Printer, ADB, and SCSI ports.

Figure 8.1 The back of a Macintosh.

Port Icons

Here are the icons above the ports on a Mac, and what they represent.

SCSI Port

This diamond shape is above the *Small Computer System Interface* port, better known as the *SCSI* (pronounced "scuzzy") port. This the port where you connect SCSI hard disks and other SCSI devices such as scanners and CD-ROM drives. These ports can have several shapes depending on the type of pin connector.

Most Macintosh desktop models have a small 25-pin connector (25 pin holes), while many hard disks and other SCSI devices have a larger 50-pin SCSI connectors (called HDI-30). Some PowerBooks have a square SCSI adapter.

Modem Port

This port is the *modem* port, which is a serial port. This is a standard serial port with 8 pins (also called a DIN-8 connector). However, 128, 512, and Plus series Macs have 9-pin connectors (called DB-9 connectors). It can be used to connect a modem to the Macintosh, or other devices such as the StyleWriter and ImageWriter printers. Other uses for this port are when you connect file transfer cables to the Macintosh, and when the Macintosh does not have a separate microphone port.

Although this is similar to the Printer port, the Modem port does not support LocalTalk, which the printer port supports—even though both are 8-pin serial ports.

 ## Printer Port

This is the *Printer* port, also known as a serial port, with an 8-pin (also referred to as a DIN-8) connector just like the Modem port. You can connect a LocalTalk (network) cable, a printer cable, or a modem cable to this port.

 ## ADB Port

This is the *Apple Desktop Bus*, also known as the *ADB* port. It is a 4-pin connector used for connecting the keyboard, mouse, and other input devices, such as drawing tablets. Some Macs have two ADB ports; others have only one ADB port.

ADB devices can be daisy-chained, so if you have only one ADB port and two or more ADB devices to connect, you can connect them to each other in a chain. For example, the standard Apple keyboard has two ADB ports on it—one on the left and another on the right. One port connects the cable to the Macintosh, and the other port connects to the mouse.

 ## Video (or Monitor) Port

This is a *Video* (or *Monitor*) port for a cable connected to a monitor; it is a 15-pin connector. Some Macs have built-in video inside the Mac, so you don't need to install a video display (monitor) card in the Macintosh; you just connect the monitor to the Monitor port.

In some cases, you may need a video card even if your Mac does have built-in video support, for monitors that have special characteristics that require a video card.

 ## Audio Output Port

This is the *Audio Output* port. You can use this port to plug in headphones, powered speakers, and other audio plugs. When you connect an audio plug to this port, the Macintosh internal speaker is disabled and all sound is projected through the audio device plugged into the audio output port.

CAUTION: Don't plug a microphone into this port. The plugs are the same, but they don't work the same.

Audio Input Port

This is the *Audio Input* port. You can connect a microphone or other sound input device into this port to bring sound into the Macintosh. Many Macs come with this port and with a microphone to directly record sounds on the Macintosh. System 7 has a Sound control panel device (in the Control Panels folder in the System Folder) that can record sounds to sound files. Some other applications support sound recording as well.

CAUTION: Don't plug an audio output device (such as headphones or speakers) into this port. The plugs are the same, but they don't work the same. You might damage the Mac's circuitry!

Disk Drive Port

This is a *Disk Drive* port, which is used to connect floppy disk drives. Disk Drive ports have a 19-pin connector.

Telephone Jack

Some Macs (such as the PowerBooks) can have internal modems installed; Macs with internal modems have a telephone jack to connect a telephone line. The standard telephone cable with a jack (RJ-11 jack) that is used with your telephone at home can be inserted in this port.

Main Power Connector

This is usually a three-pronged *main power connector* port to connect a power cord to the Macintosh. Desktop Macs have another port to connect the monitor directly to the Macintosh, so when you turn on the Macintosh the monitor is powered on as well. You can leave the monitor power switch on all the time, and the monitor will only be powered on when the Macintosh is powered on.

 ## Power On/Off Switch

This is a *Power* or *On/Off* icon, which varies depending on the type of Macintosh you own. If you own a Macintosh that can be powered on from the keyboard, you might not use this button very often. On some Macs (such as the IIsi and IIci), the switch can be rotated to lock the power in the on position.

 ## Security Slot

This is a security slot for a lock and chain. You can protect the Macintosh from relocation or theft by inserting a narrow connector here; locks and steel cables can be attached to the connector. Security kits are available from authorized dealers and Apple.

Problems With Ports

There are some problems you can experience with these ports if you are not careful. Here are some problems you might experience, and possible solutions.

Forced Cable Connections

If a cable connector does not fit in a port, but is forced in by accident, this can damage the cable connector and the port. A damaged (broken or bent) pin on a connector will prevent a port from working.

Changing Connections With The Power On

Turn off all devices, as well as the Macintosh, before connecting and disconnecting cables from the ports. If the power is on while connecting and disconnecting cables, you risk damaging the connected devices and the Macintosh.

Testing The Ports

If you have more than one of the same port (such as Macs that have two ADB ports) then you can test the other port by connecting the cable to the other port to verify if the problem is just in one of the ports. If using the other port doesn't solve the problem, try testing a new cable. If that isn't the problem, try testing the setup on another Mac's port.

Make sure you have ruled out any problems with the cables and devices. Go through all the procedures for testing a device and the cables used to connect the device to the Macintosh. Check the firmness of the cable connections and the power cables as well.

Even if you have checked the cables, devices, and the Mac, the problem could be on the Macintosh logic board. The data travels from the cable through the port and on to the logic board. The problem could be a cable connection inside the Macintosh or a component directly on the logic board that is failing, and not the port that is failing.

If you feel industrious, you can test to see if a port is working by testing the voltage reading off of the port, using a voltmeter (from Radio Shack or an electronics store). For more information on the port pin assignments and voltages, refer to the manuals that came with your Macintosh.

Going Under The Macintosh Hood

There are a number of reasons why you might want or need to open the Macintosh case. For example, you may want to add a video card, upgrade the memory (RAM) on the logic board, clean the inside of the case and the logic board or add a larger internal hard drive to your Macintosh.

WARNING: Before you do any installation, upgrading or fixing, back up all your valuable data.

Opening The Mac Case Safely

Opening a Macintosh can be a daunting experience if you have never taken the lid off of a computer before. It is not that difficult, though, as long as you take precautions to avoid damaging the electronic circuitry and other hardware inside the Mac case, and avoid areas that might hurt you. Follow these steps to open up a Macintosh successfully.

WARNING: Modifying your Macintosh yourself while your Mac is under Apple's warranty voids the warranty (Apple's current warranty is one year and the Mac must be brought to an authorized Apple service provider). If you damage your computer while the Mac is open, the warranty will not cover the repair costs and Apple will void the warranty. So if you don't feel comfortable taking the risk, bring your Macintosh to an authorized Apple service provider.

* Shut down the Macintosh safely by choosing Shut Down from the Special menu in the Finder.

* Power down the Macintosh and all connected devices.

* Unplug the Mac from the wall or power strip, and disconnect all devices connected to the Mac.

* Move all food, liquids, and metal objects out of the area. Take off all metal jewelry. Prepare a working surface that cannot conduct electricity (a wood or paper surface). You can buy anti-static mats from computer and office suppliers. Avoid working on carpeted areas, and avoid wool, plastic and silk clothing.

* Reduce the possibility of damaging the circuitry in the Macintosh by eliminating static charges. Wear a wrist or grounding strap to dissipate static electricity. You can use a grounding strap to ground the Macintosh by attaching it to a ground. Touch the power supply inside the Macintosh when you first open the Mac case to dissipate static electricity.

* Handle circuit boards (logic and other boards that have wiring etched into the surface) and other components along the edges. Do not touch the face of the circuit boards, and do not touch high-voltage areas inside the Macintosh. High voltage areas include the video tubes (also called CRT for Cathode Ray Tube) inside the compact Macs (Mac Plus, SE and Classic), and components attached to the video tube by wires.

 WARNING: Be careful when opening up a compact Macintosh because the built-in monitor (video) holds electrical charge even after the Mac has been turned off. You can discharge any electricity on the video tube by using a discharge tool (CRT discharge tool) which connects the video tube to a grounded object. You can order a specially made tool from mail order houses and parts suppliers. See Appendix C, "Product Information."

Opening Compact Macs

Compact Macs have all the components within one case—the monitor is built with the rest of the computer in one case. These are the trickiest to open. Examples of compact Macs are the Mac Plus, SE, SE/30, Classic, and Classic II.

Tools To Use

To open the case of a compact Mac the following tools are recommended:

* A #15 Torx Screwdriver (with a long handle). Many hardware and electronics stores (such as Radio Shack) carry these, as do Mac mail order houses that supply PC tool kits.

✳ A Case Spreader (also referred to as a Mac Cracker). This is necessary if you don't want to blemish the outside case when separating the back of the case from the front of the case. You can do it without the spreader, but it takes a lot of patience.

✳ An anti-static Wrist Strap. The Mac's internal components can be damaged by static electrical discharge. If you do not have this, the metal chassis (metal frame inside the Mac) can be touched before touching other parts.

✳ Flat-Blade Screwdriver. This may be handy to pry the case open as well as pry other things inside the case. Use it with care!

Opening A Compact Macintosh Step-by-Step

Because compact Macs (Mac 128, 512, Plus, SE, or Classic) are somewhat challenging to open, here are the steps to follow when opening the case:

1. Take all necessary precautions as mentioned previously to reduce damage to your Mac and yourself. See the section entitled "Going Under The Macintosh Hood" before returning here.

2. Put the Macintosh on your work surface with the monitor face down.

3. Remove the screws. There are two screws near the ports (bottom) and two more in the handle on the top. Check for screws in other areas (like in the battery compartment) on the older Macs. Put the screws in a safe place so they will not be lost!

4. Remove the programmer's switch, if it has been installed. It will be on the left side of the Mac.

5. Spread the case open using the case spreader and the back of the case, lift it off and set it aside. Place the Macintosh face down (video to the floor), carefully so you don't scratch or damage the front of the tube.

6. Ground yourself as described above—either with a wrist strap or by touching the metal chassis (the metal frame inside the Mac).

7. Remove the Radio Frequency Shield, which looks like metal foil. (This prevents the Mac from transmitting radio interference to other electronic devices.)

8. To separate the logic board from other components, you will have to disconnect some cables (Remember or sketch out which cables are connected where so you can put them back when you close the case).

There are ribbon cables that connect the disk drive(s) to the logic board—disconnect them. There is a video cable connected from the logic board to the video analog board—disconnect it. There may be other cables that need to be disconnected, such as the speaker cable and cables connecting the internal hard drive or video card.

Opening Modular Macs

Opening a modular Macintosh is much easier. There are a few screws at most; they can be removed with a regular Philips screwdriver. The cover can then be lifted off the top of the case.

Opening The Macintosh Portable

The Macintosh Portable is simple to open. The cover can be removed by pressing the two release buttons on the back of the Portable.

Opening PowerBooks

The methods vary depending on the PowerBook model you own. Here are two examples: how to open the PowerBook 100, and how to open the 140 or 170.

For the PowerBook 100, the first step is to remove the battery from the PowerBook. Then, place the PowerBook upside down and remove the screws and rubber pads on the bottom of the case (near the screen hinge). The screws can be removed with a Philips screwdriver. Turn the PowerBook over again, release the monitor fastener, and open the case. You should now be able to lay the monitor down and remove the keyboard.

To open the PowerBook 140 or 170, remove the battery and turn the PowerBook face down. You will need a #10 and #8 Torx screwdriver to remove the screws on the back of the PowerBook and one screw under the modem port on the back panel. You can now lift and tilt the top section of the PowerBook at an angle to expose the inside of the PowerBook.

Memory

There are different types of memory on the Macintosh, and they all have different functions. The three main types are *RAM* (Random Access Memory), *ROM* (Read Only Memory) and *disk space*. Other types include *PRAM* (Parameter RAM), *virtual memory, Video RAM,* and *Parity RAM.*

Measuring Memory

Both the RAM and the disk space you have are measured in terms of bytes. Storage is commonly measured in kilobytes (thousands of bytes; abbreviated as K), megabytes (millions of bytes; abbreviated as M) and sometimes even gigabytes (billions of bytes; abbreviated as G).

One byte is essentially equal to one character, so 1,000 characters takes up approximately 1,000 bytes, or one kilobyte (1K). One kilobyte is actually equal to 1,024 characters, because the number of kilobytes is calculated in the base 2 system math system, as 2 to the tenth power (2^{10}). Table 8.1 diagrams the actual and approximated equivalences of kilobytes, megabytes, and gigabytes.

Table 8.1   File size equivalents and approximations

Abbreviation		Equivalent		Approximated as
1 kilobyte (1K)	=	1,024 bytes	≈	1,000 bytes
1 megabyte (1M)	=	1,048,576 bytes	≈	1,000,000 bytes
1 gigabyte (1G)	=	1,073,741,824 bytes	≈	1,000,000,000 bytes

As an example of memory measurement, look at the RAM in your Macintosh by selecting About This Macintosh (or About The Finder) from the Apple menu in the Finder (see figure 8.2).

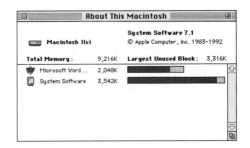

Figure 8.2 This Macintosh IIsi has 9M (which is 9,216K, which is 9,437,184 bytes) of RAM installed.

RAM (Random Access Memory)

RAM is temporary memory used to store information while the Macintosh is powered on. When the Mac is turned off, all information stored in RAM that has not been saved to a disk is lost (except for the Macintosh Portable and PowerBook 100).

What is stored in RAM? Application information, documents, and system information are all stored in RAM while you are using the Macintosh. When you save a document, the document information stored in RAM is copied to the disk (the disk you saved the file to).

What Is A SIMM?

Memory chips mounted on circuit boards are called *SIMM*s (Single In-Line Memory Module). A SIMM has several memory chips (see figure 8.3) which add up to a certain amount of RAM.

SIMM Sizes

SIMMs come in various sizes and speeds, and plug into special slots on the Macintosh logic board. Depending on the type of Macintosh, you can use SIMM sizes of 256K, 1M, 2M, 4M and 16M.

Figure 8.3   A SIMM (Single In-line Memory Module).

 CAUTION: SIMMs can be damaged by static electricity. Ground yourself (by touching something metal or by wearing an anti-static wrist band) before you touch the SIMM, and hold it along the edges to avoid touching the memory chips.

RAM Speeds

RAM typically comes in 150 ns (nanoseconds), 120 ns, 100 ns and 80 ns speeds. The number represents the time it takes the computer to retrieve information on the SIMM; the smaller the number the faster the speed, and faster Macs require faster RAM.

Adding faster RAM to a slow Mac will not hurt, but it will not speed up processes. However, you do want to have at least the minimum speed required for your Macintosh. If you do add faster RAM than necessary you can use the RAM later if you upgrade to a faster Macintosh.

Table 8.2 shows the types of SIMM speed and size the Macintosh models support.

Table 8.2 Macintosh SIMM Requirements

Macintosh	Hardwired RAM (in M)	SIMM Sizes[1]	Speed Required
Plus	0	256, 1	150 ns
SE	0	256, 1	150 ns
Classic	1	256, 1	150 ns
Classic II (Performa 200)	2	1, 2, 4	100 ns
Color Classic	4	1, 4	80 ns
SE/30	0	256, 1, 4, 16	120 ns
II	0	256, 1, 4, 16	120 ns
IIx	0	256, 1, 4, 16	120 ns
IIfx[2]	0	1, 4, 16	80 ns
IIcx	0	256, 1, 4, 16	120 ns
IIci	0	256, 1, 4, 16	80 ns
LC	2	1, 2, 4, 16	100 ns
LC II (Performa 400)	4	1, 2, 4, 16	100 ns
LC III[3]	4	1, 2, 4, 8, 16, 32	80 ns
IIsi	1	256, 1, 2, 4, 16	100 ns
IIvx (Performa 600)	4	256, 1, 2, 4, 16	80 ns
IIvi	4	256, 1, 4	80 ns
Centris 610[3]	4	4, 8, 16, 32	80 ns
Centris 650[3]	4	4, 8, 16, 32	80 ns
Quadra 700	4	1, 4, 16	80 ns
Quadra 900/950	0	1, 4, 16	80 ns
Quadra 800[3]	8	4, 8, 16, 32	80 ns
Portable[4]	1		100 ns

Macintosh	Hardwired RAM (in M)	SIMM Sizes[1]	Speed Required
PowerBook 100[5]	2		
PowerBook 140/145[5]	4		
PowerBook 160[5]	4		
PowerBook 170[5]	2		
PowerBook 180[5]	4		
PowerBook 165c[5]	4		
PowerBook Duo 210[5]	4		
PowerBook Duo 230[5]	4		

1 SIMM sizes are 256K, 1M, 2M, 4M, and 16M.

2 The Mac IIfx requires different SIMMs that have 64-pin connectors instead of the usual 30-pin connectors.

3 The Macintosh Centris 610 and 650, Macintosh LC III, and Macintosh Quadra 800 use 72-pin SIMMs.

4 Memory is added to the Portable with a special expansion card.

5 Memory is added to the PowerBooks with a special expansion card.

Installing And Upgrading RAM

The price of memory has decreased substantially in the last few years. There are some benefits to increasing the amount of RAM in your Macintosh:

✳ You can have more applications open at the same time under MultiFinder and System 7; you can use MultiFinder or System 7 if you aren't yet.

* You can increase the amount of RAM an application uses in order to improve the performance of the application. Many applications load information and a large portion (or all) of the document into RAM.

* You can upgrade to a more recent version of software that requires more RAM than your Mac currently has.

If you want to upgrade the RAM in your Macintosh, read "Going Under The Macintosh Hood" (earlier in this chapter) to take proper precautions when opening up your Macintosh.

It is also suggested that you purchase the SIMMs from a mail order house or dealer that offers installation help in the form of free illustrated instructions, a video tape, and/or free technical support when you purchase RAM from them.

Macintosh Plus and SE

When you are installing SIMMs on the Plus or SE, you will find the SIMMs must be placed in special combinations and you may need to cut some resistors (use a wire clipper to do so).

On the Plus and older SEs, there are two labeled resistors on the logic board. On the Plus they are R8 and R9; on the SE they are R35 and R36. They are labeled "256KB" and "1 ROW." Depending on the RAM configuration, you may need to cut one or both of the resistors (see table 8.3).

Table 8.3 RAM Configurations for the Mac Plus and SE (old)

Amount Of RAM	SIMMs	Resistor
512K	two 256K	keep both
1M	four 256K	keep both
2M	two 1M	keep 1 ROW, cut 256K
2.5M	two 1M and two 256K	cut both
4M	four 1M	cut both

TIP: If you cut the resistors, save them in case you down-grade the RAM and need to solder the resistors back on to the logic board.

On the newer SE, you do not need to cut the resistors because they are jumper resistors, so instead you can simply move or remove the jumper resistors, depending on the RAM configuration (see table 8.4).

Table 8.4 RAM Configuration for the Newer Macintosh SE

Amount Of RAM	SIMMs	Resistor
512K	two 256K	resistor stays on
1M	four 256K	resistor stays on
2M	two 1M	move resistor to 2 MB
2.5M	two 1M and two 256K	remove the resistor
4M	four 1M	remove the resistor

The logic board will have four slots, one for each SIMM. If you are installing 2M or less in the Plus or SE (old), fill slots 1 and 2. For 2M or less in the newer SE, fill slots 3 and 4.

Macintosh Classic

The Macintosh Classic has 1M of RAM soldered on the logic board. To upgrade the memory a special memory expansion card must be installed in the Classic. Apple sells a card which has 1M of memory on it and then two SIMM slots for SIMMs. Table 8.5 shows the possible RAM configurations for the Classic.

Table 8.5 Macintosh Classic RAM Configurations

Amount Of RAM	SIMMs	Jumper
1M	on-board RAM	
2M	expansion card with SIMM slots empty	set to SIMM NOT INSTALLED
2.5M	expansion card with two 256K SIMMs	set to SIMM INSTALLED
4M	expansion card with two 1M SIMMs	set to SIMM INSTALLED

You can expand a Macintosh Classic beyond 4M by installing a 68030-based accelerator card and Connectix Compact Virtual 3.0 (see Connectix in Appendix C, "Product Information"). The accelerator card can support 4M SIMMs, so you can bring the total RAM up to 16M.

Macintosh Classic II (and the Performa 200)

The Classic II has 2M of RAM soldered on the logic board and then you can add SIMMs to the two SIMM slots on the logic board. Figure 5.19 shows the possible configuration for the Classic II. The SIMM slots can support 1, 2 or 4M SIMMs.

TIP: 32-bit addressing must be turned on for the Macintosh to recognize more than 8M of memory. So, if you install 4M SIMMs, go to the Memory control panel and turn on 32-bit addressing (you will need to restart the Mac as well). For more information, see the section later in this chapter entitled "Installing More Than 8M Of RAM (32-Bit Addressing)."

Table 8.6 Classic II RAM Configurations

Amount Of RAM	SIMMs Added
2M	none
4M	two 1M
6M	two 2M
10M	two 4M

Macintosh Color Classic

The Macintosh Color Classic comes with 4M of RAM soldered on to the logic board and two empty SIMM slots. Table 8.7 shows the possible configurations for the Color Classic. The SIMM slots can support 1M or 4M SIMMs and must be either both full or empty.

Table 8.7 Color Classic RAM Configurations

Amount Of RAM	SIMMs Added
4M	none
6M	two 1M
10M	two 4M

Macintosh SE/30, II, IIx, IIcx

The Macintosh SE/30, II, IIx, and IIcx have 8 SIMM slots on the logic board, in two banks (called Bank A and Bank B) with four SIMM slots each. When upgrading these Macs, you must have each bank (A and B) either completely filled or empty with SIMMs, and Bank A must always be filled, while Bank B can be empty. Table 8.8 shows the RAM configurations for these Macs.

Table 8.8 Mac SE/30, II, IIx, IIcx RAM Configurations

Amount Of RAM	SIMMs Added	Bank Location
1M	four 256K SIMMs	A
2M	eight 256K SIMMs	A and B
4M	four 1M SIMMs	A
5M	four 1M SIMMs four 256K SIMMs	A B
8M	eight 1M SIMMs	A and B

 TIP: To recognize more than 8M of RAM (4M or 16M SIMMs) in the Mac SE/30, II, IIx, or IIcx, you will need System 7, and a file called MODE32. This is because these Macs do not support 32-bit addressing. For more information on 32-bit addressing, see section entitled "Installing More Than 8M Of RAM (32-Bit Addressing)" later in this chapter. Apple is planning on releasing an updated 32-Bit Enabler that will replace MODE32.

Macintosh IIci

The Macintosh IIci has two banks of SIMM slots (Bank A and B), with four slots in each bank for a total of 8 SIMM slots. How you install memory depends on whether you are using the built-in video feature in the IIci.

* If you are using the built-in video (also referred to as on-board video), where you do not use a separate card for the monitor, install the smaller size SIMMs (1M or less) in Bank A. Bank B gets the larger size SIMMs.

* If you are not using the built-in video feature (if you have installed a separate monitor card), then place the larger size SIMMs in Bank A.

WARNING: If you place 2M, 4M or 16M SIMMs in Bank A while using built-in video, this will slow down the IIci and possibly cause intermittent crashing. To avoid this, only install 1M or smaller SIMMs in Bank A when built-in video is being used. Table 8.9 shows RAM configurations for the IIci.

Table 8.9 RAM Configurations For Macintosh IIci

Amount Of RAM	SIMMs	Bank
1M	four 256K	A or B
2M	eight 256K	A and B
4M	four 1M	A or B
5M	four 256K	A
	four 1M	B
8M	eight 1M	A and B
17 M	four 256 K	A
	four 4 M	B
20 M	four 1 M	A
	four 4 M	B
32 M	eight 4 M	A and B

The IIci can also support optional *Parity RAM* , which is special RAM that supports memory error detection and is used mostly with government applications.

TIP: The IIci supports 32-bit addressing; however, if you are running System 6 you will need a software product called OPTIMA or MAXIMA from Connectix (see Appendix C, "Product Information").

Macintosh IIfx

The Mac IIfx has 8 SIMM slots, in two banks of four SIMM slots (Bank A and Bank B). The two banks are separated, with Bank A near the back of the Mac and Bank B near the CPU chip. The SIMM slots on the IIfx have 64 connectors instead of 30, so you need special SIMMs that support the 64-connector slot. Table 8.10 shows RAM configurations for the IIfx.

Table 8.10 Mac IIfx RAM Configurations

Amount Of RAM	SIMMs	Bank
4M	four 1M	A
8M	eight 1M	A and B
16M	four 4M	A
20M	four 4M	A
	four 1M	B
32M	eight 4M	A and B

TIP: The IIfx supports 32-bit addressing; however, if you are running System 6 you will need a software product called OPTIMA or MAXIMA from Connectix (see Appendix C, "Product Information").

Macintosh IIvx

The Macintosh IIvx has 4M of RAM soldered on the logic board, and four SIMM slots. The SIMM slots must be either all filled or all empty. Table 8.11 shows RAM configurations for the Macintosh IIvx.

Table 8.11 Macintosh IIvx RAM Configurations

Amount Of RAM	SIMMs Added
4M	none
5M	four 256K
8M	four 1M
20M	four 4M
36M	four 8M
68M	four 16M

Macintosh IIvi

The Macintosh IIvi has 4M of RAM soldered on the logic board, and four SIMM slots. The SIMM slots must be either all filled or all empty. Table 8.12 shows RAM configurations for the Macintosh IIvi.

Table 8.12 Macintosh IIvi RAM Configurations

Amount Of RAM	SIMMs Added
4M	none
5M	four 256K
8M	four 1M
20M	four 4M
36 M	four 8 M
68 M	four 16 M

DESPERATELY SEEKING SOLUTIONS

Macintosh Quadra 700

The Macintosh Quadra 700 has 4M of RAM soldered on the logic board, and four SIMM slots in a single bank. The Quadra 700 requires SIMMs with a 80 ns speed. Do not mix SIMMs of different speeds on the Quadra, and the bank should be full of SIMMs or entirely empty. Table 8.13 shows RAM configurations for the Quadra 700.

Table 8.13 Quadra 700 RAM Configurations

Amount Of RAM	SIMMs Added
4M	none
8M	four 1M
20M	four 4M
68M	four 16M

Quadra 900 and 950

The Quadra 900 and 950 have four banks (A, B, C and D) of SIMMs slots with four slots in each bank, for a total of 16 SIMM slots. These Quadras are highly expandable and can support up to 256M of RAM. Keep in mind that each bank must have SIMMs of the same size, and the larger SIMMs go in the lower banks first (Bank A). Table 8.14 shows some of the possible configurations for the Quadra 900 and 950.

Table 8.14 Some RAM Configurations For The Quadra 900 and 950

Amount Of RAM	SIMMs Added
4M	none
8M	four 1M
12M	eight 1M
16M	twelve 1M

Amount Of RAM	SIMMs Added
20M	four 4M
36M	eight 4M
68M	four 16M
132M	eight 16M

Quadra 800

The Quadra 800 has 8M of RAM soldered on the logic board, and four SIMM slots which must be all filled or all empty. Table 8.15 shows possible configurations for the Quadra 800.

Table 8.15 RAM Configurations For The Quadra 800

Amount Of RAM	SIMMs Added
8M	none
24M	four 4M
40M	four 8M
72M	four 16M
136M	four 32M

Macintosh IIsi

The Macintosh IIsi has 1M of RAM soldered on the logic board, and four SIMM slots in a bank. The bank must either be empty or entirely filled with SIMMs of the same size. Table 8.16 shows RAM configurations for the IIsi.

Table 8.16 Mac IIsi RAM Configuration

Amount Of RAM	SIMMs Added
1M	none
2M	four 256K
5M	four 1M
9M	four 2M
17M	four 4M
65M	four 16M

Mac LC

The Mac LC comes with 2M of RAM soldered on the logic board, and one bank with two SIMM slots. The bank must either be empty or full with SIMMs of the same size. Table 8.17 shows RAM configurations of the Mac LC.

Table 8.17 Mac LC RAM Configurations

Amount Of RAM	SIMMs Added
2M	none
4M	two 1M
10M	two 4M

Mac LC II (and the Performa 400)

The Mac LC II comes with 4M of RAM soldered on the logic board, and one bank with two SIMM slots. The SIMM slots must either be empty or full with SIMMs of the same size. Table 8.18 shows the RAM configuration of the Mac LC II.

Table 8.18 Mac LC II RAM Configurations

Amount Of RAM	SIMMs Added
4M	none
6M	two 1M
10M	two 4M

WARNING: Although you may have installed two 4M SIMMs thinking that this will give you a total of 12M of RAM (2 X 4M + 4M of on-board RAM), the Mac LC II can only address a maximum of 10M, even with 32-bit addressing turned on.

Macintosh LC III

The Macintosh LC III comes with 4M of RAM soldered on the logic board, and one 72-pin SIMM slot. Table 8.19 shows RAM configurations of the Mac LC III.

Table 8.19 Mac LC III RAM Configurations

Amount Of RAM	SIMM Added
4M	none
5M	one 1M
6M	one 2M
8M	one 4M
12M	one 8M
20M	one 16M
36M	one 32M

Macintosh Centris 610

The Macintosh Centris 610 has 4M of RAM soldered on to the logic board and two SIMM slots which should be all filled or all empty. Table 8.20 shows RAM configurations of the Centris 610.

Table 8.20 Centris 610 RAM Configurations

Amount Of RAM	SIMM Added
4M	none
12M	two 4M
20M	two 8M
36M	two 16M
68M	two 32M

CAUTION: Remember that 72-pin RAM SIMMs are required for this Macintosh.

Macintosh Centris 650

The Macintosh Centris 650 has 4M of RAM soldered onto the logic board and four SIMM slots which should be all filled or all empty. Table 8.21 shows RAM configurations of the Centris 650.

Table 8.21 Centris 610 RAM Configurations

Amount Of RAM	SIMM Added
4M	none
20M	four 4M
36M	four 8M

Amount Of RAM	SIMM Added
68M	four 16M
132M	four 32M

CAUTION: Remember that 72-pin RAM SIMMs are required for this Macintosh.

Macintosh Portable

The Mac Portable comes with 1M of RAM soldered on the logic board and uses a special expansion card. There are two Mac Portables: the original Portable and the backlit (screen) Portable.

The original Portable uses expensive *static RAM* (SRAM), and the backlit Portable (a later Portable model) uses less expensive *pseudo-static RAM*. The expansion card can support 1, 2, 3 or 4M of RAM, so you can have up to 5M of RAM installed in a Mac Portable.

PowerBook 100, 140,145, and 170

The PowerBook 100, 140, 145, and 170 come with 2M of RAM soldered on the logic board, and require a special expansion module to add more RAM. The expansion card can support 2, 4, or 6M of RAM, so you can have up to 8M of RAM in these PowerBooks.

PowerBook 160,180 and 165c

The PowerBook 160, 180, and 165c come with 4M of RAM soldered on the logic board, and require a special expansion module to add more RAM. The expansion card can support 4M for a total of 8M. Some third parties sell expansion cards that add up to 10M, for a total of 14M.

PowerBook Duo 210 and 230

The PowerBook 210 and 230 come with 4M of RAM soldered on the logic board, and require a special expansion module to add more RAM. The expansion card can support 4 or 8M, for a total of up to 12M. Some third parties sell expansion cards that add up to 20M, for a total of 24M.

RAM Problems

When the Macintosh is first powered on, it runs through a memory testing sequence, testing (among other things) the RAM installed on the Macintosh. The full restart, when the Mac is totally powered off, does a more comprehensive check than when you restart the Mac from the Special menu in the Finder.

If all goes well, you hear the normal chime or musical tone (see "The Macintosh Startup" in this chapter for more information). If something is wrong with the RAM, you may hear a chime unlike the one you normally hear when the Mac starts up successfully (the "death tones"), and/or you may see an unhappy Mac on the monitor.

Here is a checklist if you suspect a RAM problem:

* Make sure the RAM SIMMs are properly "seated" or securely in the SIMM slot. It is important that SIMMs snap in the slot all the way and the wires on the edge of the SIMM touch the connectors in the slot. Overheating has been known to "unseat" SIMMs.

* Make sure the SIMMs have been placed in the correct configuration. Some Macs require that certain sizes and types of SIMMs be placed in a certain way. Check for the proper SIMM speed, type, size, and bank location.

* You may have a defective SIMM. Install the SIMM(s) on another Mac to test them. (Contact the vendor if this is recently purchased RAM.) It may not be the SIMMs, but instead something else triggered an error chord during startup, or something is damaged elsewhere in the Macintosh.

* In theory, you should be able to mix SIMM brands; however, you may encounter problems mixing different brands of SIMMs. You cannot use IBM PS/2 SIMMs in a Macintosh, but some PC-based SIMMs have been known to work in Macs.

* You cannot exchange memory expansion cards between the PowerBook 100 or Portable and other PowerBooks.

* If your Macintosh is crashing at startup as well as during use, you could have a RAM problem. Even though your system may have passed the Macintosh startup self-test, you may still be experiencing a RAM problem. RAM problems can show up after your Macintosh has been on for a while. For example, a SIMM's speed is normal when cool and then slows down after warming up. All SIMMs do this to a certain extent, but you may have a SIMM with a lower threshold. You must replace the SIMM to fix this problem.

Installing More Than 8M Of RAM (32-Bit Addressing)

If you are installing more than 8M of RAM on your Macintosh you will need to know about the limitations of your Mac and the system software version you are using. For the Macintosh system to recognize memory beyond the 8M of RAM installed, the system software and the Macintosh must support *32-bit addressing*.

Your Macintosh must also support 32-bit addressing, and not all Macs do so. Macs that use a 68000 CPU chip (such as the Mac Plus, SE and the Classic) do not support 32-bit addressing. If you are using a Mac (and System 7) that does not support 32-bit addressing, you can only access up to 8M of RAM.

Some Macintoshes need a system extension (INIT), called *MODE32*, to support 32-bit addressing. The Macintosh SE/30, II, IIx, and IIcx need MODE32 to recognize more than 8M of RAM with System 7 installed. MODE32 is free and can be obtained from Connectix, Apple, or online services and user groups. See Appendix C, "Product Information." Apple is planning on releasing a 32-Bit Enabler which will replace MODE32.

To turn on 32-bit addressing, go to the Memory control panel in the Control Panels folder in the System Folder. Turn the 32-bit addressing on and restart the Macintosh. Figure 8.4 shows the Memory control panel window.

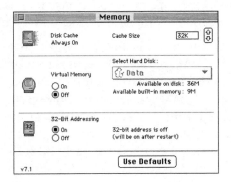

Figure 8.4   32-bit addressing in the Memory control panel.

TIP: The 32-bit addressing section does not appear in the Memory control panel if the Macintosh cannot support 32-bit addressing, even with MODE32.

WARNING: Applications must be 32-bit compatible ("32-bit clean") to work well when 32-bit addressing is turned on. If an application is not 32-bit clean it will crash; you will have to turn 32-bit addressing off to use the application.

TIP: Connectix sells software to help work around the limitations of 32-bit addressing. For more information, see Appendix C, "Product Information."

Virtual Memory

Virtual memory is a feature, available in System 7, which allows you to take some of your hard disk space and use it as RAM. Only certain Macs can support this feature. Macs that have a 68030 or 68040 CPU can support virtual memory, but Macs with a 68000 CPU cannot (such as the Mac Plus, SE, Portable, Classic, and the PowerBook 100).

The Macintosh II has a 68020 CPU, so to support virtual memory, a *PMMU* (paged memory management unit) must be added to the Mac II. This takes the form of a Motorola 68851 PMMU chip added to the logic board. The Macintosh LC cannot support a PMMU chip, so to support virtual memory it needs a 68030- or 68040-based accelerator card installed.

To turn on virtual memory in System 7, choose the Memory control panel in the Control Panels folder. Figure 8.5 shows the control panel window.

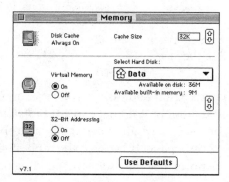

Figure 8.5 Virtual memory settings in the Memory control panel.

You can select which hard disk to use for virtual memory and the Memory control panel will set the amount of virtual memory. The Memory control shows you the amount of RAM you have installed in the Mac and the amount of hard disk space available on the currently selected disk (shown on the pop-up menu). Click on the pop-up menu to change the disk used for virtual memory.

The Memory control panel automatically sets aside the same amount of virtual memory as there is RAM installed on the Mac (so the total memory is equal to twice the size of the physical RAM in your Mac). For example, if your Mac has 9M of RAM installed and you turn on virtual memory, it will automatically set the total memory to 18M. Figure 8.6 shows this example in the Memory control panel.

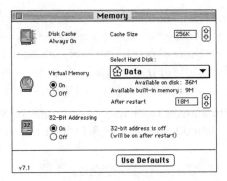

Figure 8.6 Virtual memory automatically sets the setting to twice the amount of RAM installed in the Mac.

If your Mac supports 32-bit addressing, you can turn on 32-bit addressing and increase the amount of RAM beyond 14M total, up to 1 gigabyte (1,000M)! It is, however, recommended that you keep the assigned setting in the Memory control panel because as the ratio of virtual to physical RAM increases, performance may suffer, depending on the applications that are running.

The virtual memory feature sets up a memory file (also referred to as a swap file or VM Storage), which is invisible. You can see the file if you use a utility which can view invisible files on the desktop. Figure 8.7 shows DiskTop (a file management utility) with the invisible virtual memory file, called VM Storage, on the hard disk.

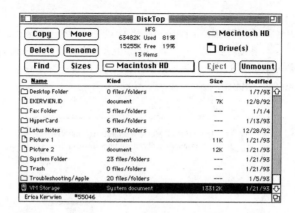

Figure 8.7 DiskTop showing the virtual memory file, called VM Storage, on the hard disk.

Virtual Memory Considerations And Problems

Some hard disks have older device drivers installed that may not be compatible with System 7's virtual memory feature. If this is the case, you need to upgrade the driver using the latest version of the hard drive's driver utility, or obtain a utility that will upgrade the drive with a System 7-compatible device driver.

If you own an Apple hard drive, you can update the hard disk driver for use with virtual memory (and System 7) by using Apple HD SC Setup utility that comes with the Macintosh system software. For more information, see Chapter 10, "Storage Devices."

Obviously, virtual memory has the advantage of giving you much more RAM to work with. There are two drawbacks to using virtual memory. Virtual memory is much slower than regular RAM, and it can take up valuable hard disk space if you are tight on space. If you have enough hard disk space, the only real issue is the performance—which can be very slow depending on the type of application you are using and how much real RAM you have installed.

CAUTION: Virtual memory will run down the battery in PowerBooks quickly because the disk is always spinning, so avoid using virtual memory on PowerBooks when running on battery power (see figure 8.8).

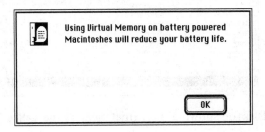

Figure 8.8 Virtual memory reduces the battery life of PowerBook batteries.

To check how much virtual memory is being used and see the largest unused block of memory (combined RAM and virtual memory), choose About This Macintosh from the Apple menu in the Finder (see figure 8.9).

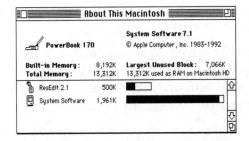

Figure 8.9 The combined memory (virtual and RAM) in the About This Macintosh window.

Checklist To Optimize Virtual Memory

Here is a checklist that will help you optimize your use of virtual memory:

* Do not use virtual memory to increase your RAM by more than 100 percent—if you have 8M of installed RAM, only use 8M of virtual memory, for a total of 16M of RAM.

* Set up virtual memory on a drive or partition that is not frequently accessed. This way the disk will not be reading and writing information on the disk, and working with the virtual memory file at the same time.

* Defragment your files (including the virtual memory file) to improve your hard disk access time (use a file utility for defragmentation). File fragmentation can slow your Macintosh's overall performance and increase wear on the drive.

* Some applications are not compatible with virtual memory.

TIP: You cannot use Virtual Memory on ejectable media (such as a Bernoulli disk) and the Memory control panel will not let you select a removable disk.

PRAM

PRAM (parameter RAM) is a separate section of memory on every Macintosh used to store some control panel settings and the time and date. The PRAM is maintained (even when the Macintosh is powered off) by a battery.

TIP: If your Macintosh is not holding the date, time and settings, the battery could be running down, or the information stored in the PRAM may be scrambled. To test this, you can "zap" (reset) the PRAM.

To zap the PRAM under System 7, restart the Macintosh and hold down the ⌘-Option-P-R keys. Press this key combination before you get to the "Welcome to Macintosh" screen.

Under System 6, while holding down the Shift, ⌘, and Option keys, open the Control Panel from the Apple menu. Click on yes to the dialog box asking if you want to zero the parameter RAM, and restart the Macintosh.

If you own a Mac128K, 512K, 512Ke, or Plus, zap the PRAM by unplugging the Macintosh and removing the battery for several minutes.

TIP: Zapping the PRAM does not change the time and date because the date and time are read from the PRAM before it is zapped, and then written back in afterwards.

Disk Cache

A disk cache is an adjustable setting which uses a part of RAM to store information most recently read from or written to a Macintosh volume (such as a hard disk). The disk cache is used to speed up retrieval of frequently accessed information.

Under System 6, you can turn the disk cache off (in the General control panel), or turn it on and increase the amount of RAM reserved for the cache. Under System 7, the disk cache is set in the Memory control panel and the amount of RAM reserved for the disk cache depends on the amount of RAM in your Macintosh—with the default set to 32K of cache for every 1M of RAM installed in the Macintosh. Figure 8.10 shows the System 7 Memory control panel; the first setting is the disk cache.

TIP: The Macintosh IIci can accept additional RAM cache, in the form of a cache card, to store information in special RAM for improved performance. The memory cache does not add to the RAM installed; however, it can make a substantial difference in computing performance when working with applications and documents. Apple, Daystar, and other third parties sell a RAM cache card that can be added to the Mac IIci logic board.

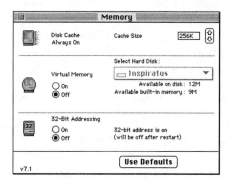

Figure 8.10   The disk cache, controlled from the Memory control panel, is always on under System 7.

 TIP: The Macintosh IIfx has 64K of built-in cache memory.

Video RAM

Many newer Macs support video RAM, which is special RAM installed for faster video refresh speeds and support for larger monitors.

Macs that can support video RAM include the Macintosh LC, LC II, IIvx, Quadras, and Duo docks.

RAM Disk

RAM Disk

With some Macs, such as the PowerBooks and the Quadras, you can create a *RAM disk*. A RAM disk is a portion of RAM that you can set aside to be used as if it were a disk; it appears on the desktop in the Finder just like a hard disk or floppy. You can store files on the RAM disk, and launch them from the RAM disk, for faster access.

A RAM disk speeds up application and document processing because the information is easier to access in RAM than from a hard disk. This means using an application and saving files is faster than if the information were retrieved from a real disk.

Macs that support the RAM disk include the Macintosh Quadras, PowerBooks, Portable, and IIvx.

The disadvantage of using a RAM disk is that, in most cases, the disk is lost when the Mac is shut down (just like other information in RAM). All the information on the disk is lost. The Macintosh PowerBooks' RAM disk is more stable. If you choose Sleep, Restart, press the reset button, or press the power button to wake up the PowerBook, the RAM disk *will* retain the information. Only the Portable and the PowerBook 100, however, do not lose RAM disk information when the Mac is shut down.

 TIP: Connectix sells a product called MAXIMA; the MAXIMA RAM disk survives after a crash or system restart (but not a shutdown).

To set up a RAM disk, choose the Memory control panel from the Control Panels folder in the System Folder. Figure 8.11 shows the RAM disk settings in the control panel window.

The slider sets the amount of RAM set aside for the RAM disk. Memory set aside for a RAM disk cannot be used to open applications, so be practical in setting this size. You should have enough memory to launch applications after you have assigned a RAM disk size.

The calculation below shows that this PowerBook is using less than half of the RAM available for the RAM disk—2M of RAM. The PowerBook has a total of 8M, 2M of which were used to load the system software. This means there will be 4M left over for applications and documents to open in regular RAM space.

2M of RAM = system software
2M of RAM = RAM disk
+   4M of RAM = application and document RAM

8M of RAM = Total RAM

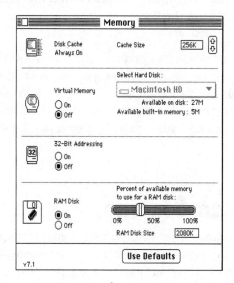

Figure 8.11   RAM disk settings in the Memory control panel.

RAM Drive

A *RAM drive* is a device that connects to the Mac just like a hard drive (through the SCSI port or into a NuBus slot), and can contain hundreds of megabytes (which is a lot of RAM!) to be used as disk storage. A RAM drive is much faster than a regular hard disk.

Just like other RAM, though, if your power fails, you will have lost the data stored in the RAM drive. So make sure you have adequate power supply backup, like a UPS (Uninterruptable Power Supply) to protect you from sudden power outages and surges.

ROMs

The *ROM* (Read Only Memory) is a chip on the Macintosh logic board that holds part of the Macintosh operating system. Since it is read-only memory, it cannot be erased or lost. This operating system information is essential for your Macintosh to operate, and the Mac relies on both the system information in the ROM as well as the System Folder on the startup disk.

The ROM in your Macintosh plays a part in your RAM memory configuration as well. For example, your ROM must support 32-bit addressing for your Macintosh to take advantage of 32-bit features such as virtual memory and installed RAM beyond 8M. (MODE 32, discussed earlier, is an extension that can add this capability if your ROM doesn't support 32-bit addressing.)

The Macintosh Startup

Every time you turn on your Macintosh, it goes through a sequence of events to test hardware and load software into memory before it arrives at the Finder desktop. If you are experiencing problems at Macintosh startup time, refer to this section and Chapter 13, "Symptoms and Solutions," to troubleshoot startup problems.

The normal (healthy startup) sequence of events goes like this:

1. You power on the Macintosh.

2. The Macintosh self-test begins by initializing and checking logic board components such as the CPU, ROM, and RAM.

3. The Macintosh operating system sequence begins by searching for a Startup disk. See below for the exact order in which it searches.

4. Once the Macintosh has found the startup disk, it searches for other SCSI devices to be mounted on the desktop.

5. The "Welcome To Macintosh" screen with the happy Macintosh appears.

6. Extensions, control panels and other startup files are loaded into RAM.

7. The Macintosh Finder is launched and the desktop appears.

The Startup Sequence Details

1. Power Up

The power is turned on and the power supply sets a voltage level for the Macintosh. The voltage level is important for the logic board electrical circuits.

If you don't hear a beep and the screen remains dark, you have a power problem. Check the power outlets, power cables, cable connections on the Macintosh and test all of these areas to confirm that the problem is not in the Mac's power supply.

2. Logic Board Testing

The Macintosh runs through self-testing (diagnostics) to check that all hardware components on the logic board are working. When all diagnostic testing is successful you hear the short, friendly chord; the Mac then continues on to look for a startup disk.

When the diagnostic sequence fails, another series of musical tones is played after the normal startup chord. Most Macintosh models have different series of tones to identify different problem areas on the logic board, such as the RAM, ROM, the SCSI chip, the PMMU chip, and the CPU. (The Mac Plus and SE do not have these error tones.) Although it is not easy to diagnose what the problem is by hearing the tones, here are the possible meanings of error tones:

* A short, harsh series of tones is played when the problem is on the logic board. This means the problem is a component on the logic board, or of the SIMMs on the board.

* A long medium-pitched series of tones, or a medium- and then high-pitched series of tones, is played when there is a problem with the SIMMs on the logic board.

＊ Four tones, from low to high, are played when there is a problem with the video hardware.

TIP: To hear the exact chords, a program called the "Diagnostic Sound Sampler" can be found on Apple's online service, AppleLink (see Chapter 14, "Technical Resources" for more on the AppleLink online service).

The Macs (except for the Mac Plus and SE) may sound the failure chord and display a sad Mac face with a code number. Quite often you can tell from the error codes whether the problem is hardware or software. If you have a software problem, the Mac displays a hexadecimal number with an F in the last digit on the top row; a Mac Plus (and earlier Macs) display a hexadecimal number with an F in the second digit location. Examples of the sad Mac icon are shown below. The error code line with the X's will show the point at which the error occurred, or Y's in the newer Mac error codes.

Error codes on a Mac Plus look like this.

0F0003

Error codes on a Mac SE and II family look like this.

0000000F
00000003

Otherwise, the problem is with the Mac hardware. Most hardware problems are on the logic board; however, sometimes the problem lies with a cable, video card, or SCSI device.

At startup, video (monitor) errors are usually accompanied by an error chord and a gray or dark monitor screen. High-resolution color monitors may have a purple haze over the screen.

Test video problems by checking the screen brightness setting, video cables and cable connections, the video card, and the slot the video card is in. If you have built-in video, test the monitor with another Macintosh or test another monitor on the problematic Macintosh.

Here is a checklist for troubleshooting the sad Mac icon:

* The startup disk is damaged. Restart the Mac with a floppy startup disk. If the Mac starts up successfully, repair the damaged startup disk with a third party disk utility or the disk utility that came with the bad disk.

* Power down the Mac and detach all external peripherals. Restart the Mac from a floppy startup disk.

If the Mac does not start up successfully from the floppy disk, there is a problem with the Macintosh hardware.

If the Mac does start up successfully from the floppy disk, there is a problem with one of the peripherals. Test each peripheral individually until the problem appears. Check SCSI cables, ID conflicts, and termination.

If you have recently added hardware such as SIMMs or a video card to the Macintosh logic board, remove the hardware and restart the Mac. The hardware may be damaged or installed improperly.

3. The Search For The Startup Disk

During the Macintosh startup process, the Macintosh looks for a startup disk with the "blessed" System folder, checking drives in this order:

* The first internal floppy drive. On a Macintosh II, IIx, and IIfx this drive is on the right side in the front of the Mac. On a Mac SE it is the lower drive.

* The second internal floppy drive or an external floppy drive. On a Macintosh II, IIx, and IIfx this drive is on the left side. On a Mac SE it is the upper drive.

* An external floppy drive on a dual-floppy Mac SE.

* The Startup device selected from the Startup Disk control panel.

* SCSI devices, starting at SCSI ID 6 and going down to SCSI ID 0.

* NuBus startup devices in the Macintosh II.

If the startup disk cannot be found or accessed, a blinking "?" icon or an "X" icon will be displayed.

 This can be either a hardware or software error. There could be a disk that does in fact have the proper system files; however, the disk itself may be causing the problems, or the system files may be incomplete or damaged.

Here is a checklist for troubleshooting the blinking question mark icon:

* Check the attached SCSI devices for proper termination, cabling and ID assignment.

* The system software might be damaged, or missing the System or Finder files. Reinstall the system software. You may need to delete the System and Finder file before reinstalling. See Chapter 4, "System Software."

* The startup information on the startup disk is damaged. Restart the Mac with a startup floppy disk and repair the disk with a disk utility such as Disk First Aid or Norton Utilities.

* The parameter RAM (PRAM) information has been scrambled and must be zapped. To zap the PRAM under System 7, restart the Macintosh and hold down the ⌘-Option-P-R keys. Press this key combination before you get to the "Welcome to Macintosh" screen.

  Under System 6, while holding down the Shift, ⌘, Option keys, open the Control Panel from the Apple menu. Click on yes to the dialog box asking if you want to zero parameter RAM and restart the Macintosh.

 Here is a checklist for troubleshooting the "Blinking X" icon:

* The system software on the startup disk is damaged, or it is missing the Finder or System file. Reinstall the system software. You may need to delete the System and Finder file before reinstalling. See Chapter 4, "System Software."

✳ The disk is damaged. The startup-disk boot blocks are damaged. Use a disk utility to repair the disk.

4. External SCSI Device Search

5. "Welcome To Macintosh" With the Happy Macintosh

6. Loading Extensions and Control Panels

7. Finder Is Launched and Desktop Appears

Upgrading To A More Powerful Macintosh

If you bought a Macintosh that you are now outgrowing due to speed, color, or other requirements, instead of buying a whole new computer consider upgrading the Mac you own. Table 8.22 shows upgrade paths for some Macintosh models. Apple offers upgrades through authorized dealers, so find a dealer near you. For more information on these upgrades, contact an authorized Apple dealer for upgrade information (see Chapter 14, "Technical Resources").

Table 8.22   Macintosh Upgrades

The Macintosh	Can be upgraded to a...	By buying a...
Classic	Classic II	Classic II logic board
LC	LC II	LC II logic board
LC II	LC III	LC III logic board
LC	LC III	LC III logic board
II	IIfx	IIfx logic board

continues

Table 8.22   Continued

The Macintosh	Can be upgraded to a...	By buying a...
IIx	IIfx	IIfx logic board
IIcx	IIci	IIci logic board
IIcx	Quadra 700	Quadra 700 logic board and case
IIvx	Centris 650	Centris 650 logic board
IIci	Quadra 700	Quadra 700 logic board and case
Quadra 900	Quadra 950	Quadra 950 logic board

Conclusion

Many problems can be traced back to the Macintosh CPU itself; however, several common problems are caused by other elements of the computer system. The next chapter covers a wide range of the basic components that connect to the Macintosh, including the mouse, keyboards, monitors, and power cables.

I Need To Know!

Chapter 9

CPU Attachments

The Macintosh CPU isn't self-sufficient; different devices and cables must be connected to it before it will work. This chapter covers them, including power sources and cables, monitors, keyboards, and mice.

Cables

Cables are used to connect all kinds of things to your Macintosh; they can be damaged by accident or improper care. Hardware problems are often linked to cable quality, damage, and setup.

Possible Problems with Cables

* Cable length. Cables do not work well when the cable length exceeds the recommended length for the type of cable connection. There are cable length limitations for network cabling, SCSI cabling, and ADB device cabling.

* Improper shielding. Shielded cables, in general, are higher quality cables because they reduce data transfer errors. A shielded cable reduces electrical interference that can cause data transfer errors along cable highways.

* Damage. Cables can be damaged in several ways.

How Cables Are Damaged

Cables and their connectors can be damaged in the following ways:

* During a power surge

* When cramped, knotted, or not fully extended

* When forced into connectors the wrong way or into the wrong connector

* By normal wear and tear

* When stepped on, nailed through, or stuck under heavy equipment

* When not properly shielded

Power

Every Macintosh has a power supply to deliver and maintain the required operating voltage. The power supply takes alternating current (AC) and converts it to direct current (DC), which the computer circuits require. The Mac circuitry is very sensitive to power fluctuations (as is all computer circuitry), so it is important that the power supply keeps the electrical current at a steady flow.

How To Prevent Damage from Power Problems

Chapter 2, "Macintosh Maintenance," talks about how to protect your Macintosh from power problems. Connecting the Mac and devices to a surge protector is one simple way to protect your computer equipment from power brownouts, blackouts, and surges.

Most devices have a *fuse* in them to prevent electrical current surges from damaging the device. If a device no longer powers on at all, check the fuse; it might have blown. You can replace most device fuses by purchasing a new fuse at a hardware or electronics store. Check the manual that came with the device to find out what fuse is required and how to replace the fuse. Make sure you replace the fuse with a fuse of the required rating, which is measured in amps.

What Causes Power Problems?

* Overloading a surge protector or electrical wall outlet

* A lack of proper grounding on the power cable, or a damaged power cable

* Disconnecting cables and devices while the power is on

Here are some troubleshooting tips for power problems you may encounter:

My Mac doesn't always power on when I press the power switch.

* Your Macintosh battery may be weak. See the section in this later in this chapter, entitled "The Macintosh Battery And PRAM."

* Your wall outlet or surge protector may be overloaded. Disconnect some devices and turn the Mac on again. Turn on just the Macintosh. If you have a monitor connected to the Mac, try connecting the monitor power cable into a separate outlet (rather than into the receptacle on the back of the CPU).

* The switch may be bad.

* The internal relay may be bad.

My Mac restarts while I'm working or instead of turning off when I select Shut Down.

* Restart your Macintosh from a floppy disk and see if Shut Down works properly. If it does, reinstall the system software by deleting the System and Finder files and then reinstalling from Apple's system software installer.

* The power supply is wearing out, or the power supplied from the wall outlet is unreliable. Test the wall outlet by plugging in a small appliance (lamp or radio) to see if the outlet is consistently working. Test the Mac from another wall outlet.

* If the Macintosh has a lockable power switch, as in the Macintosh IIci and Macintosh IIsi, make sure the switch is not locked in the On position.

* Detach the keyboard and restart with the AC power switch. The keyboard power-on key might be stuck or defective.

* Try zapping the PRAM to reset control panel settings. See the section in this chapter entitled "The Macintosh Battery And PRAM."

Conserving Power

You do not need to turn on all your Macintosh devices unless you are using them. For example, keep your printer turned off until you need to print. Then, if you intend to do more printing leave it on; otherwise turn it off.

You wouldn't want to turn the Mac on and off a few times a day, though, because cycling a power supply (powering on and off) does stress the circuitry, possibly shortening the life of the device.

Using Your Macintosh Internationally

If you will be using your U.S.-made Macintosh or peripheral device outside the United States, you may need an electrical outlet adapter to convert the power to a configuration your Mac can use.

The first thing to do is find out the *voltage* and *frequency* of the power supplied in the other country. Depending on the type of Macintosh and/or peripherals you are using, your hardware may be universal, which means it can be used anywhere. As an example, the U.S. voltage is typically 110V, 60 Hz, while European Macs have power supplies designed to handle 220V at 50 Hz.

Universal Macintosh hardware can work within a wider range of voltages and frequencies. For example, the PowerBook 100, 140, and 170 can work with a frequency of 50 Hz or 60 Hz and voltage between 100V and 240V.

Alternatively, your Macintosh hardware may operate at around 110 volts, at either 50 Hz or 60 Hz. In countries that supply a different standard, you will need to compensate for the voltage differences by using a grounded (it has a third prong on the outlet plug) voltage transformer (which looks like a power adapter) to convert 220V to 110V.

Table 9.1 shows various types of plug adapters. Whether you need a voltage transformer or not, you will most likely need a plug adapter, which can be used with your power adapter.

Table 9.1 Outlet Types And Locations

Outlet Type	Location
(I I) (I.I)	the United States; Canada; parts of Latin America; Japan; Korea; the Philippines; Taiwan
(· ·)	the former Soviet Union; most of Europe; parts of Latin America; the Middle East; parts of Africa; Hong Kong; India; most of South Asia
(I __)	Mexico; the United Kingdom; Ireland; Malaysia; Singapore; parts of Africa
(\ /) (I)	China; Australia; New Zealand

To connect a device that is not designed for the U.S. market to your Macintosh, find out from the device's manufacturer if it is frequency-independent. If it is, you can use the device with your computer, but you will still need to compensate for the voltage differences and use an adapter to plug it into your wall outlet. Otherwise, you must purchase a device that is suitable to the Mac's required frequency. Table 9.2 shows common Macintosh voltages and frequencies.

Table 9.2   Common Macintosh Voltages and Frequencies

Macintosh Hardware	Frequency (Hz)	Voltage (AC)
AppleColor Hi-Res RGB	47-63	85-270
Apple Hi-Res Monochrome	47-63	85-270
Macintosh 12" Monochrome Display	47-63	90-132 and 190-270
Macintosh 12" RGB Display	50-60	100-120
Apple Two-Page Monochrome Monitor	47-63	90-270
Apple Macintosh Portrait Display	47-63	90-270
Macintosh 16" Color Display	47-63	90-270
Macintosh 21" Color Display	47-63	85-135 and 170-270
Mac Plus	50-60	105-125
Macintosh Classic	47-63	120
Macintosh Classic II	47-63	120
Macintosh SE	47-63	90-140 and 170-270
Macintosh SE/30	47-62	120-240
Macintosh II	48-62	90-140 and 170-270
Macintosh IIx	48-62	100-240
Macintosh IIcx	50-60	100-240
Macintosh IIci	50-60	100-240

Macintosh Hardware	Frequency (Hz)	Voltage (AC)
Macintosh Portable	48-62	85-270
Macintosh IIfx	47-62	100-240
Macintosh IIsi	47-63	120
Macintosh LC	47-63	90-240
Macintosh LC II	47-63	90-240
Macintosh PowerBook 100	50-60	100-220
Macintosh PowerBook 140	50-60	100-220
Macintosh PowerBook 145	50-60	100-220
Macintosh PowerBook 160	50-60	110-220
Macintosh PowerBook 170	50-60	100-220
Macintosh PowerBook 180	50-60	110-220
Macintosh PowerBook Duo 210	47-63	85-270
Macintosh PowerBook Duo 230	47-63	85-270
Macintosh Quadra 700	50-60	100-240
Macintosh Quadra 900	50-60	100-240
Macintosh Quadra 950	50-60	100-240
Macintosh IIvx	50-60	100-240
LaserWriter IINTX	50-60	90-126
ImageWriter II	60	120

Service and Repair When Traveling Abroad

Service and repair becomes an issue when traveling abroad. Apple's warranty is valid only in the country of purchase, so a defective Macintosh or Apple peripheral must be returned to a dealer in the country of purchase for service under the Apple warranty. Apple dealers overseas will service hardware designed only for their country.

It is a good idea to buy and use a Macintosh hardware product for a while before you leave the country. Hopefully any problems that might exist will crop up before you leave.

About Airport X-Rays

Although it is not a good idea to pass computers through airport x-ray equipment, the X-rays will not damage your data or equipment. The baggage inspection equipment at airports produce X-rays, which will damage photographic film but not magnetic computer media. (However, magnets and magnetic fields *do* damage magnetic media on computer disks.)

The best way to handle laptops and disks when traveling is to separate them from the rest of your luggage and carry them separately with you through the inspection area. Hold on to the power cord or battery to make sure you can turn your computer on for the airport security folks.

 TIP: If you are traveling with a PowerBook, don't check your computer as baggage, carry it with you. And don't shut it down—select Sleep from the Special menu in the Finder, in case the security personnel want to see the computer work as you pass through security.

The Macintosh Battery and PRAM

Even when your Macintosh is not powered on, the Mac has to save settings such as keyboard, mouse, and other Control Panel settings. It does this by storing the information in *PRAM* (which stands for Parameter RAM). PRAM is a small portion of memory in your Macintosh which is always powered, thanks to a small battery in the Mac.

Although most of the time you don't need to think about the PRAM or do anything to maintain it, if the PRAM settings become scrambled due to a crash or other mishaps, some strange problems can occur. To reset the PRAM to default settings, you can do what is referred to as "zapping the PRAM."

To zap the PRAM under System 7, restart the Macintosh and hold down the ⌘-Option-P-R keys. Press this key combination before you get to the "Welcome to Macintosh" screen.

Under System 6, while holding down the Shift, ⌘, and Option keys, open the Control Panel from the Apple menu. A dialog box appears, asking if you want to zap parameter RAM and restart the Macintosh; click on Yes.

If you have a Macintosh 128K, 512K, 512Ke, or Plus, zap the PRAM by unplugging the Macintosh and removing the battery for 15 seconds or so.

 TIP: PRAM is also referred to as non-volatile RAM because when you turn the Mac off, the information in PRAM is not lost. Zapping the PRAM does not change the time and date. The Macintosh reads the time and date before zapping the PRAM and restores them after completing the process.

Here are some troubleshooting tips and questions regarding the PRAM:

When should I zap the PRAM?

* When you notice that your Macintosh is not holding the settings, the correct date or time, or the settings are off. If zapping the PRAM doesn't fix this, the battery may need to be replaced.

* If you notice strange behavior with control panel settings such as the PowerBook's battery and performance settings, or scrambled characters in the control panels.

* If you are having difficulty starting up the Macintosh, a device attached to the Mac or the monitor connected to the Mac.

* If your file creation dates are looking very off, such as the year 1904! This could also indicate a dying battery.

How do I replace the battery?

If the Macintosh is a Mac Plus (or a Macintosh 128K, 512K, or 512Ke), you can simply take out the battery from the back of the case (behind a panel above the power cable plug) and replace it with a 4.5 volt battery, which you can purchase from your local electronics store.

Other Macs have lithium batteries either soldered or snapped on the logic board. Newer Macs have a snap-on battery box that lets you simply pop the batteries out to replace them. On older Macs the original batteries are soldered in, which means you should take this Mac to an authorized Apple service technician to replace the battery.

My Macintosh keeps resetting the system date to January 1, 1904.

Either the battery in your Mac is dying, or the information stored in the PRAM is scrambled and you will need to zap (reset) the PRAM.

If PRAM is memory, how much PRAM do Macs have?

All Apple Macintosh computers and LaserWriter printers have PRAM. LaserWriter PRAM holds configuration settings such as page count, emulation mode, and data transmission rate of the printing port.

The Macintosh 128K, Macintosh 512K, and Macintosh 512Ke have 20 bytes of PRAM. The Macintosh Portable has 128 bytes of PRAM; and all other Macs have 256 bytes of PRAM.

The Macintosh Interrupt and Reset Switches

Most Macintosh computers have two switches called the *Interrupt* and *Reset* switches. These switches are really meant to be used by Macintosh developers; however, you may find them useful in troubleshooting situations.

The Reset switch will restart the Macintosh computer as if you had turned the power switch off and then back on again. The Reset switch can be used when you are frozen or have crashed and have no other way of restarting the Macintosh, except to power down the Mac.

The Interrupt switch is for software programmers who want to interrupt a process to debug the software they are programming. It is to be used with debugging software. (An example of debugging software is Apple's debugger, called MacsBug.)

TIP: The Reset switch has a small triangle icon above it, while the Interrupt switch has a small circle with a line in it.

These switches are sometimes placed on the side of the computer, as in the case of the Mac Plus, SE, II, IIx, and IIfx. Alternatively they are placed in the bottom left corner of some Macs, as in the case of the Mac IIcx and IIci. PowerBooks have two small switches on the back or left side of the computer. Check your Macintosh computer manual to locate where these switches are.

TIP: The Macintosh IIsi does not have hardware switches for these two settings; however, you can reset the IIsi by pressing ⌘-Control-Power On, and interrupt by pressing ⌘-Power On. (Power On refers to the Power On key on the key-board, which is normally pressed to start up the Macintosh.)

PowerBook Battery

Most Macintosh PowerBooks (except for the Duos and the PowerBook 100) have a nickel-cadmium battery (NiCad). The PowerBook 100 has a lead-acid battery, and the PowerBook Duos have a nickel-hydride battery (see table 9.3).

Table 9.3   PowerBook Battery Types

Battery Type	PowerBook Model	Recharge Time
lead-acid	PowerBook 100	3 hours
nickel-cadmium (NiCad)	PowerBook 140, 145, 160, 165c,170, and 180	3 hours
nickel-hydride (NiHy)	PowerBook Duo 210 and Duo 230	1 hour

The PowerBook batteries can be used for anywhere between one and a half to four hours; however, this varies depending on what measures you take to reduce power usage and what kind of computing you are doing. The NiCad batteries last between one and a half to two hours before recharge is necessary. The nickel-hydride battery lasts between two and a half and four hours.

The battery should be completely discharged and recharged on a regular basis (once a month) to fully cycle the battery through its charge and discharge phase. To fully recharge the battery, you must fully drain the battery.

The PowerBook Duos have a quick-recharge battery as a backup battery, as well as an internal lithium backup battery. So if you have a spare battery and one battery has run out, you can pull the dead battery out and slip in a fresh one without shutting down the PowerBook (the quick-recharge battery saves you from losing the data while you are swapping batteries).

For more information on caring for your PowerBook battery, see the PowerBook manual.

Troubleshooting PowerBook Problems

Here are some tips and troubleshooting help for PowerBook users:

What is the life of my battery?

NiCad batteries last through about 500 recharges.

I cannot fully recharge my battery.

Your battery may be reaching the end of its life span, or it may be damaged. Remember to fully discharge and recharge your battery once a month.

Can I connect a mouse to the PowerBook?

Yes. PowerBooks have one ADB (Apple Desktop Bus) port; however, the port is a low-power ADB port and cannot support the older ADB mouse.

The mouse must be designed to connect into the low-power ADB port. There are a few companies that make small mice that can be stuffed away in your PowerBook carrying case. Two mice that can do this are Appoint's Thumbelina Mac and MicroSpeed's MicroTRAC.

What about a free protective battery case?

To prevent batteries from electrically shorting and starting a fire, place idle batteries in the protective case that came with your PowerBook. You can order a free case by calling Apple at (800) 377-4127.

How can I conserve battery power?

* Set up a RAM disk. You probably need at least 6 MB of RAM to do this, but reading information from RAM instead of from the disk will save power. Reading from and writing to the disk drive in your PowerBook takes up precious battery power.

* The PowerBook screen backlighting draws a lot of energy from your battery. Turn down the screen as much as possible.

* Run applications that don't require a lot of RAM and that don't access the hard drive frequently.

* In the PowerBook control panel (in System 7.1 and above), you can slow the processor speed, which slows down the battery drain (see figure 9.1). Under System 7.01, hold down the Option key while clicking on the word Automatic to bring up a dialog box to turn on the system-rest feature.

* Turn off AppleTalk if you are not connected to a network or printer. AppleTalk keeps the computer processor constantly active, which drains the battery.

Is it safe to move the PowerBook when it is in sleep mode?

The PowerBook hard disk is locked when it is not spinning, so it is safe. Be careful not to jar or drop a PowerBook while the hard disk is spinning up or spinning down.

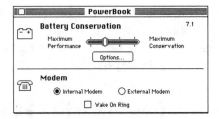

Figure 9.1 The PowerBook's battery settings in the PowerBook control panel.

How can I transfer data from my PowerBook to another Macintosh?

* With a SCSI cable connection. For more information, check your PowerBook manual; see Chapter 10, "Storage Devices," for more information about SCSI connections.

* You can use LocalTalk or PhoneNET connectors to connect the printer port from the PowerBook to the printer port in the desktop Macintosh. Then make sure AppleTalk is enabled in the Chooser, turn on File Sharing for either Macintosh, and share the PowerBook or Macintosh disk. See Chapter 4, "System Software" for more information about File Sharing.

Monitors

Usually, the Macintosh monitor isn't very troublesome. This section discusses a few techniques for diagnosing and fixing monitor problems.

Monitor Testing

You can test your monitor for accurate screen geometry, focus, and color quality in several ways. Take an image that you have seen on a monitor that you know to be good and view the image through the monitor you want to test. This is a rudimentary form of testing, but it may be all you are looking for.

If you want to perform a battery of screen tests you can use a shareware program by Larry Pina called Test Pattern Generator (available from online services and user groups). There are some commercial programs that will run through tests as well, such as Snooper (see figure 9.2).

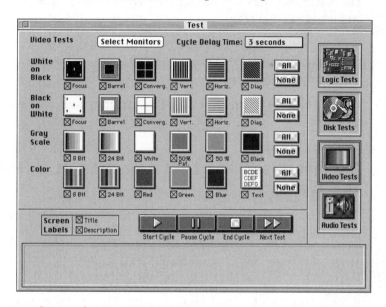

Figure 9.2 Snooper's monitor testing screen.

Macintosh monitors are built into some models, while other models are separate from the monitor. The compact Macs, such as the Mac Plus, SE, and Classic, have the computer and monitor in one case. The portable Macs, such as the PowerBooks and Mac Portable, also have the monitor built into the Mac case.

Compact Macintosh Monitor Problems

In the Macintosh Plus (and older Macs), the power supply and video (monitor) circuitry are combined, so if something goes wrong it is critical to both the power supply and the monitor.

The Mac Plus also does not have a fan cooling the inside circuitry, so overheating is a problem with the Mac Plus and can increase failure of the Mac Plus video. If the power goes off unexpectedly on a Mac Plus, it might indicate that the video has gone. The Macintosh Classic has a similar design, combining the video circuitry and power supply; however, it has a cooling fan.

The Macintosh SE family has seperate video circuitry and power supply, and it has a cooling fan.

Because of the danger in repairing the high-voltage video components in these Macs, it is suggested that you bring the compact Mac to a qualified Apple service technician.

Here are some problems and questions you may have with a compact Mac monitor:

My Macintosh has only a horizontal line across the screen.

This horizontal line usually means the video is not receiving enough power, or it is dying.

To test if it is not receiving enough power, try another wall outlet and test the power cables and the outlet for appropriate voltage.

If the power supply or the video circuitry is bad (referred to as a blown flyback transformer), you will need to bring the Mac to a qualified service technician.

The monitor is out of focus.

If you cannot correct the focus with the available settings, the video circuitry is damaged or the video tube parts need cleaning. Bring the Mac to a qualified service technician.

My monitor picture is dark.

Check the brightness setting. One other possibility is that the video circuitry is wearing out. If changing the brightness setting doesn't fix the problem, take the Macintosh to a qualified Apple service technician.

All-Around Monitor First Aid

Here are a host of problems, questions and solutions for monitors of all kinds.

How does the resolution affect the screen image?

If you want the size of objects on the screen to reflect their printed size, you want to use a monitor with a resolution of 72 dpi (dots per inch). A 72-dpi monitor is known as a WYSIWYG (pronounced "wizzy-wig," for What You See Is What You Get). On monitors with higher resolution the image appears smaller and more of the image fits on to the screen. Of course, this skews the actual size of the image and can make text more difficult to read.

Monitor Cables

Make sure you have the correct cable for the Monitor you are using. There are cables to support different monitor types, like the Apple High Resolution Monochrome monitor and the High Resolution RGB monitor (color).

Can I attach a color monitor to my Mac SE/30, Mac IIfx, IIx, II, or IIcx?

Yes; however, you will also need a color video card because these Macs do not have built-in video support. The Mac IIci, Quadras, and other desktop Macs have built-in color video support, so you don't necessarily need a video card—depending on the monitor you are attaching to the Mac. You do have to make sure the monitor and video card are compatible, and obtain the correct cable to attach the card to the monitor.

Should I use built-in video support or buy a video card?

The Macintosh IIci, Quadras, and other desktop Macs have built-in video support, which means you can connect a monitor directly into the monitor port on the back of the Macintosh without installing a video card. The advantages here are that you do not need a video card and you free up a card slot for another card. The disadvantages are that it uses up more RAM, can slow down the Macintosh (in the case of the Mac IIsi), and only certain monitors can be connected to the monitor port.

How can I tell if my screen is warped?

A good monitor displays circles, straight lines and squares accurately. Sometimes there is distortion at the edges of the screen because the light beam that draws the screen image travels farther to get to the edges of the screen.

Do I need an anti-glare screen over my monitor?

Some monitors have an anti-glare agent built into the screen (usually invisibly etched in the glass) to cut down on glare. You can also purchase an anti-glare screen from a third-party manufacturer; however, make sure the screen doesn't reduce your visibility or distort the screen colors and image resolution.

Can I clean my monitor?

Yes you can clean the glass screen and the case. Use a damp, lint free cotton cloth. Do not use sprays, solvents (be careful about some glass cleaners that have harsh solvents) or abrasive soaps. Special anti-static cloth and solvents are sold specifically for cleaning monitors.

How can I reduce the flickering from my monitor?

Screen flicker is caused by the beams of light that rapidly draw and redraw the screen image, both vertically and horizontally.

To reduce screen flicker when buying a monitor, look for a monitor with a refresh rate (vertical scan rate) greater than 60 Hz (around 75 Hz if possible). Some of Apple's newer monitors have vertical scan rates of 75 Hz.

Also reduce the amount of direct light shining on the monitor and don't use fluorescent lighting if possible. Fluorescent lights flicker, but not at the same speed as the monitor, so the combined flickers can create an even greater disturbance. Soft white lights are a bit gentler on the eyes as well.

Can I connect more than one monitor to my Mac?

You can if the Mac can support more than one monitor connected at the same time. The Mac II series supports more than one monitor with a video card slot(s) and the built-in video support. You can have as many as six monitors hooked up at the same time; you can arrange them using the Monitors control panel.

To specify which monitor will show the Startup screen, choose Monitors from the Control Panel and hold down the Option key. When the Happy Mac icon appears, drag it to the monitor you want to be the main monitor and then restart the Mac.

Can I connect an external monitor to the PowerBook?

Some of the PowerBooks, like the PowerBook 160 and 180, have a video port and built-in monitor support for up to 256 colors. You will have to confirm that the monitor you want to connect to the PowerBook is supported. In general, the built-in video supports Apple's 12-inch Monochrome, 12-inch RGB, High Resolution RGB, Color, and 16-inch Color, Portrait, and some VGA (commonly connected to PCs) and SVGA (Super VGA) monitors. You can even display the screen image on both the PowerBook and external monitor screens.

The PowerBook 100, 140, 145, and 170 were not designed to support external monitors, so you will have to buy a monitor adapter. Many different companies supply adapters for these PowerBooks. See Appendix C, "Product Information," for more details. Be aware that some adapters support only monochrome display imaging; performance suffers a bit, too.

The screen is slightly rotated.

The monitor needs to be adjusted from inside the monitor case. Take the monitor to a qualified technician.

The image is fuzzy.

Either the contrast and other focus control settings need to be adjusted, or the monitor is aging. If the controls are inside the monitor, take it to a qualified service technician.

The screen image appears wavy or distorted.

There are many environmental factors that can distort the monitor's screen image, including the earth's electromagnetic field. Monitors are adjusted at the factory for accuracy; however, the accuracy can be different when the monitor is unpacked. The extent of the distortion depends on the location of the monitor; you can test this by rotating the monitor or moving it to another location. Your goal is to reduce the interference affecting the quality of the screen image. Here are some ways to do this:

* There are magnets inside the monitor that align the light beams to display the image on the screen. As a result, objects with magnets or objects that generate magnetic fields can disrupt the monitor. Move these objects (such as phones or another monitor) away from the monitor.

  If you have placed two monitors side-by-side, they are both creating magnetic fields and one is probably interfering with the other.

  Move the monitor to a different location. If the display changes when the monitor is moved or rotated, the monitor's environment is the source of the image distortion. Rearrange your work area so that large metal objects (such as file cabinets) are as far from the monitor as possible.

* Turn off electrical appliances, or other electrical devices, such as other devices connected to the Mac, to see if the distortion goes away. Fluorescent lighting is also a cause of interference. Turn the lights off to see if there is a difference.

* The monitor may need to be *degaussed*. Degaussing the monitor clears up magnetic field distortion and interference. Many monitors (including Apple monitors) have a button specifically for degaussing the monitor.

✳ Adjust the contrast, vertical, and horizontal image controls. This sometimes solves ghosting or shadowing problems.

My monitor picture is rolling.

Adjust the vertical hold on the monitor if the setting is on the outside of the monitor. Otherwise you will have to open the monitor case or take the monitor to a service technician.

My color monitor has a purple haze over the screen.

This purple haze usually indicates a problem with the monitor cable or the video card.

Check the monitor cables, untwist them (if they are twisted or cramped), or try another cable. Also test another video card, or change the slot the video card is in if you have more than one slot. If you are using built-in video (no monitor card is installed), test the monitor with another Macintosh, or test another monitor on the same Macintosh.

My Mac II won't start with a color video card installed.

If you have an old Mac II, you may confront this problem. The initial Mac II's (from 1987) experienced problems with add-on cards (NuBus card slots) that have 1M or more of memory on them. The problem was fixed in the ROM; upgrades to the new ROM are available at no charge from any authorized Apple Dealer. All Macintosh IIs manufactured since then have been fixed.

A crackling noise is coming from inside my monitor.

Turn off the Monitor and unplug it. The monitor tube may be cracked or damaged, or an electrical connection is damaged. Bring the monitor to a qualified service technician.

My monitor's picture is snowy or distorted.

The monitor may need to be *degaussed*. Degaussing the monitor clears up magnetic field distortion and interference. Many monitors (including Apple monitors) have a button specifically for deguassing the monitor.

My monitor is dark and there is no power.

If the power light on the monitor does not light up when you turn on the monitor, check the power cables (secure the connections), the monitor cables (untwist them) and the monitor power switch. If the monitor power cord is connected directly to the Mac, make sure that the Mac is on.

* The monitor fuse may have blown. Check the fuse (refer to the monitor manual for its location) and replace it if it is blown. Most fuses can be purchased at an electronics or hardware store.

* Adjust the brightness controls and other settings to make sure the monitor settings are not turned down.

* Check the position of the video card (if there is one) and try another video card slot or another monitor cable.

What does "picture burn-in" mean?

If you were to leave the same image on your Mac monitor for a long period of time (a couple of days) the image would eventually burn in to the screen. What is really happening is the phosphors in the tube for displaying the image are permanently stuck with that image. The image appears as a ghost—and this is permanent!

This can be prevented; turn the screen brightness down when you're not using the machine. Another solution is to purchase a screen saver, which replaces the normal picture on your monitor with a moving image when the computer isn't in use. Two popular screen savers are After Dark and Pyro.

There is a thin black line across my color monitor.

This is not actually a problem; it is due to a specific design in some color monitors, notably monitors using a Sony tube. The design for this monitor's tube causes a single thin black horizontal line to appear one-third of the way up from the bottom of the screen. So there is nothing you can do about it; however, this is in fact a high-quality color tube.

How do I adjust the color setting for my monitor?

In System 7, open the Monitor control panel from the Control Panels Folder (see figure 9.3). Under System 6, go to the Control Panel and select the Monitor setting.

Figure 9.3   The Monitor control panel.

I cannot change the color settings on my monitor.

Make sure your video card and the monitor support color. If you have tried changing the setting in the Monitor control panel to no avail, try zapping the PRAM (parameter RAM), which holds several system settings, including the monitor settings.

To zap the PRAM under System 7, restart the Macintosh and hold down the ⌘-Option-P-R keys. Press this key combination before you get to the "Welcome to Macintosh" screen.

Under System 6, while holding down the Shift, ⌘, and Option keys, open the Control Panel from the Apple menu. A dialog box appears, asking if you want to zap parameter RAM and restart the Macintosh; click Yes.

If you have a Macintosh 128K, 512K, 512Ke, or Plus, zap the PRAM by unplugging the Macintosh and removing the battery for 15 seconds or so.

Also try reinstalling the Monitor control panel by deleting the file in the System Folder and then installing a new file with the system software installer.

My Macintosh IIci won't start up with the monitor attached.

If you are using the built-in video (not a separate video card) with the monitor, the Mac IIci's built-in video requires that with only 1 MB of RAM installed, the RAM must be in Bank A. If the RAM is in Bank B, the Mac IIci ignores the video port. See Chapter 8, "The Macintosh CPU," for more details on Macintosh IIci RAM requirements.

If you have installed the memory properly, then check other areas of the monitor such as the video card, the slot the card is in, and the monitor cable, and make sure that model of monitor is supported by the Mac IIci's built-in video.

Monitor (Video) Cards and Built-In Video

There are two ways to install a monitor on a Macintosh. If the Mac has built-in video support, the Mac does not require a video card installed for the monitor. The only trick here is the built-in video must support the monitor you are attaching. Most Macintosh monitors are supported, such as the Apple 12-inch color and monochrome monitors, the Apple 13-inch High Resolution color and monochrome monitors, and others. Check with your Macintosh manual for the monitors it supports.

If the Mac does not have built-in video or the monitor requires a video card anyway, then you will need an open card slot. Most Macs have slots that support the *NuBus* standard, while others support alternative slots.

Macintosh computers that have card slots which support alternative slot standards include the PowerBooks, SE, SE/30, LC, LC II, and the Classic II (for an optional math coprocessor). The Mac IIsi can support a NuBus or 030 Direct slot, but both require that a special adapter be installed. The

Macintosh LC has an 020 Direct Slot. So when buying a video card or any other card for Macs, specify the kind of Mac you are buying the card for.

Apple Desktop Bus (ADB) Devices

There is at least one *Apple Desktop Bus* (ADB) port on the back of every Mac, except for the Mac Plus and earlier Macs (which have separate ports for the mouse and keyboard).

The ADB port is designed to support devices such as the mouse, keyboard, graphics tablets, touch screens, and electronic pens. In some unique cases, the ADB port is used for modems and portable hard drive power.

Although the claim is that up to 16 ADB devices can be chained together, realistically only about three can be attached successfully before you can notice communications problems with the ADB devices.

CAUTION: To prevent damage to ADB devices and the Macintosh, only disconnect and reconnect them when the Macintosh power is off.

Keyboard

The keyboard is an ADB device. Most keyboards also have an extra ADB port on the side to daisy-chain (connect) another ADB device to the keyboard, rather than directly to the Macintosh CPU.

Figure 9.4 shows the System 7 Keyboard control panel window. You can change the settings and select a keyboard type; in this case the American keyboard type is selected.

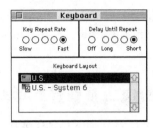

Figure 9.4   The Keyboard control panel.

The Keyboard control panel controls the Key Repeat. When a key is held down, that character is repeatedly typed, which saves you from pressing the key over and over. The Key Repeat Rate controls how fast the character is typed when the key is held down. The Delay Until Repeat controls how soon the computer will repeatedly type the character when the key is pressed. If the Delay Until Repeat is too short, you will often type mulitiple characters without intending to.

Here are some common keyboard problems and questions.

The control panel is not holding my keyboard settings.

* Is your clock time incorrect as well? This is a sign that the battery is going on your Macintosh.

* It is also possible the *parameter RAM* (PRAM) information has been scrambled and must be zapped.

   To zap the PRAM under System 7, restart the Macintosh and hold down the ⌘-Option-P-R keys. Press this key combination before you get to the "Welcome to Macintosh" screen.

   Under System 6, while holding down the Shift, ⌘, and Option keys, open the Control Panel from the Apple menu. A dialog box appears, asking if you want to zap parameter RAM and restart the Macintosh; click Yes.

   If you have a Mac Plus or earlier Mac, zap the PRAM by unplugging the Macintosh and removing the battery for 15 seconds or so.

Can I use an ADB Device on the Mac Plus?

No, unfortunately you cannot. However manufacturers of some ADB devices, such as trackballs and tablets, do make Mac Plus versions of their products. The Mac Plus (and the Mac 128K, 512K, and 512Ke) do not have ADB ports. They have an RJ-11 connector in the front bottom right corner which connects the keyboard with what looks like a telephone cord; this cord uses slightly different connectors than telephone wire.

WARNING: You can damage the keyboard by trying to use a telephone wire to connect the keyboard.

The keyboard is not responding.

There are a couple of things to check to make sure that it is actually the keyboard that is causing the problem.

* Make sure the ADB cables are firmly connected at all points. The entire length of the ADB chain should not exceed 16 feet, and even 16 feet is pushing it. Try another cable and test both ADB ports on the keyboard.

* The problem could actually be an ADB device between the keyboard and the Macintosh, so connect the keyboard and cable directly to the Mac (rather than through another ADB device) to check just the cable and the keyboard connection.

* Make sure the problem isn't with the ADB port on the Macintosh. Connect the keyboard to another ADB port if your Mac has one, or try the keyboard on another Mac. Also connect another device, like your mouse, into the ADB port.

* If no devices work when attached to one or more of the ADB ports, then there could be a problem with the ADB circuitry on the Mac's logic board. At this point, you probably need an authorized Apple technician to look at the Mac.

✳ Restart the Macintosh from another startup disk and test the keyboard. If the keyboard works with this startup disk, you need to reinstall the Keyboard control panel or the system software.

My mouse responds but my keyboard doesn't.

Power down the Mac, unplug the cables and plug them into the ports again. This sometimes solves the problem. In most cases, the mouse is working because it is plugged into another ADB port; however, if it is plugged into the keyboard it could be just a temporary power problem across the ADB bus (electronic path). The problem could also be with the keyboard cable; try using another cable to connect the keyboard to the Mac.

Keyboard response is slow.

There are a few things to check here:

✳ Check the settings in the Keyboard control panel to speed up the response rate.

✳ If you use a non-Apple keyboard, there could be a problem with support for the keyboard, or a conflict with an extension or system software. Disable extensions by holding down the Shift key while restarting the Macintosh, test a regular keyboard with the Mac, or call the keyboard maker.

✳ Your ADB cables may be too long, damaged, or suffering from electrical interference. Try another cable, another ADB port, or disconnect an ADB device if you have more than two connected to one ADB port.

✳ It is also possible the *parameter RAM* (PRAM) information has been scrambled and must be zapped.

To zap the PRAM under System 7, restart the Macintosh and hold down the ⌘ -Option-P-R keys. Press this key combination before you get to the "Welcome to Macintosh" screen.

Under System 6, while holding down the Shift, ⌘ , and Option keys, open the Control Panel from the Apple menu. A dialog box appears, asking if you want to zap parameter RAM and restart the Macintosh; click Yes.

If you have a Mac Plus or earlier Mac, zap the PRAM by unplugging the Macintosh and removing the battery for 15 seconds or so.

How should I connect my mouse and keyboard?

Since you can daisy chain ADB devices, you have some options depending on what is most comfortable for you. You can connect your keyboard into the ADB port on the back of the Mac and connect the mouse to the ADB port on the right or left side of the keyboard. If you use your mouse with your right hand, then plug the mouse into the port on the right side of the keyboard and plug the cable from the keyboard to the Mac into the left side of the keyboard. Reverse this if you use the mouse with your left hand.

If your Mac has two ADB ports you can plug the mouse into one ADB port and the keyboard into another; however, if your mouse cord is short you might not want to do this.

An option that will help avoid cable tangle is to buy a cordless mouse.

I spilled liquid on the keyboard!

If you spilled a drink or other liquid on the keyboard, shut down the Macintosh and disconnect the keyboard. Hold the keyboard upside down and empty the liquid out. Let the keyboard dry out.

When it dries, you will need to test it to see if the spill damaged the keyboard. Liquids interfere with the keys making contact when pressed, so you will find the keys will not work while they are wet.

You can also open the keyboard to clean it.

How do I clean the keyboard?

You can open up the keyboard by unscrewing the screw(s) on the bottom or side of the keyboard, and then separating the top from the bottom. Wipe the keyboard clean with a non-conductive cleaning solution (such as distilled water) and an anti-static cloth. Let the keyboard dry before closing it, reconnecting it, and restarting the Macintosh.

Some keys are stuck.

If a key is sticking, there is probably dirt between the key and the contact point. The best solution is to clean the keyboard. See above on how to clean the keyboard.

Mouse

Besides the keyboard, the mouse is the most common ADB device. Quite often the mouse is connected to the ADB port in the keyboard, and then the keyboard is attached to the ADB port in the back of the Mac. Other times the mouse is connected directly to the ADB port on the back of the Mac.

You can adjust the mouse settings in the Mouse control panel. Figure 9.5 shows the System 7 Mouse control panel. The Mouse Tracking options control how fast the mouse pointer will move across the screen when you move the mouse. If the setting is too slow, getting to where you want to go will take forever; if the setting is too fast, correctly positioning the mouse will be difficult. The Double-Click Speed options control how fast you have to click twice to double-click. A slow setting will lead to unintentional double-clicks, while a fast setting will make more of your double-clicks go unrecognized.

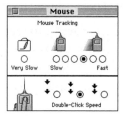

Figure 9.5 The Mouse control panel.

Here are some common mouse problems and questions.

Cleaning The Mouse

The standard Apple mouse has a exposed mouse ball on the bottom of the mouse. To clean these mice, remove the bottom lid around the mouse ball by turning the lid (the exact process varies depending on the model you own) until the lid lifts off and the ball falls out.

There are metal or plastic rollers inside where the ball rolls; you can clean these rollers with cotton lightly dipped in alcohol. The rollers and the mouse ball should be completely clean of all dirt and lint build-up. Clean out all the pet hair, threads, and other particles which can interfere with the mouse ball rolling action. Blowing air into the ball cavity can clear out excess dust that settles inside the mouse—but close your eyes before you blow!

You can follow this cleaning regimen for trackballs as well. Just lift the trackball out of the top of the unit and follow the same procedures.

How do I clean a PowerBook trackball?

To clean a PowerBook trackball, remove the plastic ring around the trackball by turning it counterclockwise until it pops out. You don't need tools; just press against the two small ridges with your fingernails. Then take the trackball out. There are rollers inside the trackball hole. Use a cotton swab or something similar to clean the rollers.

The mouse jumps erratically across the screen.

* The mouse probably needs a cleaning.

* Check the mouse cable connections; try connecting it to a different ADB port on the keyboard or the Macintosh.

* Restart the Macintosh with another startup disk. If the problem goes away, reinstall the Mouse control panel or the system software.

* Power down the Macintosh and check all the ADB cabling, and try another ADB port if necessary.

I can't use the mouse.

There is a control panel called Easy Access, which comes with the Macintosh system software, that allows you to use the keyboard for both keyboard and mousing functions. Figure 9.6 shows System 7's Easy Access control panel with settings for Mouse Keys, Slow Keys, And Sticky Keys.

Mouse Keys controls the settings for keys assigned to work like the mouse. Slow Keys lets you set the delay at which a key is accepted or registered for action. Sticky Keys allows you to type combinations of two or more keys with one hand.

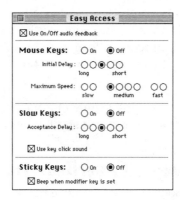

Figure 9.6   The Easy Access control panel.

Conclusion

This chapter has dealt with the most common components that plug into the Macintosh CPU, including the power cables, the monitor, and ADB devices such as mice and keyboards. The next chapter covers another integral part of the Macintosh: storage, including hard disks, floppy disks, and CD-ROM drives.

I Need To Know!

Chapter 10

Storage Devices

This chapter covers problems with the most common types of storage media: hard disks, floppy disks, and CD-ROMs. General coverage of SCSI devices is also included, as hard disks and CD-ROMs use the SCSI interface to connect to the Macintosh.

SCSI (Small Computer System Interface) Devices

SCSI (pronounced "skuh-zee") is a standard port used to connect devices such as hard disks, CD-ROM drives and scanners to the Macintosh. The SCSI port on the back of a Macintosh identifies the port with a SCSI icon. From the Macintosh Plus and on, all Macs have a SCSI port.

Three essential parts to getting your SCSI devices connected successfully include SCSI addressing (SCSI ID), SCSI configuration (SCSI cables), and SCSI termination.

What Is a SCSI ID?

Every SCSI device requires a unique ID number, sometimes referred to as an address. The *SCSI ID* identifies each device regardless of where it's connected to the *SCSI bus*. The SCSI bus is the data path along the chain of SCSI devices connected to the Macintosh. The higher the SCSI ID number assigned to a device, the higher the priority of the device on the SCSI bus.

The Macintosh CPU itself always has an ID of 7, so don't set any SCSI devices to ID 7. An internal hard disk always has an ID of 0. Everything else on the chain is numbered between 1 and 6. If an internal hard disk is not present in the Macintosh, you can number external devices between 0 and 6.

TIP: It is not necessary to follow a numbering sequence. For example, you can have a hard drive with an ID of 5 and a scanner with an ID of 3, without using the ID number 2 in the chain.

Assign a startup hard disk with a high SCSI ID number (ID 6) so that it will be recognized by the Macintosh before other devices. You can also override a SCSI ID startup order by selecting a startup device in the Startup Disk control panel.

SCSI devices usually have a switch on the back of the device to set the SCSI ID number, such as a push button, thumbwheel, or DIP switch; in rare cases the ID is set with software. Avoid buying devices that do not have a hardware switch on the back panel to change the ID number.

SCSI Cables And Connectors

Cable and connectors can be a source of problems, and the SCSI cable in no exception.

Types Of Connectors And Cables

SCSI connectors on the back of a device vary in size and shape. Most Macs have a 25-pin connector on the back panel; however, PowerBooks have a 30-pin connector. SCSI peripherals, such as hard disks, usually have a 50-pin connector.

Connectors either have a number of pins coming out of the connector or holes for another connector's pins. These types of connectors are sometimes referred to as *male* and *female* connectors. The male connectors have pins and the female connectors have pin holes.

The cables connect SCSI devices together to create a *SCSI chain* or *SCSI bus*. There are two types of SCSI cables on the SCSI chain: the SCSI System Cable and the SCSI Peripheral Interface Cable.

The *SCSI System Cable* (also referred to as a Macintosh-to-SCSI cable) connects the Macintosh to an external SCSI device. This cable has 25-pin male connector on one end to connect to the Mac, and a 50-pin male connector on the other end to connect to a SCSI device.

The *SCSI Peripheral Interface Cable* (also referred to as a SCSI-to-SCSI cable or a 50-to-50 cable) is used to daisy-chain SCSI devices. It connects an external SCSI device to another external device. Both ends have a 50-pin male connector that is plugged into the SCSI port on the device.

There are SCSI Peripheral Cables designed to connect non-standard SCSI connectors, including cables with 25-pin male connectors on both ends and cables with a 25-pin male connector on one end and a 50-pin male connector on the other end. You can figure out if you need a non-standard cable by examining the SCSI connectors on the SCSI devices.

How To Connect SCSI Cables

1. Power down the Macintosh and all peripherals before attaching cables and devices.

2. Determine which cables you will need to connect all of your SCSI devices. Your total cable (or chain) length cannot exceed 20 feet. Exceeding this limit causes SCSI signals to deteriorate, resulting in problems with device recognition and reliability.

3. Attach the proper cables to the SCSI devices. Secure all metal clamps and thumbscrews on the cables to insure reliable connections.

Testing For Bad SCSI Cables And Connectors

The easiest way to determine if a cable is bad is to replace the suspect cable with a cable that you know is good. Alternatively, bring the suspect cable to another Macintosh and test the cable with other SCSI devices. If the cable works with another device or Macintosh, you know the problem is not the cable. Remember to turn off the Macintosh and all peripherals before connecting or disconnecting cables.

If the cable isn't the problem, the SCSI connector on the device may be damaged. If there are two connectors on the back of the SCSI device, connect the cable to the other connector to see if it works. Make sure you test an alternative external terminator and other SCSI connections along the SCSI chain as well. Try attaching one SCSI device alone, and then add devices on one at a time until the problem reappears.

SCSI Termination

A *SCSI terminator* absorbs electrical signals at either end of a SCSI chain (see figure 10.1).

TIP: The basic rule is this: No matter how many SCSI devices are on the chain, you should have two terminators on a SCSI chain at all times—a terminator on both the first and the last device in the chain.

Termination is an important part of setting up your SCSI devices. An improperly terminated SCSI setup can cause damage to the SCSI circuits on the Macintosh logic board and other SCSI devices; corrupt data; prevent the Macintosh from starting; and cause sporadic hardware problems.

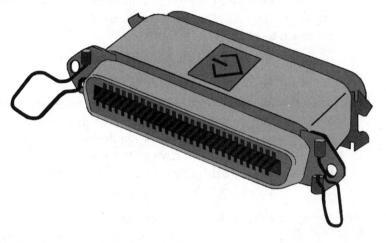

Figure 10.1 An external SCSI terminator.

Types Of Termination

SCSI termination can be installed internally in a SCSI device, such as an internally terminated hard disk, or you can attach an external terminator to a SCSI device or cable.

There is one type of external termination and two types of internal termination you can encounter with SCSI devices:

* External termination uses an external terminator, which looks like two cable connectors stuck together. An external terminator is placed at the beginning and/or end of a SCSI chain. All other devices on the chain should not be terminated.

* Internal termination with a termination switch on the back of the device allows you to enable or disable termination by moving the switch to the terminated or non-terminated position. This is the most user-friendly termination for a SCSI device.

✳ Another form of internal termination uses a termination resistor inside the device. The case must be opened to access the termination resistor and disable termination. Some vendors tell you how to remove the internal terminator in their device, and some request that you send the device back to the vendor to have it removed. Avoid buying SCSI devices that have this form of internal termination; they are much more difficult to configure.

SCSI Termination Scenarios

Most Macs require one terminator for one SCSI device, and two terminators for two or more SCSI devices. The termination in PowerBooks and the Mac Portable is weak enough that they require two terminators for one to six external SCSI devices. If you have a Macintosh IIfx or PowerBook, refer to the sections following this one for terminating these Macs.

WARNING: The Macintosh Plus does not provide termination power as do the other Macintosh computers (except for the PowerBooks which do not provide adequate termination power). Usually the SCSI device supplies termination power so the Mac Plus can work with the device. If you are having difficulty with a SCSI device connected to a Mac Plus and the SCSI device works fine on another Macintosh model, you can repair the SCSI device so that it provides termination, connect another SCSI device that provides termination power, or use this SCSI device on another Mac that provides termination.

Here are some SCSI configurations for a Macintosh:

Macintosh IIfx Termination

Termination on a SCSI chain with a Macintosh IIfx requires special attention. A *black* external terminator must be used when connecting SCSI devices to the system. This is because a unique SCSI chip was used in the Mac IIfx to offer data transfer rates up to 3M per second, the fastest rate possible when the Mac IIfx was first released. Do not use more than one black SCSI terminator on a SCSI chain—this could damage the Mac IIfx logic board or the device providing termination.

Macintosh IIfx systems shipped before March 19, 1990 did not have proper internal termination for the internal hard disk or the Macintosh. After that date, Apple hard disk drives shipped with the proper termination.

For proper termination of the Mac IIfx, a special internal SCSI Filter and a SCSI Termination Block can be obtained from an Apple dealer to internally terminate the Macintosh IIfx, and any hard drives or any non-Apple hard drives that do not offer internal termination. The filter has a 50-pin female connector on one end and a 50-pin male connector on the other. When connected to an internal drive, the drive cable is connected directly into the logic board and the internal SCSI Filter block is plugged in between the drive cable and the 50-pin connector on the hard drive. When there is no hard drive, the SCSI Filter is connected to the logic board and the internal SCSI Termination block is connected to the filter.

If you have a hard drive which is internally terminated, you can remove the internal SCSI Termination block, but leave the internal SCSI Filter connected to the logic board.

PowerBook Termination

The Apple HDI-30 SCSI System Cable is used to connect an external SCSI device to a Macintosh PowerBook. This cable is 19 inches long and has a standard 50-pin male SCSI connector to plug into a external SCSI device.

The PowerBooks have a different kind of internal termination, so PowerBooks require two terminators when attaching from one to six SCSI devices.

The PowerBook 100 has internal hard disk termination; however, the SCSI termination resistor provides only a minimal amount of termination. So, even though the system has internal termination, it requires an external terminator at the beginning and end of the SCSI chain.

The PowerBook As An External Hard Disk

PowerBooks, such as the 100, 160, 180, and Duo 210 and 230, can be connected to another Macintosh with the PowerBook SCSI port. By doing this, the PowerBook appears as an external hard disk on the Macintosh system's desktop.

To attach one of the PowerBooks to be used as a hard disk, the HDI-30 SCSI Disk Adapter cable is required. Once the PowerBook appears on the other Macintosh desktop, you can exchange, copy, and rename files from the desktop Macintosh as if the PowerBook were another hard disk.

SCSI Checklists

Here are checklists to help you determine if you have covered all the possible SCSI problems.

SCSI Power On Checklist

✻ It is recommended that all SCSI devices be turned on before the Macintosh. This is a good rule to follow, but it's not always necessary.

If you are having difficulty with SCSI devices being recognized at startup, and you must restart the Macintosh for the device to be recognized, then this is a case where you want to turn on the SCSI device before the Macintosh. You may need to turn on the first and last SCSI device along the SCSI chain.

✻ Do not adjust cables or connections while any devices or the Macintosh are turned on.

✻ Secure all cable connections before turning on the devices and the Macintosh.

SCSI ID Checklist

✻ In general, assign higher ID numbers to startup devices. For example, set an external hard drive that's used as the startup disk to ID number 6 or 5.

✻ After assigning IDs to startup devices, set other ID numbers according to how often they are used. For example, set a scanner or tape backup drive to a lower number, like 2 or 1.

✻ Don't set a SCSI device to an ID of 7, because ID 7 is reserved for the Macintosh CPU.

SCSI Cable Checklist

* Buy SCSI cables that are double-shielded. Double-shielded cables have two layers of metal shielding surrounding the data wires. The shielding protects the wires from electrical interference, preventing data loss.

* Keep the SCSI cable length as short as possible. The longer the cable is, the greater the chance of data errors. Avoid using cables longer than a few feet between SCSI devices. If you don't need the length, then go as short as possible. Don't go over 20 feet (6 meters) in total SCSI chain length; even this length is risky.

SCSI Termination Checklist

* In most cases, you need two terminators on the SCSI chain, one at the beginning and one at the end. They can be internal or external terminators.

* All Macintosh models except the Mac Plus, Macintosh Portable, and the PowerBooks provide internal SCSI termination power. The PowerBooks and Mac Portable require two terminators for one to six external SCSI devices. The other Macintosh computers require one terminator for one device, and two terminators for two or more SCSI devices.

* Power down the computer and all peripherals before attaching or removing terminators.

* Use the correct type of terminator. Terminators are usually gray or black. Use the gray one for any Macintosh except the Macintosh IIfx. The Macintosh IIfx requires the black external terminator to terminate the SCSI chain. The black terminator can be used on other SCSI devices; however, use only one black terminator on a SCSI chain (make the other a gray terminator).

 WARNING: Do not use more than one black SCSI terminator on a SCSI chain. This can damage the Mac IIfx logic board or the device providing termination.

✳ If the Macintosh has an internal hard drive which is terminated, terminate only the other end of the SCSI chain. All Apple internal SCSI hard drives have built-in terminators. For non-Apple hard drives, check with the hard drive manual or the vendor to make sure your internal hard drive has internal termination.

✳ If your Macintosh does not have an internal hard drive or the internal hard drive is not terminated, terminate both ends of the SCSI chain. Place a terminator between the device and the cable into the first SCSI device, and one terminator in the empty connector on last SCSI device.

✳ Some SCSI devices have only one SCSI port on the back panel. Place this device on the end of the SCSI chain if the device has internal termination.

If the device does not have internal termination, add the terminator between the cable and the device. Avoid buying peripherals which have only one SCSI port on the back panel.

✳ If you want to remove the internal termination from a SCSI device, check the manual for instructions on how to remove the internal terminator. Some internal termination requires that the device be sent to the vendor for removal.

SCSI Troubleshooting Tools

Besides using the SCSI checklists (and Chapter 13, "Symptoms and Solutions") to troubleshoot problems, there are SCSI utilities that will help mount SCSI devices that are not showing up on the Finder's desktop.

There are several commercial, shareware and freeware SCSI-mounting utilities. Shareware is software that you pay for on the honor system—if you use it, then you pay for it. Freeware is software that is free. Most of these utilities work with hard disks, tape drives, removable drives, and CD-ROM drives.

One freeware SCSI utility is included on the disk that accompanies this book; it is called SCSIProbe, by Robert Polic (see figure 10.2). SCSIProbe can identify and mount devices connected to your SCSI bus, and it includes a startup extension that can mount SCSI volumes without having SCSIProbe open.

Figure 10.2 SCSIProbe's window, showing attached SCSI devices.

Some of the commercial disk utilities, such as Silverlining and Hard Disk ToolKit, include a small utility to mount SCSI disks that have been formatted with their hard disk utility or have their SCSI driver installed (see the next section, "Hard Disks," for more information).

A utility called Drive7rem by Casa Blanca Works allows you to mount SCSI devices regardless of what utility formatted the drive or is needed to mount the drive (in the case of removable drives). This is handy when you do not have the driver for a particular drive, such as Bernoulli and Syquest drives, which normally requires a driver be present in the System Folder to mount the drive.

Hard Disks

Most hard disks are SCSI devices. There are two types of hard disks, internal and external. Internal hard disks are connected to the SCSI bus inside the Macintosh, while external hard disks are connected to the SCSI port on the back of the Macintosh (or another SCSI device in a chain of SCSI devices).

Connecting And Disconnecting Hard Disks

When disconnecting a hard disk, turn off the hard disk, the Macintosh and other connected devices before disconnecting the hard disk.

When connecting a hard disk, follow all the advice for connecting SCSI devices in the previous section on SCSI devices.

When turning on your Macintosh setup, the hard disk must come to full speed before the Macintosh will recognize and mount the disk on the desktop. If you have an internal hard disk it will be powered on when the Macintosh is turned on.

Hard Disk Backup

You don't know what you've got till it's gone—but don't wait until it's gone! Back up your hard disk as frequently as possible. For more information on hard disk backup see Chapter 2, "Macintosh Maintenance."

Formatting Your Hard Disk

There are two types of hard disk formats: low-level and initialization. A low-level format divides and maps out the disk, and gets the disk ready to be initialized for data. The initialization prepares the disk to accept hard drive information and software. If you have already initialized your disk, then re-initializing will erase all data on the disk by changing the disk directory.

A disk must be low-level formatted first, and then the disk can be initialized. When you first buy your hard disk, the disk has already been low-level formatted. The disk may also be initialized and contain a System Folder.

You can initialize your disk by using software that came with the drive or other commercial software, or you can initialize the disk by choosing Erase Disk from the Special menu in the Finder.

What's On The Disk After Initialization

When the Macintosh initializes a disk for data storage, the disk is organized into several areas: the boot blocks, the volume information block, the volume bitmap, the catalog tree, the extents tree, and the data region. There may also be a partition region to store partition information if the disk has been partitioned. The only area of the disk visible to you (from the Finder) is the data region, where you store your files and applications.

Boot Blocks

The first two blocks of the disk are reserved for the system startup or boot information (hence the term "boot blocks"). The boot blocks have information used to configure the Macintosh at startup and to locate system file information.

Boot blocks are found on a disk that is a startup disk. A startup disk is any Macintosh volume that has a System folder and is the designated startup disk (chosen in the Startup Disk control panel). Disks that are not bootable or startup disks will not have boot blocks.

Volume Information Block

The Volume Information Block stores information about the disk, such as the name, size and space free on the disk.

Volume Bitmap

The Volume Bitmap region keeps track of occupied and free space on the disk, which helps the Macintosh find free space to write file information.

Extents Tree

The Extents tree keeps track of where pieces of a file (fragments) are stored. Since there may not be enough room in one sector to store a file, the file is written to more than one sector of the disk, or fragmented.

Catalog Tree

The Catalog tree (also referred to as the directory) keeps track of the location of each file and folder on the Macintosh volume. The Macintosh uses the catalog to find files on the volume.

Data Region

The data region is where all the files that you write to disk are stored. This is the area where all your working applications, documents, and the invisible Desktop file are stored.

SCSI Driver

The SCSI driver software is installed when the disk is initialized. This driver manages the communication between your Macintosh and the hard disk. If the hard disk's SCSI driver is corrupted, the Macintosh will not be able to mount the hard disk on the desktop or read data from the disk. To fix this, use the software that came with the drive to reinstall the SCSI driver.

How To Install a SCSI Driver

Every hard disk has a SCSI disk driver (not visible to you as a file) which is installed on the disk so that the Macintosh can interact with the hard disk. The driver is installed by the software that came with your disk. If it is an Apple drive, you install the driver using the utility called *Apple HD SC Setup* (see figure 10.3). Apple HD SC Setup comes with your Macintosh system software and can be found on the Disk Tools disk.

Figure 10.3 Apple's HD SC Setup window.

The driver can become damaged in a crash or power interruption, in which case the disk will not show up (mount) on the desktop. To update the driver using Apple HD SC Setup, double-click on the application, choose the hard disk on which to install the driver and then click the Update button.

WARNING: The software you use to install the driver is also the software you initialize the hard disk with, so be careful not to initialize your hard disk!

System 7-Compatible SCSI Driver

Is the driver you are installing compatible with the version of Macintosh system software you are using? Many hard disks formatted while running System 6 will need a new driver installed for System 7.

Your hard disk utility may not be able to install a System 7-compatible SCSI driver. If this is the case, you have three options for upgrading the SCSI driver on your hard disk so it is System 7-compatible:

1. Use the System version of the Apple HD SC Setup if you have an Apple hard disk,

2. Upgrade the disk utility for your drive by contacting the hard drive maker, or

3. You can purchase a commercial disk utility that will install its own SCSI driver on your hard disk. Make sure you do not have to reformat your hard disk to install their driver.

Two products that can install a System 7-compatible SCSI driver on your hard disk without formatting it are Drive7 from Casa Blanca Works and Silverlining from La Cie. For more information on upgrading to System 7, see Chapter 4, "System Software."

Hard Disk Problems

The following are hard disk problems you might encounter. For more solutions for hard disk problems, see Chapter 13, "Symptoms And Solutions."

Hard Disk Hardware Problems

These are some problems you might encounter with the hard disk hardware.

What Is A Disk Crash?

Today a hard disk crash means the hard disk has failed somehow. A disk crash originally referred to the head of the disk crashing or falling on the disk itself. The disk head, like a stereo turntable needle, reads and writes to the magnetic disk. If the disk head failed or was not "parked" in place, the head hit the disk. Today all hard disks have automatic head parking when powered down, but we still use the catch-all phrase "disk crash."

Blown Fuse

If the hard disk is not receiving power, it could be because the hard disk has blown the fuse. The fuse is a protective device designed to melt or blow when there is a current overload.

Some drive fuses are on the outside of the drive, while others require that you open up the drive to replace the fuse. Most drives use a standard fuse like those found in cars and appliances.

If you are connecting other devices to the hard drive, you may need a fuse with a higher rating (measured in amps). Check the manual that came with the hard drive on how to replace the fuse and fuse requirements, or call the hard drive vendor.

Hard Drive Ventilation

Don't block vents on a hard drive, because the drive needs these vents to circulate air and maintain the correct temperature. If the vents are blocked, the drive may overheat and damage components and the disk media inside the drive.

Hard Drive Fan

Some drives have fans and some don't, and some fans are noisier than others. The fan is in there to maintain the temperature inside the drive case.

Hard Drive Cleaning

If your hard drive comes with a filter, then clean or replace the filter if recommended by the drive maker. The filter keeps dust and dirt particles from accumulating inside the drive. If dirt accumulates inside the case, the drive can overheat. You can wipe down the outside case with a mild soap and cloth—but make sure to turn the drive off before cleaning it.

Extreme Temperatures

Avoid storing or operating your hard drive in extremely low and high temperatures. If the drive has been in a temperature range outside of the suggested range (check you drive manual for the range) then wait until the drive has returned to room temperature before turning it on.

Hard Disk Software Problems

For most hard disk problems, you will want a software repair utility and an emergency floppy disk. (See Chapter 3, "Troubleshooting Tactics," for instructions on how to make an emergency disk.)

Sometimes it may be helpful to own more than one hard disk utility if the utility you own is not fixing a particular problem. Disk utilities have their strengths and weaknesses, but look for a disk utility that has a combination of disk repair and file recovery features.

Hard Disk First Aid

When you are having trouble accessing a disk, or you are receiving error messages when using the disk, the first thing to try is to repair the disk with a disk repair utility. If the repair utility cannot fix the disk, the next step is to recover the data from the disk. If you have a recent disk backup then you don't have to worry about data recovery.

CAUTION: Before you do any troubleshooting, if you can, backup all your valuable data.

Earlier in this chapter some unique parts of an initialized disk were described, such as the SCSI driver and the Volume Information Block. If one or more of these areas of the disk is damaged, there are disk repair utilities that can take a shot at fixing them. These utilities include: Norton Utilities For The Macintosh, Public Utilities, MacTools, and Disk First Aid.

Some of these utilities can also recover data from a damaged hard disk. Norton Utilities, MacTools and Public Utilities can recover data (Disk First Aid cannot). For more information on obtaining these disk utilities, see Appendix C, "Product Information."

 CAUTION: Software utilities that perform operations on one of your disks must be installed on a separate disk in most cases. Depending on the operation the utility is performing, you may receive a message saying the disk or the application is busy if the utility is stored on the disk you want to repair.

You can run a disk utility from a special floppy disk, like the ones created in Chapter 3, or you can run it from another hard disk, other than the damaged disk. Disk repair utilities may also include an "emergency" floppy disk with the disk repair software on the disk.

Here are some system messages that signal the need for hard disk repair. For more information on disk problems and solutions, see Chapter 13, "Symptoms And Solutions."

"This is not a Macintosh disk. Do you want to initialize it?"

Your hard disk should be showing up on the desktop, but instead you get this message. You do *not* want to initialize it—that will erase all your data! The volume information block or related areas of the hard disk are damaged. Use a utility to repair the disk.

"This disk needs minor repairs. Do you want to repair it?"

The hard disk catalog area is damaged. Click on OK. If this fails to fix the disk you can use Disk First Aid; however, it will most likely report that a problem exists that it cannot fix. Your best bet here are repair utilities that say they fix the catalog or directory, such as Public Utilities, MacTools, and Norton Utilities. If you cannot fix the disk, most utilities should be able to recover all or some of the files on the disk.

The hard disk is on the desktop, but the Mac cannot start up from it.

This hard disk was a startup disk and has a System Folder installed on it, but it cannot be used as a startup disk now, even though it mounts on the desktop. The hard disk's boot blocks are damaged; a disk utility such as Disk First Aid or Norton Utilities can repair the boot blocks.

One other possibility here is that the System and/or Finder file is damaged or missing. If this is the case, you will need to reinstall the system software.

A message says the disk is full, but it's not.

The disk directory and disk information are damaged. Use a disk utility to repair the disk. Also, try rebuilding the disk's Desktop by holding down the Option and ⌘ keys while restarting the Macintosh.

The hard disk does not show on the desktop.

The hard disk might have power, cable, or SCSI problems, but it is also possible that the disk is damaged.

Check the power cables for all SCSI devices in the SCSI chain. A SCSI device may not be powered on or receiving power. With some SCSI devices, all SCSI devices must be powered on for the devices to work.

Try a SCSI mounting utility (such as SCSIProbe, which is included on the disk with this book) to mount the disk on the desktop. You may have to install another SCSI driver to do this. Use a utility to help with mounting disks, such as Drive7.

The desktop file could also be damaged. Rebuild the desktop file by holding down the ⌘ and Option keys while restarting the Mac.

Finally, the disk's Volume Information Block may be damaged. Repair the disk with a disk repair utility.

"The disk could not be opened."

The disk information is damaged. Use a disk repair utility to repair the disk. If the disk cannot be repaired, use a file recovery program to recover the data.

Hard Disk File Recovery

If a disk repair utility cannot repair the disk, your next bet is to recover as much data as possible. If you have a recent backup, you may not need to sweat this out; just restore your disk from the backup.

You will need a file recovery tool, and most disk repair utilities include a file recovery feature. Here are some utilities that can recover files from a damaged disk: Norton Utilities For The Macintosh, Public Utilities, MacTools, and 911 Utilities.

 TIP: Don't copy the file recovery utility to the damaged hard disk, and *don't* recover files to the damaged disk. You will need a "safe" disk to save your recovered files on; saving them back to the damaged disk won't work. You can recover files to a removable disk, floppy disk, or hard disk, or a network volume.

If you are not able to recover data from the hard disk, there are professional data recovery services that will charge you to recover the data from your hard disk. Drive Savers is one such company. For more information, see Appendix C, "Product Information," or check the classified section of trade publications.

After you have recovered the data from the damaged disk, you can initialize the disk (remember—all data will be permanently erased!). After initializing the disk, but before copying data to the newly initialized disk, run a disk utility that can test the disk media. Checking the media will lock out bad areas of the disk so you won't copy files to those areas anymore. Some disk utilities check the disk media as a part of initializing the disk.

Hard Disk Partition Recovery

If you have partitioned your hard disk and a partition is giving you trouble, use the partitioning software to solve the problem as well as trying the repair utilities. If the partition software cannot fix or mount the partition, then take out the disk repair and file recovery software.

Recovering Deleted Files From A Hard Disk

If you have erased files from a hard disk by placing the file in the trash and emptying it, you have a very good chance of recovering the file(s). This is possible because although the file no longer appears on the disk, the file is still on the disk until the disk is initialized or another file takes its place. If you want to recover a deleted file, don't copy any files to the disk until you have recovered the deleted file(s)—copying a new file could overwrite the space where the deleted file is stored.

 WARNING: When you have accidentally deleted files by emptying the trash, do not copy anything to that disk and do not install the undelete utility on that disk. By doing so, you could be permanently erasing the deleted file by copying over it.

Here are utilities that can assist you in recovering deleted files: Norton Utilities, Public Utilities, MacTools, Complete Undelete, and 911 Utilities.

Many disk utilities offer a system extension which tracks deleted files. This makes the deleted files easier to recover, thereby offering a better chance of recovering deleted files.

File recovery and undelete utilities can recover files when:

* The deleted file space has not been used for a new file.

* The hard disk has not been reformatted with a low-level formatting program.

* In the case of a floppy disk, if the floppy disk has not been reformatted (if it has not been erased in the Finder).

Hard Disk Formatting Utilities

Whether you are formatting your disk to optimize your disk, or you are formatting a damaged disk, here are some formatting utilities that you may find helpful: Silverlining, Hard Disk ToolKit, Apple HD SC Setup, and Disk Café.

You can, of course, use the utility that came with your hard disk to initialize your disk, but the independent formatting utilities are designed to optimize the disk's performance. Some of the above utilities are bundled with hard drives, and Apple HD SC Setup comes with the Macintosh system software. (However, Apple HD SC Setup only works with Apple hard disks.)

Hard Disk Interleave

The performance of your hard disk is directly related to its *interleave factor* and the type of Macintosh computer you are using. The interleave is set during the hard disk formatting procedure.

The Mac Plus performs optimally with an interleave factor of 3:1. The 68020-based and higher Macs have an optimal factor of 1:1, and the Macintosh SE works best with an interleave factor of 2:1.

For the optimal performance for a hard disk, the formatting utility matches the interleave to the Macintosh attached to the disk.

Where and when do I set the interleave factor?

Fortunately, disk formatting software automatically determines which interleave is the best for your Macintosh when you are formatting a disk.

There are utilities that can tell you the interleave factor of a hard disk. FWB's Hard Disk ToolKit, Apple HD SC Setup, La Cie's Silverlining and others can format and set the interleave for a hard disk.

To check what the interleave is on your disk using the Apple HD SC Setup (and to change the interleave), use the latest system version and the latest version of the Apple HD SC Setup application. Press the ⌘-I keys after you arrive at the Apple HD SC Setup window to access the interleave dialog box (see figure 10.4).

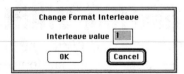

Figure 10.4   Changing the interleave with the Apple HD SC Setup program.

What are interleave considerations when formatting a hard disk?

* Use the program that came with your disk, or a disk utility program that can format your disk. Many utilities work with almost any disk.

* Format the hard disk from the type of Macintosh the drive will be connected to. If more than one type of Macintosh will access the SCSI hard disk, it is best to format the disk on the slowest Macintosh for the best average performance.

* Consider changing the interleave factor when you attach a hard disk to a different Macintosh model or add an accelerator card to speed up the Macintosh CPU (central processing unit) performance.

You may need to reformat the disk to adjust the interleave factor to the new setup. For example, a hard disk may have been attached to a Mac Plus (1:1 interleave factor), and is now attached to a Mac IIci.

 WARNING: Remember to back up your entire disk before changing the interleave. Changing the interleave requires reformatting the disk—an operation that erases all the data on the disk.

Floppy Disks

The problems with floppy disks are similar to hard disk problems, on a smaller scale. The disk media can be damaged, the software on it can be damaged, or the disk hardware can be damaged.

Formatting A Floppy Disk

Formatting a floppy disk is different from formatting a hard disk when using the Finder's Erase Disk command (see figure 10.5). When you select the floppy disk and choose Erase Disk from the Special menu, the floppy disk is both formatted and initialized, so data is not recoverable—even with a file recovery utility.

Figure 10.5   The Finder's Erase Disk command under the Special menu.

If you select Erase Disk... while a hard disk is selected, you stand a better chance of recovering data from the hard disk because the disk is only initialized. It doesn't hurt to try and recover the data from an erased floppy disk, but the chances of recovery are slim.

Floppy Disk First Aid

Disk repair utilities that you have for your hard disk can also fix floppy disks. Buy a disk utility that has both disk repair and file recover features for floppy disks as well. The following disk repair utilities also fix floppy disks: Norton Utilities, MacTools, Public Utilities, and Disk First Aid. For more information on how to obtain these utilities, see Appendix C, "Product Directory."

If you think a floppy disk is in need of repair, make sure the problem is not with the floppy drive (see the next section for more information on floppy drives). If the problems are occurring with more than one floppy disk, this is a sign that the problem may be with the floppy drive or a bad batch of floppy disks.

Here are some signs of floppy disk damage and what to do in each case.

"This is not a Macintosh disk. Do you want to initialize it?"

You normally receive this message if your disk has not been initialized (a new disk). You will also receive this message if the disk is has been formatted with a computer other than a Macintosh, if you have inserted a high-density disk into an 800K floppy drive, or a high-density or 800K disk into a 400K floppy drive; damaged disks can lead to this message as well. Click Eject, unless you are *sure* that you want to erase the disk.

To fix the disk, launch your disk repair utility and then insert the floppy disk. If the utility cannot repair the floppy disk, then recover the files on the disk to a safe disk. You can try reformatting the floppy disk, but don't trust a disk if this has happened to this disk before.

 WARNING: Don't format an 800K disk as a 1.4M high-density disk or vice-versa (see figure 10.6). Although it seems like you can format an 800K as a high-density disk and visa versa, this is not a good idea. The disks are specifically designed for a certain format size and will eventually (if not immediately) cause problems when reading the data from the disk.

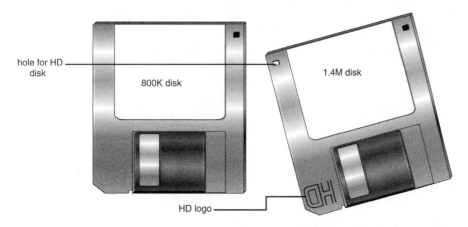

Figure 10.6   An 800K disk and a 1.4M disk.

If you must read a high-density disk that has been formatted as an 800K disk, block the top left hole in the disk with tape and copy the contents of the disk onto another disk that is properly formatted.

"This disk needs minor repairs. Do you want to repair it?"

Click OK. If this fails to fix the disk, your best bet here are repair utilities such as Public Utilities, MacTools, and Norton Utilities. If you cannot fix the disk, most utilities should be able to recover all or some of the files on the disk.

"Due to a disk error, the file could not be copied. Continue copy?"

The disk you are copying the file to is damaged, the disk area the file resides on is bad, or the file itself may be damaged. Make a backup of the file if possible and then try copying the file to another disk. If you are not able to copy the file to another disk, run a disk repair utility on the disk storing the file, and repair the disk. If the disk is bad or an area of the disk is damaged, move the file to a good disk or a safe area of the same disk.

A message says the disk is full.

Most floppy disks have some space taken up by invisible files such as the Desktop file and disk directory. Even when you format a disk, you don't really get to use all the space. Figure 10.7 shows the window of a floppy disk that has been formatted but does not have any files on it (0 items).

Figure 10.7 An empty floppy disk window.

Notice that there is already 1K of space taken up on the disk. This space grows as you add more files to the disk. To recover some of the space taken up by invisible files, you can rebuild the desktop or reformat the disk.

It is possible that the disk is not full, but in fact the disk directory and disk information are damaged. In this case, use a disk repair utility to repair the disk.

The floppy disk does not show up on the desktop.

The Desktop file could be damaged. Rebuild the desktop file by holding down the ⌘ and Option keys while inserting the disk into the floppy drive (see figure 10.8), or while restarting the Mac. If this doesn't work, repair the disk with a disk repair utility.

> ⚠️ Are you sure you want to rebuild the desktop file on the disk "Floppy Disk"? Comments in info windows will be lost.
>
> [Cancel] [OK]

Figure 10.8   Holding down the ⌘ and Option keys when you insert a disk brings up the dialog box to rebuild the desktop.

A message says the disk could not be opened.

The disk information is damaged. Use a disk repair utility to repair the disk. If the disk cannot be repaired, use a file recovery program to recover the data on the disk.

Once you have recovered any data from the floppy disk you may want to reformat the floppy disk to start over and clean up the disk. Under System 6, if a portion of the disk is damaged, the operating system will not allow you to reformat the disk. Under System 7, the operating system will reformat and block out bad areas of the floppy disk so you can use the disk again. Some disk utilities, such as Public Utilities, offer a floppy formatting feature which will format and repair bad disk media regardless of whether you are running System 6 or 7.

Recovering Deleted Files From A Floppy Disk

If you have erased files from a floppy disk by placing the file in the trash and emptying it, you have a very good chance of recovering the file(s). This is possible because although the file no longer appears on the disk, the file is still on the disk until the disk is initialized, or another file takes its place. If you want to recover a deleted file, don't copy any files to the floppy until you have recovered the deleted file(s)—copying a new file could write over the space where the deleted file is stored.

WARNING: When you have accidentally deleted files by emptying the trash, do not copy anything to that disk and do not install the undelete utility on that disk. By doing so, you could be permanently erasing the deleted file by copying over it.

Here are utilities that can assist you in recovering deleted files: Norton Utilities, Public Utilities, MacTools, Complete Undelete, and 911 Utilities.

Many disk utilities offer a system extension which tracks deleted files. This makes the deleted files easier to recover, thereby offering a better chance of recovering deleted files.

File recovery and undelete utilities can recover files when:

* The deleted file space has not been used for a new file.

* The hard disk has not been reformatted with a low-level formatting program.

* In the case of a floppy disk, if the floppy disk has not been reformatted (if it has not been erased in the Finder).

As an example, MacTools offers a separate program for recovering files, called CP Undelete. Figure 10.9 shows the CP Undelete window and some deleted files from my hard disk.

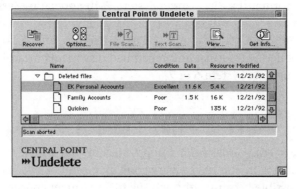

Figure 10.9 MacTools' CP Undelete program for recovering deleted files.

Floppy Disk Spring And Shutter

There is metal shutter on your floppy disk which is kept in place with a tiny metal spring. The shutter covers the disk media while it is not inserted in the floppy disk drive.

If these pieces should fall off, you may have a chance at putting them back together again. Reinsert the spring into the disk and then latch the shutter back on to the spring. It may take some work, but it's not impossible.

If you can't manage it, just insert the disk into the floppy drive without the shutter on, copy the data to another disk and then throw the disk in the (real) trash.

Floppy Disk Formats

The Macintosh uses 3 1/2-inch floppy disks that can be formatted as double-sided (800K) or high-density (1440K or 1.4M). The original Macs use single-sided floppy disks (400K).

High-density disks, like the one in figure 10.10, are usually labeled as such and have an extra hole in the top left corner of the floppy disk (besides the write-protect tab on the top right corner of the disk).

Some disk drives can read all three disk formats, and others can read only 800K and 400K disks. The Apple SuperDrive can read all disk types, whereas older Mac disk drives (on the Mac Plus and older Mac SEs) are able to read only 800 and 400K formatted disks. The Macintosh 128K and 512K have 400K disk drives, and therefore read only 400K disks.

Don't Format 800K disks As 1.4M disks!

Don't format 800K disks as 1.4M (high-density disks)! Although it seems that you can format an 800K as a high-density and visa versa, this is not a good idea. The disks are specifically designed for a certain format size and will eventually (if not immediately) cause problems when reading the data from the disk.

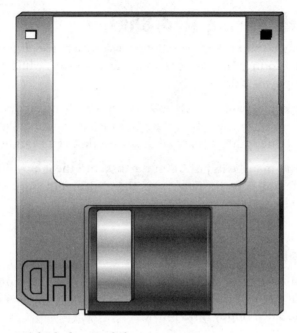

Figure 10.10 A high-density disk.

If you must read a high-density disk that has been formatted as an 800K disk, block the top left hole in the disk with tape and copy the contents of the disk onto another disk that is properly formatted.

There are three different formatting sizes for floppy disks: 400K, 800K and 1440K. Table 10.1 shows which disk formats require which floppy disk drives.

Table 10.1 Disk size and floppy disk drive required to read it

Disk	Capacity (in K)	Floppy Drive Required
Single-Sided	400	400K or 800K or 1440K
Double-Sided	800	800K or 1440K
High-Density	1440K (1.4M)	1440K (SuperDrive)

If you insert a high-density disk to be formatted in an 800K disk drive, the disk will be formatted at 800K, and will not be reliable. A high-density disk should only be formatted in a high-density disk drive, called a SuperDrive (previously called Apple FDHD SuperDrive).

On the other hand, if you insert an 800K disk in a SuperDrive, the disk will be formatted properly, as an 800K disk.

A Floppy Disk That Won't Eject

Do not force a disk to eject by pulling on it. You will damage the floppy disk and the floppy drive's read/write mechanism because the disk shutter is open while the disk is in the floppy drive.

Here are several ways to eject a floppy disk:

* Highlight the floppy disk and press ⌘-E, which is the same as choosing Eject Disk from the Special menu in the Finder.

* In System 7, pressing ⌘-Y will eject the highlighted floppy disk and remove the icon of the disk from the desktop as well. This is the same as dragging the disk over the Trash icon; it works with network volumes as well. Pressing ⌘-Y will also get rid of the remaining disk icon after you have ejected a floppy disk.

* Press ⌘-Shift-1 for the first internal floppy drive, or ⌘-Shift-2 for the second floppy drive.

* Hold the mouse button down while restarting the Macintosh.

* Insert the end of a paper clip into the small hole on the side of the floppy drive. You are manually forcing the disk to eject by exerting pressure on the ejection mechanism in the floppy drive.

Floppy Disk Drives

Floppy disk drives are included in most Macintosh computers (some of the exceptions are the PowerBook 100 and Duo 210 and 230). All Macs (except for the Mac Plus, older Mac SEs, and Mac IIs) come with an Apple SuperDrive.

Most of the problems associated with floppy disks are due to dust and dirt buildup, but there occasions where a part in the disk mechanism will fail.

Most dirt enters through the same slot that you insert the disk. Dirt can damage the disk read/write head that sits on the disk media—and the result is that your disks become unreadable or have high failure rates when writing files to floppy disks. You can prevent this by cleaning your floppy drive. For more information on disk drive cleaning, see Chapter 2, "Macintosh Maintenance."

Here are some signs of disk problems, both disk hardware damage and the signs of dirt accumulation inside the drive.

Strange Sounds

If your disk is making a grinding or other strange sound, check to see if it is happening with all floppy disks. It may just be with one or two damaged floppy disks. If not, then the read/write heads on the drive are probably damaged. Have the disk drive replaced by a qualified service technician.

Disks Don't Eject Easily

If disks are getting stuck frequently or don't eject easily, you may have to have the disk drive replaced. Bring the Macintosh (or the disk drive if it is an external disk drive) to a qualified service technician.

This disk is unreadable or not a Macintosh disk. Initialize?

If this is happening to several of your disks, the disk might be dirty, the read/write heads misaligned, or you may have a bad batch of floppy disks. Clean the disk with a commercial disk cleaner.

The Drive Is Slow

Clean the disk drive with a commercial cleaner. If the lack of speed persists, bring the Macintosh (or the disk drive if it is an external disk drive) to a qualified service technician.

Upgrading To A SuperDrive

If you have an older Mac SE (*not* the Mac SE/30) or Mac II, you can upgrade the floppy disk drive from an 800K to a 1.4M SuperDrive.

To upgrade the Macintosh SE or Mac II floppy drive to a SuperDrive, you will need the upgrade kit from an Apple authorized dealer, which includes the ROM replacement, a *SWIM* chip kit (the disk controller for the SuperDrive) and the SuperDrive. Unless you know what you are doing, it is suggested that you have an authorized Apple service technician perform the upgrade.

In the case of the Macintosh II, if you upgrade the Macintosh II to a Mac IIfx, you will replace the entire logic board and need only purchase the SuperDrive. For some more money you will have a Mac IIfx and a SuperDrive.

How Many Floppy Disk Drives Can I Connect To My Macintosh?

A Macintosh computer can support one external floppy drive connection. Table 10.2 lists the floppy drive configurations supported by Macintosh computers.

Table 10.2 Floppy disk drive configurations of Macintosh computers

Macintosh	Floppy Disk Drive Configuration
Plus	1 internal (800K) and 1 external (400K or 800K)
SE	1 or 2 internal (800K or SuperDrive if upgraded) and 1 external (400K, 800K or SuperDrive if upgraded)
SE w/SuperDrive	1 or 2 internal (SuperDrive) and 1 external (800K or SuperDrive)
SE/30	1 internal (SuperDrive) and 1 external (800K or SuperDrive)

continues

Table 10.2   Continued

Macintosh	Floppy Disk Drive Configuration
Classic	1 internal (SuperDrive) and 1 external (800K or SuperDrive)
Classic II	1 internal (SuperDrive) and 1 external (800K or SuperDrive)
II	1 or 2 internal (800K or SuperDrive) and no external
IIx	1 or 2 internal (800K or SuperDrive) and no external
IIcx	1 internal (SuperDrive) and 1 external (800K or SuperDrive)
IIci	1 internal (SuperDrive) and 1 external (800K or SuperDrive)
IIfx	1 or 2 internal (800K or SuperDrive) and no external
LC	1 or 2 internal (SuperDrive) and no external
LC II	1 internal (SuperDrive) and no external
IIsi	1 internal (SuperDrive) and 1 external (800K or SuperDrive)
Quadra 700	1 internal (SuperDrive) and no external
Quadra 900	1 internal (SuperDrive) and no external
Quadra 950	1 internal (SuperDrive) and no external
Portable	1 or 2 internal (SuperDrive) and 1 external (800K or SuperDrive)
PowerBook 100	No internal and 1 external HDI-20 1.4M drive
PowerBook 140	1 internal (SuperDrive) and no external
PowerBook 145	1 internal (SuperDrive) and no external
PowerBook 170	1 internal (SuperDrive) and no external
PowerBook 160	1 internal (SuperDrive) and no external

Macintosh	Floppy Disk Drive Configuration
PowerBook 180	1 internal (SuperDrive) and no external
PowerBook Duo 210	No internal and 1 external (one internal on Duo Dock)
PowerBook Duo 230	No internal and 1 external (one internal on Duo Dock)
Performa 200	1 internal and no external
Performa 400	1 internal and no external
Performa 600	1 internal and no external
IIvx	1 internal and no external

CD-ROM Drives

A CD-ROM drive plays CD-ROM disks which look just like audio CDs; they contain the same computer information that you can store on regular hard disks. The only difference is the data cannot be erased. CD-ROM disks are based on a master disk and mass-produced with CD-ROM pressing technology.

CD-ROM disks can hold, on average, 550M of data—equal to over 680 800K floppy disks. This vast amount of storage space makes CD-ROMs really handy for storing large files and lots of files that can then be distributed on the CD-ROM disk.

CD-ROM drives are SCSI devices that allow you to read CD-ROM disks. The CD-ROM drive comes with a set of files to be installed in the System Folder.

CD-ROM drives also come with the capability to play CD audio disks. You can connect headphones or a hi-fi system to your CD-ROM drive if there is software support that enables the drive to play sound from audio CDs.

Here are some common CD-ROM drive questions and troubleshooting tips:

What kinds of CDs can I read with my CD-ROM drive?

The CD-ROM driver software determines the computer's ability to read a CD-ROM disk. Apple ships software with its CD-ROM drives that enables it to read the following formats:

* HFS (Hierarchical File System). This is the Mac's native filing system.

* High Sierra. This is the first CD-ROM standard.

* ISO 9660. The current CD-ROM standard, derived from the High Sierra standard.

* Audio CDs. Standard audio (musical) CDs.

Can I use my Mac CD-ROM player on a PC?

You need software drivers for the PC to be able to read from the Mac CD-ROM. To find out if you can do this with your drive, contact the drive manufacturer.

Can I read CD-ROM disks for PCs on my Mac?

CD-ROMs intended for use across platforms (Mac and PC included) are written in the High Sierra or ISO 9660 formats, which both Mac and PC can read. HFS CD-ROMs typically contain files and programs specific to the Macintosh. However, the Macintosh cannot read DOS files or run DOS programs without special software.

One solution is to use a product called SoftPC. SoftPC allows you to mount PC drives and use PC software from a DOS partition the software sets up. For more information, see Appendix C, "Product Information."

I can't hear sounds I copied from a CD-ROM disk.

Macintosh sound files are different from the audio sounds on a CD. If the sound you are copying is a CD audio recording (only audible from the sound outputs of the CD player), then the actual sound cannot be copied. The icon you see is only a placeholder.

I can't unmount my CD-ROM disk when File Sharing is turned on.

When File Sharing starts up, it remembers all the volumes available on the current desktop. All volumes (excluding floppies, which cannot be shared) are considered shared, even if you have not selected to share the volume.

If a CD-ROM disk isn't inserted into the drive when you start File Sharing, you can't share the CD-ROM disk. The reverse works as well, so if you turn on File Sharing while a CD-ROM disk is inserted into the drive, you can't eject the CD-ROM disk.

To unmount the CD-ROM disk you will have to turn File Sharing off in the Sharing Setup control panel (in the System Folder), unmount the CD-ROM disk, and then turn File Sharing back on. Alternatively, you can restart the Macintosh and the CD-ROM disk will be ejected at restart.

Can I share a CD-ROM drive on an AppleShare File Server?

AppleShare File Server version 3.0 allows you to set up and exchange removable media, including CD-ROM disks. Earlier versions of the AppleShare File Server can have one or more CD-ROM disks as shared volumes; however, they do not support the exchanging of removable media while the server is active. On earlier versions, you have to shut the server down to change the disk in the CD-ROM drive.

To start a disk as a volume on an AppleShare server, bring the server down, insert the CD-ROM disk (the CD-ROM drive is attached to the server), and then restart the server so it examine all the volumes attached to it.

Conclusion

This chapter has covered problems with the most common types of storage media: hard disks, floppy disks, and CD-ROMs. The next chapter covers peripherals that deal with the printed page: printers and scanners.

I Need To Know!

Chapter 11

Printers and Scanners

Despite predictions of the "paperless office," printed communication is alive and well. Computers interact with the world of paper by converting electronic files to images on paper (through printers) and by converting images on paper to electronic files (through scanners). This chapter covers common problems that are found in both processes.

Printers

There a several types of printers that can be used with the Macintosh, including daisy-wheel, dot-matrix, inkjet, thermal, and laser printers.

Of all the printers mentioned here, the laser printer is the most commonly used with a Macintosh; Table 11.1 shows a comparison of the printers and their advantages and disadvantages.

Table 11.1   Printer Comparison

Printer Type	Pros	Cons
dot-matrix	affordable	average output (just adequate for letter quality); noisy
daisy-wheel	good for producing forms; inexpensive	slow; noisy; no real graphics capability
inkjet	quiet; good resolution (300 dots per inch); affordable	print can look smudged; slow
thermal	quiet; inexpensive; portable	printout poor; slow; uses special paper
laser	fast; quiet; uses standard paper; high-quality output; upgrade paths; flexible	expensive but worth it (prices are coming down)

Printer Resolution

The *resolution* of a printer refers to the quality of the printout and is measured in the number of dots per inch (or dpi) that the printer can print. You should look for a resolution of 300 dpi or better if you looking for business letter or better quality. The higher the density of dots (resolution) the better and sharper the output.

If you are printing graphics, you should consider what kind of printer you need to work with your graphics software. Many laser printers support PostScript, which is required to print out documents from advanced layout and high-end graphics applications (for applications such as QuarkXpress, PageMaker, Aldus FreeHand, and Adobe Illustrator), and also if you are using PostScript fonts.

If you don't need PostScript support in a printer, you still need to make sure the printer can work with the Macintosh.

Plugging In A Printer

Printers connect to the Macintosh by way of the modem port, the printer port, or (in a few cases) the SCSI port.

What makes the printer port different from the modem port on the back of the Macintosh is that the printer port supports *AppleTalk*. AppleTalk is the Mac's built-in set of networking protocols that enable Macs to be connected into a network.

If a printer has support for AppleTalk, it can also be networked, so other Macintosh users can use the printer as well. An example of a printer with AppleTalk support is Apple's LaserWriter series of printers. Some printers, such as Apple's LaserWriter IIg, also have EtherTalk support, and can be connected to an Ethernet network. Personal printers designed for individual use, such as Apple's StyleWriter, do not have AppleTalk support.

Upgrading Printer Memory

Here are some good reasons to upgrade the RAM in your printer:

* More printer RAM will decrease the printing time when printing complex documents, such as graphics and layout documents. Some documents may not print at all without more memory.

* More printer RAM will decrease printing time when using downloaded fonts in a document. More memory allows more fonts to be downloaded (sent over the network) to the printer at one time. The printer is less likely to need to retrieve large font files (improving network performance).

* More memory will decrease the printing time of documents that have been scaled down from larger originals.

* More memory will increase the imageable area of a document.

* More memory gives your printer more space to store and compute calculations it performs to print large and complex documents.

You can upgrade or expand the amount of memory on many printers if the printers have the memory slots to support RAM upgrades. Table 11.2 shows the memory upgrade path for some Apple printers. In most cases, the printer RAM is different than your Macintosh RAM, so you cannot use RAM from your computer in your printer.

Table 11.2   Printer SIMM Configurations

Printer	RAM Size	SIMM Slots	Memory Possibilities	RAM Speed Required
ImageWriter II	32K Memory Card[1]	n/a	n/a	
LaserWriter		n/a	1.5M on board[2]	n/a
LaserWriter Plus		n/a	1.5M on board[2]	n/a
LaserWriter NT		n/a	2M on board[2]	n/a
LaserWriter NTX	256K, 1 MB	12	2, 3, 4, 5, 8, 9 or12M	120 ns
LaserWriter IISC	256K	4	1M	120 ns
LaserWriter IIf	256K, 1 MB, 4 MB	8	2, 4, 5, 8, 16, 17, 20, or 32M	80 ns
LaserWriter IIg	256K, 1 MB, or 32M	8	5, 8, 16, 17, or 20M	80 ns
Personal LaserWriter SC	256K	4	1M	120 ns
Personal LaserWriterLS	256K	4	500K or1M	100 ns
Personal LaserWriter NT	1M, 4M	2	2 or 8M	120 ns
Personal LaserWriter NTR	1M, 2M	1	3 or 4M (2M on board)[3]	80 ns

[1] This upgrade allows you to continue working while the printer is printing; for ImageWriter II printers numbered A9M0320 and earlier.

[2] These LaserWriter printers have the RAM soldered on the board. RAM upgrades are not possible.

[3] The Personal LaserWriter NT printer's two SIMM slots are treated as one bank, so you cannot combine 1M and 4M SIMMs to get 5M.

If you own a printer other than an Apple brand, it is quite possible that your non-Apple printer memory can be upgraded. To find out how to upgrade your printer's memory, contact the printer manufacturer.

Upgrading Printers

If you bought an Apple printer that you are now outgrowing due to speed, memory, or other needs, instead of buying a whole new printer consider upgrading the printer you own. Table 11.3 shows upgrade paths for some Apple printers. Apple offers the upgrade through authorized dealers, so find a dealer near you. For more information on these upgrades, contact an authorized Apple dealer for upgrade information (see Chapter 14, "Technical Resources").

Table 11.3   Apple Printer Upgrades

Printer	Can be upgraded to a...	By buying a...
Personal LaserWriterSC	Personal LaserWriter NTR	Personal LaserWriter NTR upgrade kit
Personal LaserWriterNT	Personal LaserWriter NTR	Personal LaserWriter NTR upgrade kit
LaserWriterSC	LaserWriterIIf	LaserWriterIIf upgrade board
LaserWriterSC	LaserWriterIIg	LaserWriterIIg upgrade board
LaserWriterIINT	LaserWriterIIf	LaserWriterIIf upgrade board
LaserWriterIINT	LaserWriterIIg	LaserWriterIIg upgrade board
LaserWriterIINTX	LaserWIIf	LaserWriterIIf upgrade board
LaserWriterIINTX	LaserWriterIIg	LaserWriterIIg upgrade board
LaserWriterIIf	LaserWriterIIg	LaserWriterIIg upgrade board
LW Select 300	LW Select 310	LW Select 310 upgrade kit

TIP: An ImageWriter II/LQ can have a LocalTalk option installed so that it can be connected to a network for group use.

Using A Non-Apple Printer With A Macintosh

You can connect a variety or printers to a Macintosh other than Apple printers; however, you will need to consider whether the printer has an AppleTalk connection and printer drivers that enable it to communicate with the Macintosh.

If the printer does not have an AppleTalk port (or some other support for AppleTalk) you will have to obtain an adapter or connect it through an intermediary device.

The printer drivers that come with the Macintosh system software support Apple's printers and most printers made for the Macintosh. If you have a non-Apple printer, you may be required to install special software drivers so that the Macintosh can communicate with the printer.

If you are connecting a printer that does not have AppleTalk support, there are commercial utilities that enable your Mac to succesfully print to the printer. Grappler IIsp from Orange Micro, PowerPrint from GDT Softworks, and MacPrint from Insight Development enable the Macintosh to print to a variety of PC dot-matrix, inkjet, and bubblejet printers. See Appendix C, "Product Information."

Printer Testing

Most printers can run a self-test to check that all is well. Laser printers typically print a test page when first powered on. You can also use some utilities that come with your printer to adjust printer settings.

Apple's LaserWriters come with a printer utility called *LaserWriter Font Utility*, which lets you turn the test, called the Start Page, on or off. Figure 11.1 shows the dialog box for changing this option in the LaserWriter Font Utility. You can find the LaserWriter Font Utility on the System 7 "Tidbits" disk.

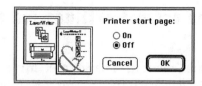

Figure 11.1   Changing the Start Page with the LaserWriter Font Utility.

The ImageWriter's self-test is performed by turning off the printer, then pressing the Form Feed button while you turn it back on. The ImageWriter prints character sets continuously across the page (so make sure you have paper in the printer!) like this:

```
!#$%&'()*+,./0123456789:;<>?@ABCDEFGHIJKLMNO
PQRSTUVWXYZ[\]^'abcdefghijklmnopqrstuvwxyz{¦}
```

You can also run self-test on the ImageWriter II in all three printing modes. Just turn the printer off and hold down the Form Feed button while turning it back on. While it's printing, deselect the printer by pushing the Line Feed button, then push the Print Quality button to select a new mode. Then reselect the printer by pushing Line Feed. When the print head begins a new line, it will print in standard quality. Repeat this step again to enter high quality mode.

To determine the self-test procedure for other printers, refer to the manual that came with the printer.

TIP: Under System 6, you can print the active window directly to the ImageWriter by pressing ⌘-Shift-4.

ImageWriter Problems

Here are some problems and questions encountered with the ImageWriter:

What are the correct settings for the ImageWriter?

For software settings, select the ImageWriter driver in the Chooser (under the ⌘ menu in the Finder). If the driver is not visible in the Chooser, make sure the ImageWriter driver is installed in the System Folder (see figure 11.2); under System 7 the driver goes in the Extensions Folder.

ImageWriter

Figure 11.2   ImageWriter driver icon.

AppleTalk should be inactive, and the port the ImageWriter cable is connected to on the back of the Mac should be selected in the Chooser—either the Modem or the Printer port.

As for the ImageWriter's hardware settings, the power should be on, the paper inserted, the top closed securely and the Select button on. Check appropriate paper settings for pin or tractor feed paper.

Can I clean the ImageWriter?

Yes, you can blow dust and dirt out of the printer with a can of compressed air, and wipe grease and dirt from moving parts with a non-conductive cleaner or alcohol and a cotton cloth or swab.

Can I connect a PC printer to my Macintosh?

You might be able to, depending on the type of printer. The printer has to be able to connect to one of the Macintosh ports (Modem, Printer, or SCSI port). If the printer has a *parallel* printer connector, it cannot directly connect to the Macintosh. You can purchase an adapter to connect the parallel connector to the Mac's SCSI port, or a custom cable to connect the printer's serial port to one of the Mac's serial ports (the Modem and Printer ports).

The other part of the picture is support for one of the Mac's *printer drivers*. The printer driver is a file that goes in the System Folder and allows the Mac to interact with the printer. Printer drivers can be found in the System Folder and include files for the ImageWriter and LaserWriter (see figure 11.3).

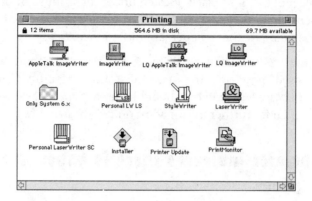

Figure 11.3   Printer driver icons (usually found in the Extensions folder).

If the printer can work with the printer drivers that come with the Macintosh system software, you're set. Otherwise, you will have to purchase a separate software driver to support the PC-based printer. Two products that provide both printer drivers and cables are MacPrint and PowerPrint. See Appendix C, "Product Information."

The ImageWriter compresses the first line of text.

If the first line of text on the page is compressed, the platen gears are out of alignment. The platen is the cylinder in the printer which the paper goes over. Turn the printer off, wait a few minutes and then turn it on again. The initialization upon powering on realigns the platen gears.

Also, make sure the ribbon is aligned well and moving as the printer prints.

The ImageWriter's red error light blinks.

* Make sure that the printer is not out of paper and that the paper has been inserted properly.

* Check to make sure that the cover is securely fastened and that the magnet is still in place (located under the front right of the cover). Sometimes the magnet becomes loosened and falls out. Also, check to make sure that a paper jam has not occurred.

* Check DIP switch 4 on Switch 2. DIP switch 4 should be set to the "closed" position if the AppleTalk Card or Memory Card is installed. Otherwise DIP switch 4 should be set to "open." See the ImageWriter manual for further information on its DIP switches.

The printer indicates there is paper when there isn't paper.

* Turn off the printer and then turn it on again. Make sure the printer is selected in the Chooser (under the menu in the Finder).

* The platen may be dirty or covered with ink. The ink build-up makes the platen surface reflect the light from the optical paper sensor. Clean the platen surface with typewriter platen cleaner.

* If the printer is an ImageWriter II, the magnet on the cover may have fallen off.

The paper jams in the tractor feed on the Imagewriter.

* Turn the power off and on again to center the feeder.

* If using tractor feed, don't switch the feed setting to friction feed. The tension on the paper is maintained, so if the paper is still on the tractor feed pins, it will be ripped off.

* The paper may be catching on the back of the paper guide.

* Try inserting a clean sheet before starting the friction feed.

* Make sure that drive select is in the proper position.

The paper jams on the ImageWriter when using the pin feed.

* The paper may be too heavy. Paper should be 15-pound or lighter. Also check the setting of the paper thickness lever.

* Make sure the paper is feeding properly and is not catching on the back of the paper guide.

* Make sure the switch is positioned to pin feed.

* Clear the paper path and start over.

The ImageWriter does not respond when turned on.

* Try another electrical outlet, test the outlet with a small appliance, or try another power cord.

* If you are traveling internationally, verify that you have the correct voltage setting or transformer.

* Check that the printer is selected in the Chooser and confirm that the port it is connected to is selected in the Chooser— either the Modem port or the Printer port.

The error light is on but the select light is off.

There isn't paper inserted or it is improperly inserted.

The ImageWriter is not printing.

Check that the printer is selected and the cable connections are secure, and verify the DIP switch settings.

The printed characters are garbled.

* Check the DIP switch settings. In particular, check DIP switch 4 on Switch 2. DIP switch 4 should be set to the "closed" position if the AppleTalk Card or Memory Card is installed. Otherwise DIP switch 4 should be set to "open". See the ImageWriter manual for further information on its DIP switches.

* Secure the cable connections.

* Try software that you know prints to the printer without a hitch—the problem could be the software.

* Reinstall the ImageWriter driver in the System Folder. Delete the old ImageWriter driver and reinstall the new one.

The paper is tearing.

* Check the setting of the paper thickness lever and check that the paper-feed lever is set to the type of paper being used (either pin feed or tractor feed).

* Check that the paper is correctly installed and, if using tractor feed paper, that the sprocket holes are aligned on the tractor sprockets.

The printing isn't dark enough.

Check the setting of the paper thickness lever, and replace the ribbon if it hasn't been replaced for a while. Also check to see if the ribbon is moving as the ImageWriter prints.

The printing is too dark.

Check the setting of the paper thickness lever.

The ImageWriter is printing stray characters.

* Try turning the printer off and on again. Also perform a printer self-test by holding down the Form Feed key and turning on the printer.

* Test the printer with other software to determine if the problem is with the software.

* Check the Chooser to see if AppleTalk is turned on (under the Apple menu). AppleTalk should be turned off when using the ImageWriter.

Can I print in color with the ImageWriter?

Yes, you can purchase a 7-color ribbon and replace the black ribbon with the color ribbon. You must also print from software that supports color printing, such as Aldus SuperPaint.

How can I prevent paper from wrapping around the platen?

If you find the paper is wrapping around the platen and jamming the printer, leave a sheet of paper hanging out of the platen, or attach a post-it to prevent the paper wrap-around.

Laser Printer Problems

Here are problems and questions encountered when using laser printers. Also check Chapter 4, "System Software," and Chapter 5, "Fonts and Sounds," for printing problems on the software end, because many times the problem originates from the Macintosh that is sending the print job.

How do I disable the startup page?

Laser printers usually print out a startup page to signify that they are ready for print jobs. The startup page can be disabled by sending a PostScript code to the printer or by using a utility to disable the startup page.

The LaserWriter Font Utility is software that comes with Apple's laser printers and Macintosh system software. This utility offers several options, one of which is to disable or enable the startup page (see figure 11.4).

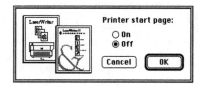

Figure 11.4   Turning the Startup Page off in the LaserWriter.

A quick and dirty way to stop the startup page from printing is to pull the paper tray out an inch or so when you start the LaserWriter. When the green light stops flashing, indicating that the printer is warmed up and ready to go, push the tray back in.

Yet another way to disable the startup page is by downloading a PostScript code to the printer if you have a PostScript printer. Using either a PostScript downloading utility or Microsoft Word, type the following and then send it to the printer:

```
serverdict begin 0 exitserver

statusdict begin false setdostartpage
```

If you are doing this in Word, set the style of the text to PostScript style and then print.

What do I need to do when traveling with a laser printer?

When you are moving or traveling with a laser printer, take out the toner cartridge and tape down the shutter that exposes the toner on the cartridge.

How can I change the name of my printer?

You can change the name of a LaserWriter printer by using Apple's *The Namer* utility, which comes with Apple's printers. Figure 11.5 shows The Namer's dialog box to change the printer name.

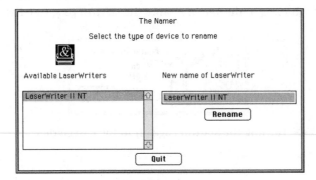

Figure 11.5 Changing the printer name with Apple's Namer utility.

What kind of care and maintenance can I perform for my laser printer?

There are a number of things you can do to maintain your printer:

* Replace the toner cartridge when necessary (check your printer manual for full instructions). To replace the toner cartridge, turn off the printer, let it cool down a bit, open the top and remove the old cartridge. Insert the new toner cartridge in place.

  Use the felt cleaner enclosed with most cartridges to clean the metal drum, usually covered by a flap that says something like "Caution, High Temperature". Place the new felt cleaning pad in place.

  Clean the inside of the printer gently with an anti-static brush or cotton swab with alcohol, being careful not to break any wires.

* Clean the outside of the printer. Unplug the power cord and wipe the printer outside with a damp cotton cloth and mild soap.

The LaserWriter icon is not listed in the Chooser.

The LaserWriter driver needs to be in the System Folder for it to appear in the Chooser. Under System 7, the LaserWriter driver goes in the Extensions Folder in the System Folder.

Make sure you don't have more than one System Folder on your disk, otherwise the Chooser will be confused. If so, consolidate everything into one folder and make sure all the files are the same software version. For more information, see Chapter 4, "System Software."

The laser printer isn't listed in the Chooser.

* Make sure the LaserWriter icon is selected and AppleTalk is active.

* Check the cables connecting the printer to the Macintosh. If you are on a network, check *all* network cable connections, especially if it is a LocalTalk network.

* Check that the printer is powered on and ready (check the status lights). Wait for a test print page to signify the printer is ready.

* Check settings and switches if you have recently upgraded the printer, added option cards, or changed the network configuration.

* If you are on a network which has zones, make sure you have selected the correct zone as well as the LaserWriter icon to see a list of the printers in that zone.

The printer isn't printing the test page.

* If the test page (or startup page) has not been disabled, then check the display lights on the printer to see if the printer is in ready state. To force a page start, try using the Apple LaserWriter Font Utility which comes with Apple Laser printers.

* Check the power and the on/off switch, and make sure the cover is closed.

* Check to see if the printer is out of paper or if there is a paper jam.

The test page is blank.

Check the toner cartridge and the status light to see if the toner is low. If you just changed the toner cartridge, make sure you pulled the plastic sealing slip out of the toner cartridge after installing the cartridge.

The printer has a paper jam.

To fix a paper jam, remove the paper tray and fix the paper stack. Remove any jammed paper gently by opening the printer and pulling the paper through the normal paper path. Be careful of wires and hot areas in the printer.

The printed document is missing elements.

* The printer may not have enough memory to process and print the entire document. Try a less complex document or try changing the size of the paper in the Page Setup dialog in the application. Test other documents from the same application as well as other printing with other applications.

* You may be using the wrong printer driver for your printer. High end graphics and layout applications include special printer drivers to be used when printing from the application.

The printed image isn't dark enough.

* Check to see if the printer is low on toner. If so, change the toner cartridge.

* Adjust the printer's print density dial (if one exists). See your printer manual for details.

* Make sure you are using the recommended paper weight for your printer. If the paper is smeared with toner or curls during printing it is not suitable for laser printing.

* If you are not low on toner, take the toner cartridge out of the printer and rock the cartridge back and forth to redistribute the toner.

* Clean the corona wire (a thin wire inside the center of the printer). To clean the corona wire, turn the printer off, open the printer and gently wipe dirt and dust off the wire with a cotton swab. See the printer's manual for the exact location of the corona wire.

The printed image is too dark.

* Adjust the printer's print density dial (if one exists). See your printer manual for details.

* Make sure you are using the recommended paper weight for your printer. If the paper is smeared with toner or curls during printing it is not suitable for laser printing.

* Take the toner cartridge out of the printer and rock the cartridge back and forth to redistribute the toner.

What kind of paper can I use with a laser printer?

In general, you can use any paper that can be used in a standard photo-copier, or typewriter paper with a weight of 16 to 20 pounds. Color paper can be used and letterhead paper can be used, as long as it can withstand high temperatures of around 165 to 180 degrees Celsius. (Some letterheads cannot withstand the high temperatures of the toner fuser inside the printer, and they will vaporize or melt off the paper.)

The printer may not print well on some paper textures as well, so test the paper before printing large print jobs.

Can I use transparency paper in a laser printer?

The high temperature inside the laser printer can cause the transparency to melt and be terminally fused to the printing mechanism if it not specifically laser printer-compatible. An alternative is take a plain-paper printout to a copier machine and create the transparencies there.

Can I print labels in the laser printer?

Most office-supply stores sell special labels (and transparency film) for use with plain-paper copiers, which are very similar to laser printers. Avery and other brands sell labels specifically for creation with a laser printer.

What do the status lights on the laser printer indicate?

* The green *Ready* light indicates the printer is ready to print a document. If it is blinking the printer is either warming up or processing a print job.

* The orange *Low Toner Level* light is steady when the toner level is low or the toner needs to be redistributed in the toner cartridge. Take the cartridge out and rock it back and forth. The orange light flashes when the toner cartridge is installed incorrectly.

* The red *Paper Out* light flashes when the printer is ready in manual feed mode. The red light is steady when the printer is out of paper or the paper tray is out or not firmly in place.

* The red *Paper Jam* light flashes when the printer needs servicing.

The LaserWriter IISC must be turned on first.

If you own a LaserWriter IISC, you will need to turn it on before starting up your Mac; leave it running as long as the Mac is turned on. This is because this printer connects via the SCSI port.

Can I print a screen dump to a laser printer?

Most 300 dpi printers—laser and inkjet—don't support ⌘-Shift-4, which sends the active window to an ImageWriter printer.

You can save the screen image to disk and then print it. If you have a black-and-white or color monitor and System 7, ⌘-Shift-3 will create an editable and printable PICT document of the current screen. Once you've created a document this way, you can open the file with TeachText or any other program than supports the PICT format, and print it out from there.

My printed documents have splotched gray marks.

You're probably running low on toner. Take out the cartridge, and rock it back and forth to redistribute the toner.

Also clean the fusion rollers (metal rollers that are very hot!). Let the printer cool down, and then gently clean the rollers with a cotton swab.

My printer has PhotoGrade, but it's not working.

PhotoGrade is the halftoning software built into Apple's newer LaserWriters. You must have atleast 5M of RAM to print a standard 8 1/2 by 11 inch page. PhotoGrade requires 8M of RAM for a legal-size page of graphics.

Another problem is that LaserWriters and other printers don't print true grays, but instead use patterns of black lines or dots, which is called halftoning. If your graphics software allows you to adjust the lines per inch, it may be set too low. PhotoGrade starts to work at about 106 lines per inch.

There is a thin line down the printed page.

* There may be some dried toner on the cleaning pad next to the fusion rollers, in which case you should just replace the cleaning pad (usually installed when you change the toner cartridge).

* Clean the corona wire, a thin wire inside the center of the printer. To clean the corona wire, turn the printer off, open the printer and gently wipe dirt and dust off the wire with a cotton swab. See the printer's manual for the exact location of the corona wire.

The toner is flaky.

The toner will not adhere well to your paper if the surface of your paper is too rough, so switch to a smoother paper stock. Try to use paper that is photocopier grade.

How do I add a hard disk to the laser printer?

You can attach a hard disk to a laser printer if the printer has a SCSI port. By attaching a hard disk storing PostScript fonts, the printer does not need them downloaded from the workstation. This decreases the time it takes to print the job and reduces the traffic across a network (if the printer is used across a network).

To attach a hard disk to a printer, you will need to follow the normal procedure for attaching a SCSI device to the Mac. Turn off the printer, attach the hard disk to the printer—with proper SCSI termination and cabling (see Chapter 10, "Storage Devices")—and then turn the printer on again. Next you will need a utility such as the LaserWriter Font Utility (which comes with Mac system software) that can download the fonts to the hard disk. Initialize the printer's hard disk from the utility and then begin downloading the fonts to the printer with this same utility.

How can I connect my laser printer to my Macintosh?

For a simple connection between a Macintosh and a printer you can use *LocalTalk* cabling, or twisted-pair wiring (regular phone wire cabling). LocalTalk cabling is sold by Apple and some third-parties, and Farallon's

PhoneNET and other twisted-pair cabling solutions can be purchased by mail order, dealers, and directly from the maker.

LocalTalk cabling is connected to the Printer port on the back of the Mac. It requires a few more pieces to set up, is more expensive, and is not as reliable as twisted-pair cabling. PhoneNET (and other twisted-pair cabling) also connects to the Printer port; PhoneNET uses one connector box for each device on the network and a simple telephone cable to daisy-chain Macs, printers, and other devices together into a network. PhoneNET can also use existing telephone wires in place in many offices. Figure 11.6 shows a printer and two Macs connected together in a network using PhoneNET connectors. For more information, see Appendix C, "Product Information."

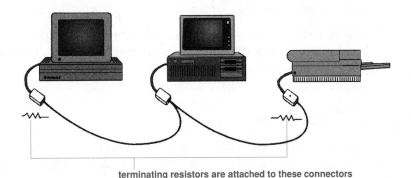

terminating resistors are attached to these connectors

Figure 11.6 Daisy chaining devices with PhoneNET connectors.

Scanners

A *scanner* is a device you can connect to the Macintosh; it converts images and text from paper to electronic files (digital information). Most scanners connect to the Mac by way of the SCSI port; some have an interface box between the scanner and the SCSI port, some require a special card, and a few scanners connect through the Modem or Printer ports.

There are several types of scanners: hand-held, flat-bed, and sheet fed are the most common. There are scanners for scanning images that are saved as picture files, and then there are scanners that can scan text and return a text file, which is referred to as OCR (Optical Character Recognition). Some scanners can do both kinds of scanning (imaging and OCR).

Scanners also require software drivers (or files) that are installed in the System Folder. The driver enables the Macintosh to communicate with the scanner.

You also need software that can interact with the scanner while you are scanning. Scanners come with software that can interact with the scanner to capture images to your disk; however, you may want to use your own software to further edit the scanned images. Adobe Photoshop is a popular image-editing application.

For OCR scanning, you will need to make sure the scanner supports OCR, whether you use the OCR software that comes with the scanner or purchase a separate OCR software package.

Scanner File Formats

For scanners that save files as images, TIFF and PICT are recognized as the standard file formats. You can take these files into most graphics, imaging and layout packages on the Macintosh.

OCR software saves text in text file formats that word processors and other text-based software can read.

Troubleshooting Scanner Setup

If you are connecting a scanner to your Macintosh and the scanner is connected by way of the SCSI port, then review Chapter 10, "Storage Devices." Just like hard disks and other SCSI devices, if you follow the rules for setting up a SCSI device you should have no problem setting up a SCSI scanner.

Also check that the scanner software is correctly installed. There may be software or extension conflicts if the software is installed and still not functioning normally. Check that you have the correct version of system software required for the software and driver.

Conclusion

Converting between electronic files and images on paper is usually a straightforward process, but sometimes it can be frustrating. This chapter has given you some tools for dealing with printer and scanner problems. The next chapter covers the means that the Macintosh uses to communicate with other computers: networks and modems.

I Need To Know!

Chapter 12

Networks and Modems

Networks and modems both give the Macintosh the capability to connect to other computers—which is very useful but which can also lead to new problems for the troubleshooter. This chapter covers common problems found with both networks and modems, and some solutions.

Networks

Every Macintosh has *AppleTalk* built into it. AppleTalk is the set of standards to allow all Macintosh computers and other network devices to communicate together across a network. A network allows groups of one or more users to share printers, files and other networked devices.

There are three physical types of networks for Macs: *LocalTalk, Ethernet,* and *Token Ring*. Macs require the addition of a network card to be connected to Ethernet or Token Ring networks, though some recent Macs have built-in Ethernet.

LocalTalk does not require a network card. All you need to have is the LocalTalk connectors and cables to chain the Macs and devices together. LocalTalk cabling is connected from one Printer port to the next on each Macintosh or other device (such as a printer) on the network.

A popular alternative to LocalTalk cabling is *PhoneNET,* made by Farallon Computing. PhoneNET connects Macs and other devices into a network with PhoneNET connectors and regular phone cable wiring. The PhoneNET connectors attach to the Printer port and the cables join the PhoneNET connectors together.

LocalTalk cabling is sold by Apple and some third parties, and Farallon's PhoneNET and other twisted-pair cabling solutions can be purchased by mail order, from dealers, and directly from the manufacturer.

Here are some common questions and problems with networking Macs:

Should I use LocalTalk cabling or PhoneNET to build a LocalTalk network?

Apple's LocalTalk cabling requires a few more pieces to set up, is more expensive, and is not as reliable as twisted-pair cabling (phone cable). LocalTalk cabling often suffers from loose connectors and is difficult to troubleshoot.

PhoneNET (and other twisted-pair cabling solutions) connects to the Printer port, uses one connector box for each device on the network, and uses simple twisted-pair telephone cable. PhoneNET can also use existing telephone wires, already in place in many offices. For more information, see Appendix C, "Product Information."

What do I need to connect a Mac to an Ethernet or Token Ring network?

❋ A network card. You will need an Ethernet (or Token Ring) card that fits into the Mac's card slot (although some of the newer Macs do come with built-in Ethernet support). Most—but not all—Macs have NuBus type slots. Ethernet cards are widely available; Token Ring cards are more rare and more expensive. If you are connecting a

PowerBook to Ethernet you need an external SCSI network adapter. When purchasing a network card, specify the Macintosh model that you want the card for.

Both Apple and third parties sell network cards to connect Macs to Ethernet and Token Ring networks. When connecting to an Ethernet network, you will also need to know what kind of network cabling is being used on your network: twisted-pair, thin coaxial, or thick coaxial cabling. Some network cards can support all three types of cabling, while others support only one or two.

✳ Network software. EtherTalk and TokenTalk drivers come with the Macintosh system software (see figure 12.1). You install this software from the system software installer disk.

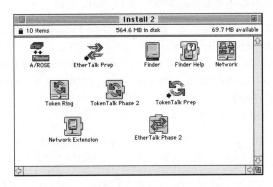

Figure 12.1   EtherTalk and TokenTalk software for the Mac.

Where do I set the network connections on the Mac?

The Network control panel is where the type of network driver is selected. In the Control Panels folder in the System Folder, double-click on the Network control panel. You can be wired to more than one network at a time, but you can only *connect* to one network at a time.

How can I select printers and file servers on the network?

In the *Chooser*, which is under the Apple menu, where you select network devices and services such as printers and file servers.

I have set up my LocalTalk network, but I cannot see the printer.

* Wait 60 seconds—a device should normally show up within 15 seconds, even on busy networks.

* Check the printer to see if it is powered on and ready, check all the network cabling, and secure all connectors.

* If you have LocalTalk, any unused jacks need to be left empty, but if you are using PhoneNET you should install a terminating resistor at the end of each network chain. If your PhoneNET network is not properly terminated you will have problems with seeing devices on the network. See the PhoneNET manual for more information on PhoneNET termination.

* Select the printer icon in the Chooser. Also, if your network is broken up into zones, make sure you are selecting the zone the printer is in.

* Turn AppleTalk off and then on again and go back to select the printer.

* Check to see if other Macs on the network can see and use the printer.

* You may need to reinstall the printer driver in the System Folder.

What are the cable length limits for LocalTalk?

The length of your LocalTalk network should not be longer than 1000 feet (300 meters). Any longer than this and data transfer will suffer and machine-to-machine data connections will be poor or nonexistent.

You can extend your LocalTalk network beyond this length by adding a bridge or a LocalTalk repeater to connect two physical LocalTalk networks together and amplify signals across both networks.

What are the limits for PhoneNET?

There are several ways to design a PhoneNET network; however, the two most popular are daisy-chaining Macs and devices, and connecting from an installed phone cable backbone (like the phone cabling jacks throughout offices).

If you are daisy-chaining the devices then the limit is 24 PhoneNET connectors and a network cable length of no longer than 1800 feet (549 meters). If you are creating a backbone, then the network cable length limit is 4500 feet (1372 meters) and you can connect and disconnect PhoneNET connectors from telephone wall jacks without disrupting other devices on the network. For more information, see the PhoneNET manual.

How can I connect an Ethernet network to a LocalTalk network?

You can purchase a router which will route (direct data) between the two networks.

How can I see the activity on the network and manage the network performance?

The Chooser is a great way to tell if something is available across the network. If you want a utility that will help you troubleshoot beyond the Chooser, there are several network utilities that you can purchase: Inter•Poll, LocalPeek, and NetMinder LocalTalk are three popular commercial network utilities.

Why is my network so slow?

* You may have too many devices (Macs and printers and so on) on one network. Break up your network into two or more segments with a bridge or router.

* If all the networked users share files with System 7's File Sharing feature, consider adding a *file server* to the network. File Sharing has a limit of 10 active users at one time. A file server is a Macintosh dedicated to sharing all user files from a common source. Apple sells

file server software, called AppleShare, which is very easy to setup and maintain. It also offers file security features and group access levels.

* There may be many print jobs going to the printer, or large, complex print jobs. You can reduce the printer traffic on a network by setting up a print server. You will need print server software and a Macintosh dedicated as a print server. With a print server, all users' print jobs are queued to the printer server and then printed as the printer is ready.

An alternative to setting up a print server is to have users enable background printing. Background printing can be set to on or off in the Chooser under the Apple menu. Background printing allows the user to continue working while the print job is held on the user's computer until the printer is ready to print the job. See Chapter 4, "System Software," for more information on background printing.

* There may be a virus on local workstations and/or on any file servers. Install a virus detection and eradication program on all workstations and the file servers.

* There may be too many *nodes* (devices) on the network. A network node is any device, Macintosh, printer or file server, connected to the network. 32 active users is the recommended limit for LocalTalk networks, however up to 254 nodes (network devices) can be on a LocalTalk network. Think about breaking your network up with bridges and/or routers to distribute network traffic.

* Check disk space availability and file fragmentation on the file server volumes. You will have to shut down the file server software to defragment the volumes and rebuild the Desktop file. Occasionally delete backup and archive files that are no longer being used.

* Improve the power of the Macintosh file server by upgrading the Mac. If you are running on LocalTalk, consider upgrading to a faster network media type such as Ethernet or Token Ring.

* Add more resources. You may not have enough printers or file server volumes for everyone accessing these services. Don't add too many network services to one Macintosh, such as a Macintosh serving as a mail, print, and file server. This will overload one Macintosh server.

❋ There may be device driver incompatibilities. All the Macs using a network device such as a printer should have the same software driver version. Incompatible printer drivers will cause the printer to be reinitialized frequently. Use a tool, such as Inter•Poll (from Apple), Status*Mac, or other network utility to check what version of printer driver and other software Macs on the network are using.

❋ Running application software from a file server will slow down the network and create excessive traffic across the network. Using an application off of a file server is slower than having the application on a local disk.

❋ Check your network design. If you have a large network with many nodes, network overhead may be contributing to the performance problems. Design networks into workgroups so that the Macs using network resources have them close to their portion of the network.

The printer is constantly reinitializing before printing.

Various Mac users on the network are using different versions of the Print driver in their system folder. The printer driver from one Mac is initializing the printer with their version of the driver, and then another user comes along to print with a different version of the printer driver in their System Folder. The solution is for all Macs to have the same printer driver version. System 7 printer drivers work with System 6.07 and 6.08.

Network devices are disappearing and reappearing in the Chooser.

❋ There may be a loose or damaged cable or network connector on the device or somewhere along the network.

❋ The network may not be sufficiently terminated.

❋ The network's total cable length may be too long.

❋ There may be too many devices (network nodes) on the network.

❋ There may be electrical interference along the network cabling or near the network device.

✳ A router may be bad, or routers may have conflicting information. Try turning off all the routers, then restart them one at a time, at one minute intervals.

Modems

Modems come in a variety of speeds and with a variety of options. There are fax/data modems that support sending faxes as well as data transmission over phone lines. Modem speed (or rate of transfer) is measured in bps (bits per second), with 1200, 2400, and 9600 bps being the most common transfer rates.

Modems on some Macs are installed internally and are designed specifically for the Macintosh. External modems are generic and work with any Macintosh. A modem that has been connected to a PC will work with a Mac as well, provided you have a Macintosh modem cable.

PowerBooks and PowerBook Duos use special internal modems such as the Apple Express Modem, or a standard modem can be connected to the Modem port. External modems from Supra Corporation, Zoom, Practical Peripherals, Hayes, Prometheus, and Intel are all Mac-compatable.

In order to connect a Macintosh to successfully communicate over a phone line, you need the following:

✳ A modem.

✳ A modem cable that connects the Macintosh to the modem.

✳ A telephone line. You can connect a modem to your phone using a regular telephone cable (a cable with RJ-11 connectors on both ends).

✳ A terminal emulator application. There are many communication software packages available for use for connecting to online services, file transfers, and dialing into networks.

Extending The Serial Port

If you need to connect more than one serial device to your Macintosh, you can also connect a modem to the Printer port. If the Printer port is also taken, you can connect a serial device to what is known as a "black box" or "AB switch box," which is then connected to a serial port.

The box connects to one of the Mac's serial ports; the box itself has two or more serial ports. The serial devices are connected into each of the serial ports on the black box, and you can switch between serial port to use that device. For information see Appendix C, "Product Information."

Modem Cables

Most external modems have a 25-pin connector for a serial cable connection. Your modem cable connects to either the modem port or the printer port on the Macintosh.

Although the regular Mac modem cables will work with all modems, high-speed modems, like 9600 bps modems can benefit from special cables, called "hardware handshaking" or "hardware flow control" cables. Some older Mac modem cables may not work well with high-speed modems.

Hayes And Hayes-Compatible Modems

Almost all modems support the Hayes modem communications language, referred to as the AT Command Set. The Hayes Standard AT Command Set (the full name) includes commands such as "ATD," which means "attention, dial the phone." You can find the full AT Command Set in most modem manuals. Do not buy a modem which is not Hayes compatible.

Communications Software

There are a number of applications that allow you to connect to another Macintosh or to an online service with a modem. For more information on communication software packages, see Appendix C, "Product Information."

AppleTalk Remote Access (ARA)

AppleTalk Remote Access (ARA) is communications software (made by Apple) used to connect one Mac to another Mac with a modem, for access to files and network resources. (Both Macs must have modems, of course.) You can use ARA to dial into another Mac from home, office or the road, as well as to dial in to an AppleTalk network. ARA can only be installed on Macs running System 7.

Troubleshooting Modem Problems

Here are troubleshooting tips for solving modem problems:

I cannot make a connection.

* If you are using AppleTalk Remote Access or another application that requires a modem script, make sure your CCL (a modem script; CCL stands for Connection Control Language) file is working with your modem. Check with the modem vendor and see if they have a customized script for the modem.

* Check the phone number you are dialing to make sure you entered the number correctly. Account for any dialing prefixes or dialing codes for a particular phone system.

* Check your modem cables and connections; power the modem off and on again to clear the modem of settings or incomplete hang-ups.

* Make sure you have entered the user name and any required password correctly.

* Check the communication settings and the speed.

I lose my connection frequently.

* Your phone lines may be noisy. Check for interference from machinery around the phone cables or contact the phone company if you hear static on the line when you use a regular phone.

* Check that your cables are secure, and not damaged. Try another cable or another phone jack.

* Make sure you are using the correct modem script in the case of ARA and other communication software.

An application says my modem port is in use or not working.

You may have another communication program open that is using the modem port. Quit all applications, reset the modem, and try dialing again. If this doesn't work, try restarting the Mac.

My modem is not responding.

* Check the power cables, secure modem cable connections, and turn the modem off and on again to clear the modem of garbled settings or incomplete hang-ups. Test the modem with another modem cable to see if the cable is damaged. Try the modem on another Macintosh to test the Modem port, or switch the cable connection to the Printer port.

* Test the phone line and the modem setup. Test the phone jack as well with a telephone to see if you hear a dial tone.

Call Waiting is disrupting my connections.

In most areas of the country you can temporarily disable the call waiting feature by dialing *70 before the rest of the phone number. Enter the phone number in the communications package as *70 and then the rest of the number: ATDT*7018005551212.

What are some standard modem commands?

Most modems used in the United States understand these basic modem commands. For more commands, including the Hayes command set, refer to your modem manual.

* 0, 1, 2, 3, 4, 5, 6, 7, 8, 9, #, * create tones for dialing.

* Placing a , anywhere in a dialing sequence will insert a momentary pause in the dialing.

* Placing a T before a number means the modem is using touch-tone dialing.

* Placing a P before a number means the modem is using pulse dialing.

Conclusion

Modem and network problems can often be confusing. Two books that provide more information about these subjects are *Yakety Mac* (for modem coverage), by Ross Scott Rubin; and *Live Wired: A Guide to Networking Macs*, by James K. Anders. Both books are published by Hayden. The next section of this book, "Prescriptions," provides additional information for fixing Macintosh problems.

Prescriptions

Chapter 13

Symptoms and Solutions

This chapter covers some common Macintosh error messages, symptoms, and questions. For more details, see earlier chapters that cover individual Macintosh software and hardware topics.

Application Problems

Here are common software messages and symptoms, along with possible solutions.

I have frequent System errors in a certain application.

Trouble in only one application indicates a problem with the application itself, or the hardware or software that interacts with the application.

* The application is damaged. Applications can be damaged during a system crash, disk failure, or a power failure. Replace the application with a good backup copy. If the problem is a disk failure, back up all the software on the disk and run a disk repair utility on the disk.

* The application is running out of memory (RAM). Quit the application and increase the memory allocated for the application in the Finder. To increase the memory, highlight the application in the Finder and choose Get Info from the File menu (or press ⌘ -I). Increase the number in the box labeled "Suggested Size," close the Get Info box, and launch the application again.

* The application conflicts with another application or extension loaded into memory. See Chapter 4, "System Software," for information about resolving extension and control panel conflicts.

* The application is written to a bad area of the disk (a bad disk sector or sectors). Use a disk repair utility such as Norton Utilities, Mac-Tools, or Public Utilities to check the integrity of the disk and lock out bad sectors. It is a good idea to remove (drag it into the trash) the application and then install it again to make sure it writes to good sectors of the disk.

I have frequent System errors, freezes, or crashes in several different applications.

Repeated system freezes, crashes, and unusual behavior in all applications—including the Finder—indicates a system software or a hardware problem. When faced with a freeze or crash under System 7, press the ⌘ -Option-Esc keys to close the application and return to the Finder. This will often allow you to save open documents in other applications and then shut down the Macintosh safely. Then try the following:

* Check your hard disk for damage (bad sectors) and other disk problems using a disk repair utility.

* You might have more than one System folder on the startup disk. You should not have more than one System folder on a disk, unless you are using a special utility such as System Picker or Blesser, which designate one System folder as the startup folder.

* The system software may be corrupted. Reinstall the system software. You may need to delete the old System and Finder before reinstalling.

* Make sure you do not attach and detach cable and power cables without first shutting down the Macintosh (by choosing Shut Down from the Special menu in the Finder).

* You may have a virus. Use a virus detection program to identify the virus and disinfect all your disks.

I get a message that says "The application has unexpectedly quit."

* Quit all other applications and restart the Macintosh. Frequently opening and closing applications leaves the memory (RAM) fragmented so another application cannot effectively use the available memory. Restarting the Mac clears the RAM for newly opened applications.

* The application may have run out of memory. Increase the memory partition for the application by highlighting the application and choosing "Get Info" from the File menu in the Finder.

* The document may be damaged. Try opening other documents to confirm that it is just the document and not the application that is damaged.

* The application may be damaged. Reinstall the application.

* The system software may be damaged. If this is happening in other applications and not just one application, reinstall the system software, especially the System and Finder.

I get an error message that says "Bus Error," "Bad F-Line," "Address Error," or "Coprocessor not installed."

* An application or other software may not be compatible with the system software version installed on your Macintosh. Contact the vendor of the software to confirm that you are using the correct version of the application, along with any hardware that is required.

* An application is not working properly and may be affecting other applications. Contact the vendor to check for known bugs or conflicts. Under System 6.07 some applications return the message "coprocessor not installed;" however, this error is often incorrectly reported by the application. Check with the vendor to correct this error message.

* A virus called WDEF may be present on your Macintosh. WDEF only infects Macs running System 6 (WDEF does not infect System 7 Desktops). Use an anti-viral program to identify and remove the WDEF virus, or rebuild the Desktop by holding down the ⌘-Option keys while restarting the Macintosh.

An application is unusually slow.

When an application is unusually slow at copying files, saving files, and other seemingly normal actions, check the following:

* The application file may be fragmented on the hard disk. Defragment the disk on which the application is installed using a disk utility which can correct the disk's file fragmentation.

* The amount of memory (RAM) remaining may be small or non-existent. Quit all applications and restart the Macintosh. Now launch the application again and compare the performance.

* The application needs more memory (RAM). Increase the memory allocated for the application.

  To do this, quit the application, go to the Finder and highlight the application icon. Choose Get Info (⌘ -I) from the File menu and increase the amount of Preferred Memory in the memory requirements box.

* The application is damaged. Reinstall the application from a good backup copy.

* If you have File Sharing turned on (a System 7 feature), check the File Sharing Monitor control panel to see if someone is using files on your Macintosh. When files are being used by another Macintosh, the Macintosh doing the sharing slows down considerably.

System and Finder Problems

The System and Finder are two essential files in the System folder that are used to run your applications and manage the desktop.

How do I rebuild the Desktop?

* On hard disks, hold down the ⌘-Option keys while restarting the Macintosh. This will work for all disks added to the desktop during startup. You will see a dialog box asking you if you want to rebuild the desktop after the Mac's startup routine and before you see the desktop.

* On floppy and removable disks, hold down the ⌘-Option keys while inserting the disk into the drive.

I get a message that says "A folder cannot be deleted" (or "The Trash cannot be emptied").

* A file in the folder is locked or in use (open) by an application. Quit any open applications and try deleting the folder again.

  To see if a file is locked, select the file and choose Get Info from the File menu (⌘-I). If the Locked check box is checked, uncheck it.

* If you see a dialog box like the one in figure 13.1, the folder is being shared and File Sharing is turned on (System 7). Choose Sharing from the File menu and a window will appear with the sharing settings for the folder. Turn off sharing for the folder; you can then throw it away.

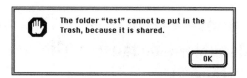

Figure 13.1 When a folder is shared with File Sharing.

* The folder is on a file server that has locked the folder or does not give you privileges to delete the folder (or files in the folder). Under System 7, select the folder and choose Sharing... from the File menu to view the access privileges for the folder.

  Under System 6, use the Get Privileges command in the File menu to see your privileges to the folder. Alternatively, you might have the

Access Privileges desk accessory installed under the Apple menu to see the folder privileges.

* The System or Finder may be damaged. Reinstall the system software by deleting the System and Finder files and then running Apple's system installer.

I cannot eject a removable disk.

* File Sharing is turned on. Turn File Sharing off with the Sharing Setup control panel and eject the disk; you can then turn File Sharing on again. If File Sharing is turned on while a removable disk is in the drive, the volume cannot be ejected until File Sharing is turned off.

* A file is open or in use by the Macintosh. Check that all documents and applications on the disk are not open or in use.

I cannot change the name of a folder or volume.

* The volume is locked, is a network volume, is on a locked disk, or is on a read-only disk such as a CD-ROM volume.

* The folder or volume is being shared with the System 7 File Sharing feature. Highlight the folder and choose Sharing... from the File menu. Turn File Sharing off; you can then change the name.

I get a message that says "You cannot replace this document because a file cannot be replaced by a folder."

You have a file and folder with the same name on the same level of a disk or folder. Change the name of either the file or the folder, or save it somewhere else (see figure 13.2).

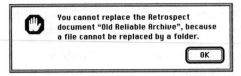

Figure 13.2 A file and folder have the same name.

The Desktop file is rebuilt during every startup.

Don't cancel this process, because chances are the Mac has not previously been able to complete the desktop rebuilding process. Here are some other possibilities.

* If you have switched between System 6 and System 7, the System is rebuilding the desktop to be compatible with the newly booted system version.

* The desktop might be damaged, or written to a damaged spot on the disk. Use a disk utility to check the disk media and repair the disk.

* Check the Option and ⌘ keys on the keyboard. These keys may be stuck, or dirt may be interfering with the keys.

I can't delete a file.

The file is usually locked or open (in use by an application). If it is not, try deleting the file with a disk or file utility.

* The file is locked. Highlight the file and choose Get Info under the File menu (⌘-I). Click the Locked checkbox to unlock the file.

  To delete the locked file in one step, hold down the Option key and choose Empty Trash from the Special menu.

* The file is open (busy). Close the file (or the application) and then delete it.

* The file is on a disk that is locked, or on a network volume which does not grant you privileges to delete files. Under System 7, check your privileges for the folder the file is in by choosing Sharing... from the File menu in the Finder. Under System 6 use the Get Privileges command in the File menu or the Access Privileges desk accessory under the Apple menu to check your folder privileges.

* If the file is an extension which is loaded at startup, you will have to drag the file out of the System folder (it may be in the Extensions or Control Panels folder) and restart the Macintosh; then you will be able to delete the file.

Files have lost their icons.

In most cases a file displays a specific icon on the desktop. However, in some cases, the icon may become generic, like a plain document or application icon. If you have documents or applications that are not displaying the appropriate icon, here are some possible solutions.

* The Desktop File is damaged. Rebuild the desktop by holding down the ⌘ and Option keys while restarting the Macintosh.

* You do not have the application that created the document.

* The application used to create the document is on a disk that is not on the desktop, such as a removable drive that is not on the desktop at the moment.

The Mac is slow when copying files and opening windows.

This indicates sluggish performance in the Finder.

* Rebuild the Desktop by holding down the ⌘ and Option keys while restarting the Macintosh..

* The Finder is running out of memory. Close disk and folder windows, and eject disks. You may even need to quit all applications and restart the Macintosh to regain memory (RAM).

* The startup disk is fragmented. Defragment the disk using a disk utility that optimizes files.

* The Finder is damaged. Reinstall the system software. You may need to delete the System and Finder files before reinstalling.

I get a message that says "The application could not be found" or "Application is busy or missing."

Normally, double-clicking on a document launches the application the document was created with, and the document is opened. Here are some reasons why this fails and the message "The application cannot be found" is displayed (see figure 13.3).

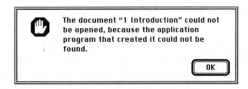

The document "1 Introduction" could not be opened, because the application program that created it could not be found.

OK

Figure 13.3 Application cannot be found message.

* The application that created the document is not installed on the disks on the desktop.

* The information linking the document to an application (the file type and creator) is missing. Open the application first and then open the document from inside the application.

* The document has been created with a different version of the application. Open the application first and then open the document from inside the application. If this doesn't open the document, contact the vendor's technical support line. You may have to upgrade the application.

* The Desktop file is damaged. Rebuild the desktop by holding down the ⌘ and Option keys while restarting the Macintosh.

The System folder cannot be trashed.

The active or startup System folder cannot be trashed (deleted). To delete a System folder, restart the Mac with another startup disk and delete the System folder.

The System or Finder file cannot be trashed.

The active System and Finder file cannot be deleted. To delete the Finder or System file, restart the Macintosh with a startup floppy disk and then delete the System or Finder file.

A folder or file is gone.

* Check that it was not moved to another location inadvertently. Use the Find utility in the Finder by choosing Find (⌘-F) from the File menu (under System 6, use the Find File desk accessory).

❋ The file may be invisible. Use a utility that can view invisible files.

❋ If you are running System 7.0 or 7.01, there is a known bug that causes files to disappear. To find the file, Use the Find feature in the Finder. To fix the problem, either install the System 7 Tune-Up (available from Apple, online services, and user groups), or upgrade to System 7.1.

The Mac freezes when I copy a file (or files).

❋ The disk you are copying the file to may be damaged. Try copying the file to a different disk.

❋ There may not be enough memory to copy the file to the disk. Quit open applications or restart the Macintosh and try copying the file again. If you are copying more than one file at once, try copying one file at a time.

❋ The Finder and/or System file is probably corrupt. Restart the Macintosh with a different startup disk and try copying the file again. If the Macintosh doesn't freeze during this copy, reinstall the System and Finder from the Macintosh system installer disks.

The Mac freezes when I empty the Trash.

❋ The Finder Preferences file may be damaged. Trash the Finder Preferences in the Preferences folder within the System folder and restart the Macintosh. The Finder will automatically create a new Preferences file with default settings.

❋ The Finder and/or System file may be corrupted. Test this by restarting the Mac with a startup floppy disk. Then empty the trash. If the Mac doesn't freeze, reinstall the system software with the system installer disks (you may need to delete the System and Finder file).

❋ The hard disk directory may be damaged. Run a disk repair utility on your disk to check the disk media and repair the disk if necessary.

13

I get a message that says "The files could not be copied, out of Finder memory."

✳ You may be copying too many files as once. Copy fewer files or one at a time, if necessary.

✳ The Finder is running out of memory. Close disk and folder windows, and eject disks. You may even need to quit all applications and restart the Macintosh to regain access to all of the memory.

✳ If you are running out of memory under System 6, increase the amount of memory allocated to the Finder. To do this, restart the Macintosh with a startup floppy disk and highlight the Finder file in the System folder. Choose Get Info (or press ⌘-I) from the File menu and increase the memory partition by 10 to 20 percent. Now, restart the Macintosh with the original startup disk.

I cannot rebuild the Desktop— out of Finder memory.

✳ This happens primarily under System 6. Increase the amount of memory allocated to the Finder. To do this, restart the Macintosh with a startup floppy disk and highlight the Finder file in the System folder. Choose Get Info (or press ⌘-I) from the File menu and increase the memory partition by 10 to 20 percent. Now, restart the Macintosh with the original startup disk.

✳ The disk may be full and/or not have enough contiguous space to write to the Desktop file. Use a disk repair utility to defragment the disk. Delete files as necessary, and check for disk damage with the disk utility.

My control panel (or other settings) are not being saved (under System 7).

✳ The Finder Preferences file may be damaged. Trash the Finder Preferences in the Preferences folder (within the System folder) and restart the Macintosh. The Finder will automatically create a new Preferences file with default settings.

* The battery in your Macintosh may be nearly dead. See Chapter 8, "The Macintosh CPU," for more about the Macintosh battery.

* The parameter RAM (PRAM) information may be scrambled; the PRAM may need to be zapped. To zap the PRAM under System 7, restart the Macintosh and hold down the ⌘-Option-P-R keys. Press this key combination before you get to the "Welcome to Macintosh" screen and then wait until you hear a second "bong" sound to let go of the keys.

   Under System 6, while holding down the Shift, ⌘, and Option keys, open the Control Panel from the Apple menu. Click Yes in the dialog box asking if you want to reset the parameter RAM. Restart the Macintosh.

 TIP: If your Mac is a 128K, 512K, 512Ke, or Plus, zap the PRAM by unplugging the Macintosh and removing the battery (located in a compartment on the back of the Macintosh) for 15 seconds or so; then place the battery back in and turn the Macintosh on again.

Printing Problems

Printing relies on printer drivers installed in the System folder, the software printing the document, and the associated hardware cables and network connections for communication between the Macintosh and the printer. Here are some commonly encountered printing problems.

The LaserWriter occasionally makes a quick jerking noise.

Don't worry—this is a power-saving feature of the LaserWriter.

The Mac freezes when printing.

* The PrintMonitor may need more memory to print the document. If you are running MultiFinder or System 7, use Find to highlight the

13

PrintMonitor file in the System folder. Select Get Info from the File menu and increase the allotted memory at least 100K. Close the dialog box and try printing again.

✳ The printer driver may be damaged. Replace the appropriate driver by deleting the driver from the System folder and reinstalling the printer driver with the system software installer disk.

✳ The application printing the document may be damaged. Test another document to see if it prints without a problem. If it doesn't print, then try replacing the application with a good copy. If the application can print other documents, the document you originally tried to print may be damaged.

I get an error message that says "Can't open the printer."

✳ The Macintosh cannot find a printer selected in the Chooser. Check to see that you have selected a printer in the Chooser (under the Apple menu).

✳ The printer selected in the Chooser may not be turned on. Check to see that the printer selected is powered on and that the network cable connections are secure.

✳ Check to see if AppleTalk is turned on or off. If you are printing across a network you will need AppleTalk turned on.

Nothing happens when I print a document.

✳ Check the Chooser (under the Apple menu) to make sure a printer is selected.

✳ You may have a different printer selected if there is more than one printer accessible from your Macintosh.

The printer has been initialized or reinitialized.

✳ If the printer is on a network with more than one user, someone else may be using a different version of the printer driver than the one you are using. You will have printer "initialization wars" until all users have the same printer driver versions installed in the System folder of each Macintosh.

✳ If you upgraded your Macintosh system software, the new printer drivers are reintializing the printer with the new printer driver software.

The printer icon isn't in the Chooser.

The printer icon(s) that appear in the Chooser are installed in the System folder. You can install the appropriate printer driver(s) using the system software installer, or other printer driver that comes with your printer.

The printer name is not listed in the Chooser.

✳ The printer is not powered on, or a cable or network connection is not secure.

✳ Check that your Macintosh network cable connections are secure.

✳ Another connection along the network may not be secure. This is particularly common with LocalTalk (or PhoneNET) networks because one loose connection anywhere on the network can disrupt the network data flow.

✳ Check to see if AppleTalk is turned on or off. If you are printing across a network you will need AppleTalk turned on.

A document printed in a different font, or the font looks "jagged."

✳ Check to see if you have the font installed in the System folder. You may be missing the printer font that matches the bitmap font you chose. You may not have the printer fonts installed properly or they are not available on your workstation or the printer. Check the printer's hard disk (if there is one attached) for installed fonts. See Chapter 5, "Fonts and Sounds," for more information.

✳ The font is damaged. Replace the printer font with a good copy. If the printer font resides on the printer's hard disk, replace the one on the hard disk by removing it and redownloading the font. See Chapter 5, "Fonts and Sounds," for more information.

✳ There is a font ID conflict. To resolve it, see Chapter 5, "Fonts and Sounds."

✳ Check to see if you have the Font Substitution option checked in the Page Setup command under the "Options" button. If the printer cannot find the printer font or a good substitute font to use, or if the Font Substitution option is not checked, then the printer will print a bitmapped version of the font.

I get a message that says "Not enough memory to print. PrintMonitor will try to print again when more memory is available."

✳ Increase the memory allocated to the PrintMonitor application in the System folder, or restart the Mac to free up memory.

✳ Print the document and then immediately quit the application. This will free up the memory the application was using; the memory can then be used by the PrintMonitor.

✳ If there is more than enough RAM when you look under "About This Macintosh…" under the Apple menu in the Finder, then the PrintMonitor file may be damaged. Throw it in the Trash and replace it with a good copy by using the system software installer.

✳ Turn background printing off in the Chooser. (Under System 6 you can gain more memory by turning off MultiFinder).

✳ If you are running System 7.0 or 7.01, upgrade to System 7.1 or install Apple's System 7 Tune-Up. Printing and memory management are improved with the Tune-Up and System 7.1.

Macintosh Startup Problems

Here are common startup errors, bombs, and other symptoms, along with possible solutions. For more information, see Chapter 8, "The Macintosh CPU."

The Mac Will Not Power On.

The Mac is not receiving enough (or any) power to start up.

✳ Secure all power cords and cables. Check the power switch on the back of the Mac. Check the battery if you have a PowerBook.

✳ Test the power outlet by plugging in a device such as a lamp or a radio into the outlet.

✳ Make sure the number of devices attached to one power source is not overloading the circuit. Disconnect a few devices and restart the Macintosh to test for circuit overload.

✳ If you have a surge protector or UPS installed, check that it has not been tripped. A power surge can damage hardware and will trip surge protectors.

✳ The power supply in the Mac may be damaged. Take the Macintosh to an Apple certified service technician.

 # I get a disk icon with a blinking "?".

The Macintosh cannot find a startup disk or the system software on your disk is damaged.

✳ Check the attached SCSI devices for proper termination, cabling, and ID assignment. (See Chapter 10, "Storage Devices.")

✳ The system software is damaged, or missing the System or Finder files. Reinstall the system software. You may need to delete the System and Finder file before reinstalling. See Chapter 4, "System Software," for more about installing the System software.

✳ The boot blocks (on the startup disk) containing startup information are damaged. Restart the Mac with a startup floppy disk and repair the disk's boot blocks with a disk utility such as Disk First Aid or Norton Utilities.

✳ The parameter RAM (PRAM) information may be scrambled; you may need to zap the PRAM. To zap the PRAM under System 7, restart the Macintosh and hold down the ⌘-Option-P-R keys. Press this key combination before you get to the "Welcome to Macintosh" screen and then let go when you hear a second "bong" sound.

Under System 6, while holding down the Shift, ⌘ , and Option keys, open the Control Panel from the Apple menu. Click Yes in the dialog box asking if you want to reset the parameter RAM. Restart the Macintosh.

TIP: If your Mac is a 128K, 512K, 512Ke, or Plus, zap the PRAM by unplugging the Macintosh and removing the battery (located in a compartment on the back of the Macintosh) for 15 seconds or so; then place the battery back in and turn the Macintosh on again.

I get a disk icon with a blinking "X."

The Macintosh found a startup disk, but the disk or the system software is corrupted or is missing a critical system file.

* The system software on the startup disk is damaged, or it is missing the Finder or System file. Reinstall the system software. You may need to delete the System and Finder file before reinstalling. If you have installed fonts or other files in your System file, make sure to create a backup copy of those files before you delete the System file. See Chapter 4, "System Software," for more about installing the System software.

* The startup disk has damaged boot blocks. Reboot the Macintosh with a startup or emergency floppy disk and use a disk utility to repair the damaged boot blocks. Disk First Aid, Norton Utilities and other disk utilities can fix boot blocks.

I get a Sad Macintosh icon.

XXXXYYYY
ZZZZZZZZ

There is a problem with the startup disk or the Macintosh hardware or software. A sad Mac icon with an error code indicates the problem was found during the Mac's startup diagnostic phase. See Chapter 8, "The Macintosh CPU," for more details.

Most error codes indicate the problem is on the logic board. If the problem is software-related, the error code (a hexadecimal number) appears with an

F in the last digit on the top row; Mac Pluses and earlier Macs display a hexadecimal number with an F in the second digit for a software problem.

* The startup disk may be damaged. Restart the Mac with a floppy startup disk. If the Mac starts up successfully, repair the damaged startup disk with a third party disk utility or the disk utility that came with the bad disk.

* Alternatively, power down the Mac and detach all external peripherals. Restart the Mac from a floppy startup disk.

   If the Mac does not start up successfully from the floppy disk, there is a problem with the Macintosh hardware.

   If you have recently added hardware to the Macintosh logic board, such as SIMMs or a video card, remove the hardware and restart the Mac. The hardware may be damaged or installed improperly.

* If the Mac *does* start up successfully from the floppy disk, there may be a problem with one of the peripherals. Test each peripheral individually until a problem appears. Check SCSI cables, ID conflicts, and termination. (See Chapter 10, "Storage Devices.")

If you cannot solve the problem with the above suggestions, take the Macintosh to a qualified Macintosh service technician.

The Macintosh plays an unusual tune at startup.

On a successful diagnostic startup you hear the normal Macintosh startup chord. If logic board components fail the startup diagnostic tests, a different chord may be played after the normal chord.

During diagnostic failures, musical notes are played on most Macintosh models (except the Mac Plus, SE, 128K, 512K, and 512Ke). Different chords identify different problem areas on the logic board. Although is not easy to diagnose what the problem is by hearing the tones, here are the possible meanings of error tones:

* A short, harsh series of tones is played when the problem is on the logic board. This means the problem is a component on the logic board, or of the SIMMs on the board.

13

* A long medium-pitched series of tones, or a medium- and then high-pitched series of tones, is played when there is a problem with the SIMMs on the logic board.

* Four tones, from low to high, are played when there is a problem with the video hardware.

TIP: To hear the exact chords, a program called the "Diagnostic Sound Sampler" can be found on Apple's online service, AppleLink (see Chapter 14, "Technical Resources" for more on the AppleLink online service).

The Macintosh powers on, but I don't hear the startup chord.

The problem may be with the logic board, an internal hard disk, or a card installed in the Macintosh.

* Restart the Mac with a startup floppy disk. If the Mac still doesn't start up successfully, the problem may be on the logic board.

* Check all NuBus or other cards installed on the logic board. Change the slot a card is in to test out the card slot, test the card on another Macintosh, or test another card in this Macintosh.

* Startup the Macintosh with a floppy disk. If you have an internal hard disk, is it showing on the desktop? If not, you have a problem with the internal hard drive. Check the SCSI cables and power cables on the internal drive, as well as other connections along the SCSI chain.

* If you have a Macintosh IIsi, there is a known problem with the speaker wire contacts inside the Mac IIsi. There are two strips of metal that make contact with the logic board to connect the speaker to the logic board. Dirt accumulates between the wire contacts and the logic board, preventing sound from playing. Plug a set of headphones in the speaker jack on the back of the Mac; if sound comes through the headphones then something is blocking the metal

contact to the speaker. To clean the speaker contacts, open the Mac IIsi, look for the metal contacts on the bottom of the logic board and polish them with a pencil eraser or steel wool.

The Mac repeatedly flashes the Happy Macintosh icon.

The Mac has found the startup disk, but it cannot get past this step in the startup sequence because of a problem with the Macintosh startup disk.

* The system software on the startup disk is damaged, or it is missing the Finder or System file. Reinstall the system software. You may need to delete the System and Finder files before reinstalling. If you have installed fonts or other files in your System file, make sure to create a backup copy of those files before you delete the System file. See Chapter 4, "System Software," for more about installing the System software.

* The boot blocks on the startup disk may be damaged. Restart the Macintosh with a startup floppy disk. If you are successful, repair the startup disk with a disk repair utility.

* There may be a SCSI ID conflict or a termination problem. Check SCSI cabling, termination, and SCSI ID assignments. Take SCSI devices off and add them back on one at a time to determine the source of the conflict.

* There may be an extension (INIT) conflict. Restart the Mac with a startup floppy disk and determine the conflict using the process of elimination (take all third party extensions and control panels out of the System folder and add them two at a time), or use an extension manager such as Extensions Manager. See Chapter 4, "System Software," for more about resolving extension and control panel conflicts.

The Mac freezes or bombs just after it shows the Happy Macintosh icon.

There is a problem with one of the SCSI devices, the startup disk, or there is an extension or control panel conflict.

13

* The boot blocks on the startup disk are damaged. Restart with a startup floppy disk and repair the original startup disk's boot blocks with a disk utility such as Disk First Aid or Norton Utilities.

* The SCSI device driver is damaged. Restart the Mac with another startup disk and reinstall the SCSI device driver on the original startup device.

   The device driver is included with hard disks, CD-ROMs, and so forth, and usually is installed with the utility software that comes with the drive. For example, if you have an Apple hard drive, update the driver with Apple HD SC Setup that comes with the Macintosh system software.

* There is an extension (INIT) or control panel conflict. Restart the Mac with a startup floppy disk. Determine the conflict using the process of elimination (take all third-party extensions and control panels out of the System Folder and test them two at a time), or use an extension manager utility such as Extensions Manager. See Chapter 4, "System Software," for more about resolving extension and control panel conflicts.

I get an error message that says "Can't load the Finder."

The Finder file (and possibly the System file) is damaged or missing on the startup disk. Restart the Mac with another startup disk and reinstall the Finder and System files using the system software installer. See Chapter 4, "System Software," for more about installing the System software.

The Mac Freezes at the Desktop.

If the Mac freezes before the startup disk appears on the desktop, you have a problem with the startup disk.

* The desktop file is damaged. Rebuild the desktop file by holding down the ⌘ and Option keys while restarting the Mac.

* The parameter RAM (PRAM) information may be scrambled; you may need to zap the PRAM. To zap the PRAM under System 7, restart the Macintosh and hold down the ⌘-Option-P-R keys. Press this key

combination before you get to the "Welcome to Macintosh" screen and then let go when you hear a second "bong" sound.

Under System 6, while holding down the Shift, ⌘, and Option keys, open the Control Panel from the Apple menu. Click Yes in the dialog box asking if you want to reset the parameter RAM. Restart the Macintosh.

 TIP: If your Mac is a 128K, 512K, 512Ke, or Plus, zap the PRAM by unplugging the Macintosh and removing the battery (located in a compartment on the back of the Macintosh) for 15 seconds or so; then place the battery back in and turn the Macintosh on again.

* The startup disk's Volume Information block is damaged. Restart the Mac with another startup disk and repair the original startup disk with a disk repair utility.

* Check SCSI device cable connections, termination, and SCSI ID assignment. (See Chapter 10, "Storage Devices," for more information about SCSI problems.)

* Check the power cables for all SCSI devices in the SCSI chain. A SCSI device may not be powered on or may not be receiving power. With some SCSI devices, all SCSI devices must be powered on for the devices to work.

* The SCSI device driver is damaged. Restart the Mac with another startup disk and reinstall the device driver for the startup device.

  The device driver is included with the purchase of that device, and is installed with the drive's utility software. For example, if you have an Apple hard drive, update the device driver with Apple HD SC Setup, which comes with the Macintosh system software.

* You may have an system extension (INIT) conflict (yes, even this late in the startup sequence). Restart the Mac and hold down the Shift key to disable the extensions. Another technique is to remove all the extensions and load them one at a time until the offending extension

becomes apparent. For more information about resolving extension and control panel conflicts, see Chapter 4, "System Software."

The Happy Macintosh icon is on the screen for a long time, or startup takes a long time.

* The last time the Macintosh was on it may have crashed, or it was not shut down properly (by choosing Shut Down from the Special menu in the Finder). The Macintosh is taking a long time "cleaning up" the disk information. This usually does not cause further problems, but if it happens after a "good" shut down then this is not the case. The disk should be checked with a disk utility just to make sure it is in good condition.

* The Desktop file is fragmented or damaged. Rebuild the desktop file by holding down the ⌘ and Option keys while restarting the Mac. You may want to optimize your startup disk to reduce the fragmentation with a disk utility such as Norton Utilities or MacTools.

Floppy Disk Problems

Here are some common problems encountered with floppy disks. For more details on floppy disk problems, see Chapter 10, "Storage Devices."

The floppy disk is stuck in the drive.

Here are methods for ejecting a floppy disk that is stuck in the drive or does not show on the desktop.

* Hold the mouse button down while restarting the Macintosh if the Mac is powered on.

* Press ⌘-Shift-1 or ⌘-Shift-2 to eject the disk.

* Stick the end of a paper clip in the small hole on the side of the floppy drive slot. You are manually forcing the ejection mechanism to eject the disk.

I get a message such as "This Disk Is unreadable," "This disk is damaged: Do you want to initialize it?," or "This disk is not a Macintosh disk: Do you want to initialize it?"

Unless you are sure you want to erase everything on this disk, *always* eject the disk and think for a minute (see figure 13.4).

Figure 13.4   The disk is not initialized, is damaged or is not a Macintosh disk. Click Eject!

* This message normally appears when you insert a disk that has not been formatted (initialized) by the Macintosh system. If you know it has been formatted already and contains data, read on.

* It has been formatted by a different operating system, such as MS-DOS. You can use a utility such as DOS Mounter, AccessPC, or other utilities to mount PC-formatted disks on the Macintosh desktop. For more information see Appendix C for product information.

   To determine if the disk has been formatted by another kind of computer, eject the disk, open Apple File Exchange, and then insert the disk into the floppy drive. Apple File Exchange recognizes disks formatted by PCs. You will be able to view the disk and its contents in Apple File Exchange.

TIP: You need a SuperDrive (also called FDHD disk drive) to do this. Apple File Exchange comes with the Macintosh system software.

* The disk may be damaged. Eject the disk and open a disk recovery utility such as Disk First Aid or Norton Utilities. Insert the disk and try to fix it with the utility.

    If it cannot be fixed, turn to a file recovery utility (this feature may be part of the same utility used for disk recovery). Recover as many files as possible and never use the disk again; back up floppy disks as well as hard drives.

* The disk is a high-density disk (1.4M capacity) and has been inserted into an 800K drive. (This message also appears when 1.4M or 800K disks are inserted into 400K drives). You will need to find a Macintosh with a SuperDrive in order to read the disk; copy the files on the disk to two 800K floppies to transfer the files to your Macintosh.

* If more than one disk you insert gives you this message, the floppy drive is dirty. Clean it with a commercial disk cleaner. See Chapter 2, "Macintosh Maintenance."

* If more than one disk you insert gives you this message, the floppy disk drive may be damaged. Insert the floppy disks into another disk drive to determine if the problem is the disk drive or the disks. Bring the floppy disk drive to a certified Apple technician.

* The drive may have overheated. Turn off the Mac and give it time to cool down. Then turn it on again to see if the message still appears.

I get a message that the floppy disk initialization failed.

When formatting or erasing a floppy disk, you might receive a message that the disk initialization failed. This indicates there is a problem with the disk or the disk drive.

* The disk format is bad or the media is damaged. Use a disk utility to run diagnostics on the disk. If the disk cannot be fixed and reformatted, throw it out.

* The disk may not be supported by the drive formatting it. For example, placing an initialized high-density (1440K) disk in an 800K disk drive will not work because high-density disks cannot be read by 800K floppy disk drives.

I can't copy files to the disk because the disk is locked.

This message indicates that the disk is locked.

* The disk is physically locked because the write-protect tab is in the locked position.

* The disk is a Read-Only disk, such as a CD-ROM disk, or a locked network volume.

The Mac is asking for a floppy that I don't have!

You probably ejected a disk without getting rid of its icon from the desktop. You can try dragging the image to the trash; if you are repeatedly asked for the disk, press ⌘-period a few times and the message will go away. (Dragging the disk icon to the Trash, or using ⌘-Y in System 7, avoids this problem.)

I get a message that the disk is full.

Either the disk is really full, or it is damaged.

* Check the size of the disk in the Finder by double-clicking on the disk to open it and choosing to view files "by Icon" under the View menu in the Finder.

* Use a disk repair utility such as Disk First Aid, Norton Utilities, or MacTools to repair the disk.

* An install program may have been interrupted and did not get a chance to erase its temporary files. Check the System folder and application folder.

* The disk's invisible Desktop file has grown very large. Rebuild the desktop by holding down the Option-⌘ keys while restarting the Macintosh.

* The disk is fragmented; there is not enough contiguous space to copy a file. Defragment and optimize your disk with a disk utility, or remove some files by deleting them from the disk after making backup copies of the removed files.

* Make sure the disk is not locked or password protected.

Can I reformat a DOS or PC disk to be used in a Mac, and vice versa?

Yes, you can reformat a 3 1/2-inch DOS disk in a Macintosh disk drive and you can reformat a Mac disk in a PC 3 1/2-inch disk drive.

PC 3 1/2-inch disk drives (not the 5 1/4-inch disk drives you may find on PCs) format Macintosh 3 1/2-inch double-density disks as 800K (double-density) PC disks. PC drives format 3 1/2-inch high-density disks as 1.44M (high-density) PC disks.

You can use a utility such as Apple File Exchange, AccessPC, or Macintosh PC Exchange (a SuperDrive or other floppy drive that can read PC disks) to mount and format PC disks on a Macintosh.

Hard Disk Problems

Hard disk problems can usually be fixed by checking the SCSI configuration, using a disk repair utility, or the utility that came with the drive. For more details on hard disk problems, see Chapter 10, "Storage Devices."

The hard disk initialization failed, or a message appears that says "Initialization failed!"

When initializing a disk, you receive a message that the disk initialization failed. This is most likely a problem with the disk and the disk may need to be reformatted. You can reformat the disk with a utility that came with the disk, or another formatting utility. Back up all data before formatting the disk—formatting erases all data!

* The disk media is damaged. Use a disk utility to run diagnostics on the disk. Use a disk utility that tests the disk media and locks out bad areas of the disk (such as Norton Utilities).

* The disk information (disk directories and data structures) may be damaged. Use a disk repair utility to try to repair the disk. Backup all data and then reformat the disk. Reformat the disk with the software that came with the drive. If it is an Apple hard disk, format it with Apple HD SC Setup.

The hard disk doesn't spin up and the LEDs (Drive Activity Lights) are dark.

This usually indicates the hard drive is not receiving power or the drive's fuse has blown. The fuse is a protective device designed to melt or blow when there is a current overload.

* ✳ Check power cables and the power outlet.

* ✳ Check the drive's fuse. Check the hard drive manual on how to replace the fuse, or call the hard drive vendor. Some drive fuses are on the outside, while some require that you open up the drive case.

* ✳ If you turn on the drive and hear nothing but the whirl of the fan, and the drive fails to mount, your hard disk's read/write heads are sticking to the surface of the inside the hard drive, or the read/write arm is stuck—the platters in the drive spin freely, but the arm can't maneuver itself to read data. Contact the vendor for information on repairing the drive.

The hard disk does not show up on the Desktop.

The hard disk may not be powered on, or it may be damaged.

* ✳ The hard disk may not have been fully powered on when the Macintosh started up. Restart the Macintosh. To avoid the problem, turn on the hard disk and let it start up before turning on the Macintosh.

* ✳ Check the power cables for all SCSI devices in the SCSI chain. A SCSI device may not be powered on or receiving power. In some cases, all SCSI devices must be powered on for the devices to work.

* ✳ Try a SCSI mounting utility (such as SCSI Probe which is included on the disk with this book) to mount the disk on the desktop. For more information, see Chapter 10, "Storage Devices."

* ✳ The Desktop file is damaged. Rebuild the Desktop file by holding down the ⌘ and Option keys while restarting the Mac.

* ✳ The startup disk's Volume Information Block is damaged. Restart the Mac with another startup disk and repair the disk with a disk repair utility.

* The parameter RAM (PRAM) information may be scrambled; you may need to zap the PRAM. To zap the PRAM under System 7, restart the Macintosh and hold down the ⌘-Option-P-R keys. Press this key combination before you get to the "Welcome to Macintosh" screen and then let go when you hear a second "bong" sound.

Under System 6, while holding down the Shift, ⌘, and Option keys, open the Control Panel from the Apple menu. Click Yes in the dialog box asking if you want to reset the parameter RAM. Restart the Macintosh.

 TIP: If your Mac is a 128K, 512K, 512Ke, or Plus, zap the PRAM by unplugging the Macintosh and removing the battery (located in a compartment on the back of the Macintosh) for 15 seconds or so; then place the battery back in and turn the Macintosh on again.

The hard disk mounts but the Mac cannot start up from the disk.

This hard disk was a startup disk and has a System Folder installed on it, but it cannot be used as a startup disk now, even though it mounts on the desktop.

* The boot blocks are damaged. Use a disk utility such as Disk First Aid or Norton Utilities to repair the boot blocks.

* The System and/or Finder file is damaged or missing. Reinstall the system software; you may need to delete the System and Finder file before reinstalling the system software. See Chapter 4, "System Software," for more information about installing System software.

A Message says the disk is full, but it isn't.

The disk information, such as directory and other invisible files, are damaged.

* Use a disk utility such as Disk First Aid, Norton Utilities or MacTools to repair the disk.

* An install program may have been interrupted before it erased its temporary files. Check the System folder and application folder.

* The disk's invisible Desktop file is taking up too much disk space. Rebuild the desktop by holding down the Option-⌘ keys while restarting the Macintosh.

* The disk is fragmented, so there is not enough contiguous space to copy a file. Defragment and optimize your disk, or back up files and then remove the files to free up some disk space.

I get a message that says "This is not a Macintosh disk. Do you want to initialize it?," or "This disk is unreadable. Do you want to initialize it?"

Do *not* click on OK! The disk information is damaged. Use a disk utility to repair the disk.

This can be tricky because when you insert the disk, it will want to initialize the disk or eject it. Eject the disk, launch the disk repair utility, and then insert the disk again so the disk utility can find the disk on the SCSI bus and open it to repair it.

My Mac's hard disk does not boot up the Mac unless I restart the Mac again.

The hard disk is not ready (the disk is not spinning up in time) for the Macintosh to read from it; however, when you reboot the Macintosh the hard disk is ready. Power on the hard disk before the Mac, wait a few seconds, and then turn on the Macintosh.

I cannot see one SCSI device when another SCSI device is turned off.

You will have to turn on all SCSI devices before turning on the Mac. Some SCSI devices do not have to be turned on for other SCSI devices to work.

You will have to test this out. At the very least, you should turn on the first and last device on the SCSI chain to ensure proper SCSI termination.

I see duplicate hard disk icons on the Desktop.

Several hard disk icons of one hard disk appear on the Desktop. You have a SCSI ID conflict.

Check all the SCSI devices attached to your Macintosh with a utility such as SCSI Probe. Look for a SCSI ID that is used twice. Each SCSI device needs a unique SCSI ID number between 0 and 6. SCSI ID 0 is used for the internal drive if there is one; otherwise, an external device can use the ID 0. SCSI ID 7 is reserved for the Macintosh computer. For more information about SCSI IDs, see Chapter 10, "Storage Devices."

I get a message that says "The disk could not be opened."

The disk information is damaged. Use a disk repair utility to repair the disk. If the disk cannot be repaired, use a file recovery program to recover the data on the disk.

How do I change the startup disk?

To change the startup disk, open the Startup control panel and choose the startup disk. Restart the Mac for the new startup setting to take effect. In System 7, the Startup Disk control panel is in the Control Panels folder. In System 6, the Startup Device setting is in the Control Panel, under the Apple menu.

Other Strange Things

And now for the more obscure and mundane problems.

Where do I set the name for my Macintosh?

Under System 7, you can set the name of your Macintosh in the Sharing Setup control panel (see figure 13.5). It is in the Control Panels folder, inside the System folder. (The Control Panels folder can usually be opened from the Apple menu.) Enter a name in the Macintosh Name field.

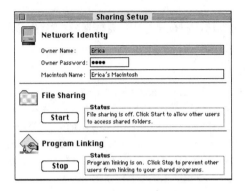

Figure 13.5 The Sharing Setup control panel in System 7.

Under System 6, you add your name in the Chooser, found under the Apple menu (see figure 13.6). The new name is not used until the Macintosh is restarted.

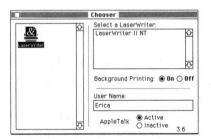

Figure 13.6 The Chooser in System 6.

How do I turn MultiFinder on?

MultiFinder is built into System 7, so you can't turn it off. Under System 6, choose Set Startup from the Special menu in the Finder.

How can I have applications automatically open at startup?

Under System 6, highlight the application icon in the Finder and then choose Set Startup from the Special menu.

Under System 7, you can place the application (or an alias of the application) in the Startup Items folder, found in the System folder. To make an alias, highlight the application in the Finder and choose Make Alias from the File menu.

How do I get a screen shot?

Under System 7, the keyboard combination is ⌘-Shift-3. The screen shots are PICT files, named Picture 0, Picture 1, Picture 2, and so on; the screen shots can be opened in TeachText or almost any graphics program.

Under System 6, you can produce screen shots only in black and white. The keyboard combination is ⌘-Shift-3. The screen shots are "paint files" called Screen 0, Screen 1, Screen 2, and so on; they can be opened with many graphics programs.

I cannot eject a disk because it is "in use."

* An application on the disk is open or a document on the disk is in use by an application. Quit the application or close the document and then eject the disk. If you are using a utility that opens suitcases and other files, such as Suitcase or MasterJuggler, check to see if the utility has any files open on the disk.

* If you are using File Sharing in System 7, you will have to turn File Sharing off before ejecting the disk. Highlight the disk and choose Sharing from the File menu. If the disk is removable, you have to turn off Sharing for the entire computer in the Sharing Setup control panel, eject the disk, and then turn sharing back on.

What is the Responder file used for?

The Responder file is added to the System folder under System 6. It is used for network administrators who need to have Macs show up in Apple's Inter•Poll network utility. The Responder is built into System 7; when you upgrade to System 7, the System 6 Responder file is automatically removed.

How can I see my access privileges under System 6?

There is a desk accessory called Access Privileges that comes with the System 6 system software and can be installed with the system installer or with the Font/DA Mover. Once it is installed, you can see privileges by highlighting a network volume and pressing ⌘ -P. You can also see privileges by selecting the Get Privileges command from the File menu.

My menu bar flashes occasionally for no apparent reason.

You have the sound turned down to 0 on your Macintosh, so instead of a hearing a beep sound, the menu bar flashes. To change this, go to the Sound control panel and increase the speaker volume.

The Apple menu icon (🍎) is flashing.

The alarm clock was set. To turn it off, open the Alarm Clock desk accessory, found under the Apple Menu. Click on the right corner handle and the window will expand (see figure 13.7). Now click on the Alarm icon to turn the alarm off (see figure 13.8).

expand the window by clicking on the handle

Figure 13.7 Alarm clock turned on.

Figure 13.8   Alarm clock off.

What is a Performa?

The Macintosh Performas include the Performa 200, Performa 400, and Performa 600. The Macintosh Performa 200 is identical to the Macintosh Classic II, and the Macintosh Performa 400 is identical to the Macintosh LC II. The Macintosh Performa 600 is equivalent to the Macintosh IIvx.

How do I get those • marks?

Press the Option and 8 key. To see more interesting Option-characters, use the Key Caps DA under the Apple Menu.

Can I use my System 6 Desk Accessories in System 7?

Usually. To do this, double-click on the desk accessory suitcase while in the System 7 Finder, and it will open up to a window showing the desk accessory as an application. Drag the application into the Apple Menu Items folder in the System Folder, and voila! It will show up under the Apple menu. You can do this with *any* application or file that you want to access from the Apple menu.

Be aware that some desk accessories may not be compatible with System 7. To find out which are not, contact the software vendor or check System 7's Compatibility Checker application that comes with the System 7 upgrade kit.

The Macintosh, the printer, or another device smells like it is burning!

The power supply is damaged, there is an electrical short somewhere in the device, or there is an overload from the electrical outlet. If the outlet looks okay, turn the device off immediately. Otherwise go to a main fuse box or electrical switch and power down the entire electrical line. Contact a electrical service technician immediately.

I'm out of memory and I need to save a file!

Try using Save As... to save the file to another disk. If you cannot insert another disk into the floppy drive, try saving to a network volume. If you are running other applications under System 7 or MultiFinder, quit the other applications and try saving the document again.

As a last resort, try printing the document out, or at least taking a screen shot of the page on the monitor (using ⌘-Shift-3).

How Do I add an FKey?

An FKey is a small resource file (that is rarely used any more) and is launched by pressing Shift-⌘ and a number key. FKey files are added to the System file with a utility such as ResEdit, or opened with a utility such as Suitcase II or MasterJuggler. An example of a built-in FKey that comes with the system software is the keyboard sequence Shift-⌘-3, which takes a screen shot.

How can I share graphics files between a PC and a Macintosh?

If the graphics file comes from an application that exists on both the Macintosh and the PC, such as Aldus FreeHand, Adobe Illustrator, or Aldus PageMaker, the files are easily opened on both the Mac and the PC. Adobe Photoshop is a handy image-editing application that can save files in either Mac or PC graphics formats so they can be opened in the native platform (Mac or PC). For example, you can save a graphics file in TIFF format; Photoshop will ask you if you want to save it for the PC or the Macintosh.

There are also file translation utilities used specifically to transfer files between Macs and PCs.

Conclusion

Don't forget to check the previous chapters for more detailed information on specific hardware and software problems. If you cannot find a solution to your problem, Chapter 14, "Technical Resources", has a host of alternative technical resources to help you solve your problem.

I Need To Know!

Technical Resources

There are technical resources that are yours to take advantage of, from the product vendors you purchase software and hardware from to the non-profit bulletin board services and user groups, and Apple Computer provides information and support in a number of ways as well.

Here is a guide to the various resources easily accessible to you by way of phone, modem, and newsstand.

Product Support

Product support is technical assistance offered by a vendor for a product you purchased from them. This is usually accessible by telephone, but it can extend further. Product support is important when you have a question that the product manual, deductive reasoning, or human intuition cannot solve.

Product Registration

The first thing to do after buying a product is to fill out the registration card and mail it back to the vendor. The vendor will know that you bought their product and will send you product and update information. Many vendors use product registration as a ticket to technical support, so keep track of serial numbers.

Avenues of Contact

When you purchase software or hardware, the manufacturer should provide you with technical support information. Most vendors offer a telephone support line; depending on the vendor, the support line may be a toll-free number (800 area code), a 900 number (a charge based on the time on the phone), or a standard phone call. Contact information is usually in the product manual or on a card with the product packaging.

Fax Support

Some vendors offer fax support. With fax support, the company provides a telephone number to call to request fax information, and then the vendor faxes information back to your fax machine.

Electronic Forums

Many vendors have electronic forums for subscribers to online services such as CompuServe, America Online, or AppleLink. The forums provide software updates, information, and Q&A areas for technical support. Vendors also may have their own BBS (Bulletin Board Service) for customers to dial and connect to for support and updates. All you need is a modem, communications software, and a telephone line. See "Online Services" later in this Chapter.

Extended Support

Many vendors offer free support for a limited time, and then charge for support after that free period. For example, some vendors may offer support for the first 90 days that you own their product, and then offer an annual contract to continue to access their support lines beyond the 90 days.

Depending on the product, many vendors offer extended support. Consider these options depending on your needs and use of the product. Pay-by-need support is a growing trend.

How to Find Company and Product Information

If you can't find the company's address or telephone number, there are alternative ways to get this information. You can search a Macintosh publication like *MacUser, MacWEEK,* or *Macworld* for a review of the product. (These publications usually list the company's name and telephone number.) Or, alternatively, you can search electronically on online services.

MacUser (a monthly magazine) publishes its MiniFinders buying guide section several times a year. There is also a HyperCard stack with the MiniFinders information, including descriptions, company contact information, and Mice ratings. You can download the MiniFinders HyperCard stack from ZiffNet on CompuServe. See Online services later in this chapter.

Computer Library is an electronic resource for information on companies, products and publication articles. It is divided into two parts: Computer Database Plus, which contains articles from all the major computer publications; and Computer Directory, which contains a comprehensive list of computer companies and products. Computer Library is available on CompuServe (type GO COMPLIB).

You can also obtain Computer Library on a CD-ROM called Computer Select. Computer Select is an annual subscription. For more information on Computer Select, call (212) 503-4400.

Hardware Repairs

What do you do when you realize your Macintosh hardware is in need of repair? Here are a number of options to consider.

* Is it under warranty? Locate a computer repair center with authorized Apple service technicians. Check newspapers and computer publications. For example, the New York Times Tuesday Science section has a classified area dedicated to computer advertisements.

* Find an authorized Apple reseller. To find an Apple Authorized reseller near you (in the U.S.) call (800) 538-9696, or (408) 996-1010.

* Repair it yourself. You may be able to obtain the part(s) you need and take it from there; this will save you money on labor costs. However, if you do not feel comfortable tinkering inside your Macintosh, or do not want to break Apple's one-year limited warranty, leave it to an authorized Apple repair technician.

* If it is third-party hardware (not from Apple), call the vendor. Approach the hardware vendor before going to a third-party repair service, because vendors know their hardware best—most of the time. If they cannot help you, ask them to suggest a qualified third-party repair service.

   If the vendor can repair it, check to see if the warranty covers the repair. If the turnaround time is lengthy, ask the vendor for a temporary replacement of your hardware.

* Find a third-party repair service. Look in the back of Macintosh publications for classified service advertisements, or check Appendix C in this book for more information. The classified sections of *MacWEEK*, *MacUser*, and *Macworld* all list hardware repair vendors.

* Approach your local Macintosh user group (see "Macintosh User Groups" later in this chapter). Members of user groups are a great resource for recommendations and technical help, and often run repair clinics.

Apple Support

Apple relies—to a large extent—on the Macintosh community of customer support specialists, authorized Apple resellers, consultants, authorized Apple Training Providers, Macintosh User Groups, and systems integrators to provide support.

* To find an Apple Authorized reseller near you (in the U.S.) call (800) 538-9696 or (800) 732-3131, or (408) 996-1010.

* To find an Apple Consultant in the U.S., call (408) 996-1010.

To complement this service community, here is what Apple provides:

The Apple Catalog

The Apple Catalog is just that: a catalog of selected products from Apple and third-party manufacturers. It contains PowerBooks, system software, accessories, printers, toner cartridges, and more. You can order any item in the catalog directly from Apple and they will deliver most items the next business day. For more information on The Apple Catalog, call (800) 795-1000 or (408) 996-1010. You will pay full retail prices.

Apple's Technical Assistance Center

If you have purchased Apple products, and the warranty still covers the product, you can call (800) 767-2775 for technical assistance.

System 7 Support

Apple offers the following assistance for System 7:

* Apple's System 7 Upgrade Kit includes 1 year of toll-free upgrade assistance and support.

* Customers who did not purchase an upgrade kit can call the System 7 Upgrade Answerline at (900) 535-APPL ($2.00 per minute).

* Customers who did not purchase an upgrade kit can call the automated Q&A system at (408) 257-7700 for the cost of the telephone call.

Apple's Toll-Free Information Number

Apple's toll-free product information number is (800) 950-2442.

Training and Support Tools

Apple also develops training courseware and support tools. The Technical Information Source CD-ROM includes support tools and technical information. For more information about these and other products, call (800) 950-2442 or (408) 996-1010.

Technical Coordinator Answerline

Apple designed this service for in-house support staffs who provide assistance to other Macintosh users. Subscribers have access to Apple support engineers for troubleshooting, including:

* Installing and administering Macintosh operating systems like System 7 and A/UX.

* Working with AppleTalk and network environments, such as Ethernet, Token-Ring, IBM, and Digital network environments.

For more information about the Answerline, call (800) 950-2442, or (408) 996-1010.

AppleLink

AppleLink is Apple's online service. This electronic service provides electronic mail, Q&A areas, utilities, and information about Apple and third-party products.

For more information about AppleLink, contact APDA (Apple Programmer's and Developer's Association) at (800) 282-2732 (in Canada call (800) 637-0029; internationally call (408) 562-3910) or order AppleLink from The Apple Catalog at (800) 795-1000. See Online Services later in this chapter for more information about AppleLink.

AppleLink CD

If you want access to the information on AppleLink without spending time online (and on the phone), you can subscribe to AppleLink CD. You will need a CD-ROM drive attached to your Mac, but no modem, communications software, or phone line is necessary.

AppleLink CD offers all the same information, software libraries and bulletin board services in CD-ROM format. Four quarterly editions are available to annual subscribers.

For more information about AppleLink CD contact an Apple dealer or Apple Online Services Helpline at (408) 974-3309.

Apple Training Providers

To locate a local authorized Apple Training Provider or for information about training and course schedules call (800) 732-3131.

The PowerBook Hotline

Owners of Apple's PowerBook models can call Apple's toll-free repair hotline. Technicians help you determine what your problem is and direct you to the nearest Apple reseller for service; or they instruct you to return the PowerBook to Apple for repair. The number is (800) 767-2775 (which is (800) SOS-APPL), or (408) 996-1010.

AppleCare

AppleCare is Apple's extended service agreement. It covers repair costs for hardware problems for as long as the length of your AppleCare contract. The service agreement is between you and the Apple authorized service provider.

If you recently purchased a Macintosh, you have a one-year warranty, so there really isn't any reason to purchase AppleCare until after the first year.

If you don't purchase AppleCare when you buy the Macintosh from an authorized reseller, the authorized service provider will require that the Macintosh hardware is inspected before the AppleCare contract is established. The only reason to purchase AppleCare when buying a Macintosh is to save yourself from having to carry the Macintosh to the service provider for inspection when you finally do purchase AppleCare.

You can purchase AppleCare month-by-month or annually. Apple bases the price on the product and configuration, but prices range from $24 annually ($2 a month) for an Apple CD to over $700 annually for a Quadra 900. Resellers offer competitive pricing between AppleCare and their own warranty, so shop around. AppleLink, Apple's online service, lists current suggested prices.

Call (800) 538-9696 or (408) 996-1010 for information about how to locate the nearest authorized reseller.

Apple Custom Support

Apple provides special support for large corporate, government, and educational customers. Contact the Apple corporate sales representative in your region, or call Apple for more information at (408) 996-1010.

Macintosh User Groups

There are Macintosh user groups nationwide, and there is probably one near you. User groups are non-profit membership groups that hold meetings, mail newsletters, maintain software libraries, provide software and hardware discounts, and most importantly, are a source of friendly technical information and support.

BMUG (Berkeley Macintosh User Group), one of the largest user groups with over 10,000 members, offers a helpline, hardware assistance, a software library, a BBS (bulletin board service), and more.

The Boston Computer Society (BCS) is another large user group that has many subdivisions to support all kinds of interests, from virtual reality to the visually impaired.

To contact BMUG, call (510) 549-2684. BMUG's ordering line for membership or products is (800) 776-BMUG. To contact the Boston Computer Society, call (617) 252-0600.

To find the Macintosh user group nearest you, contact Apple at (800) 538-9696, or (408) 996-1010.

Online Services

Online services offer subscribers with a modem, communications package, and a telephone line the opportunity to dial into a plenitude of online information. Sometimes the communication package is a customized "front end," as in the case of AppleLink and America Online.

Online services offer the latest technical information. These services provide public-domain and commercial software libraries, discussion

forums, Q&A and support forums that can help you find solutions to technical problems. Many software and hardware vendors also have forums on online services so you can contact them online.

AppleLink

As mentioned earlier, AppleLink is Apple's online service. This electronic service provides electronic mail, Q&A areas, utilities, and information about Apple and third-party products.

Figure 14.1 shows the main window when you dial into AppleLink. Figure 14.2 shows the support forum containing Apple's technical notes covering hardware and software problems.

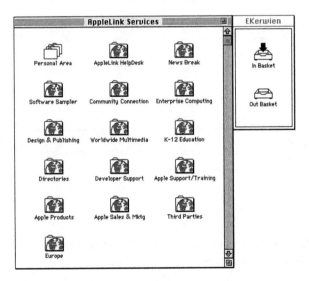

Figure 14.1 AppleLink's main window.

Figure 14.3 shows third-party vendors, from the letters H to O, who have forums on AppleLink.

For more information about AppleLink, contact APDA (Apple Programmer and Developer Association) at (800) 282-2732, or (408) 996-1010, or order AppleLink from The Apple Catalog at (800) 795-1000.

Figure 14.2   AppleLink's support forum.

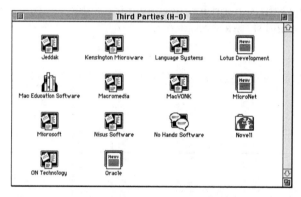

Figure 14.3   Some of AppleLink's Third Party forums.

CompuServe

CompuServe Information Service (CIS) has several areas from which to
obtain Macintosh technical information.

MAUG (Micronetworked Apple Users Group)

MAUG (Micronetworked Apple Users Group) is one area on CIS to find
Macintosh forums where you can leave messages or browse libraries and
download files. Figure 14.4 shows the various forums offered under MAUG
using CompuServe's interactive software called CIM (CompuServe Information Manager).

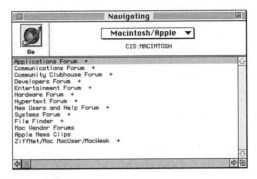

Figure 14.4 MAUG forums on CompuServe.

Figure 14.5 shows an inside view of the New Users and Help Forum, where you can ask questions, respond to others, and read other technical threads. For example, the Disk Clinic section is for disk questions, and the System Clinic is for system questions.

Figure 14.5 New Users & Help forums on MAUG.

For more information on CIM and CompuServe, call (800) 848-8990, or (614) 457-8600.

Vendors On CompuServe

Many software and hardware vendors have forums on CompuServe that offer software updates, technical notes, and Q&A areas. The Mac vendor forums are broken down into three areas: Mac Vendor Forums A, B, and C. Figure 14.6 shows a view of the vendors in forum A.

Figure 14.6   Mac Vendor Forum A on CompuServe.

To get to the Vendor Forums section on CompuServe, type at the prompt: GO APPVENA (for forum A), GO APPVENB (for forum B), or GO APPVENC (for forum C); to get the MAUG forum, type GO MACINTOSH and navigate from there.

ZiffNet/Mac

ZiffNet/Mac is another area of CompuServe sponsored by Ziff Communications—the publisher of several computer publications, including *MacUser* and *MacWEEK*. ZiffNet/Mac offers discussion forums, software libraries, news and topical forums, as well as sections for technical support and troubleshooting.

Using ZiffNet/Mac's main window in CIM (CompuServe Information Manager; this is interactive software used as an alternative to your own communications package) shown in figure 14.7, has a section devoted to software and support entitled Download Software & Tech Support. Underneath this heading, shown in figure 14.8, are sections for support and technical questions, a topical Tech Support database, and access to another area of ZiffNet—Ziff's electronic support product called Support On Site.

Support On Site is a database of technical support information that covers over 36 software products, including software publishers' manuals, technical notes, and reference books. It is primarily MS-DOS and Windows-based; however, there are Macintosh applications in this database from companies such as Aldus, Microsoft, Lotus, Claris, and Symantec.

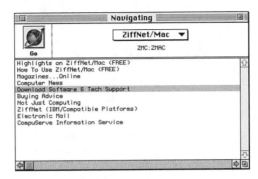

Figure 14.7 ZiffNet's main window.

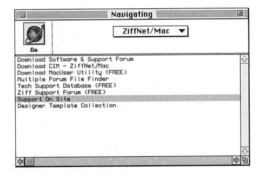

Figure 14.8 ZiffNet's technical support forums.

For more information on ZiffNet/Mac, call (800) 666-0330, or (617) 252-5000. If you are already a member of CompuServe, type GO: ZMAC when prompted to respond in CompuServe. *MacUser* magazine also contains full sign-up instructions.

America Online

America Online (AOL) is another popular online service providing technical and topical online forums, including computing forums for Macintosh users. The AOL software is a custom icon-driven front end to the system. *Macworld* magazine also is present on America Online. Figure 14.9 shows the "departments" or areas in a navigational window of America Online.

Figure 14.9   America Online Departments window.

One example of the many forums on AOL in which to find answers to technical questions is in the PowerBook Resource Center. Figure 14.10 shows the window listing folders for specific PowerBook information. The PowerBook Message Center is a place to post messages, read and reply to other messages. Figure 14.11 shows the PowerBook Message Center window.

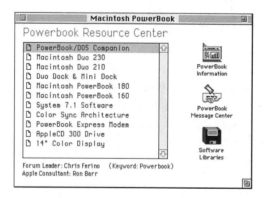

Figure 14.10   The PowerBook Resource Center on AOL.

For more information on America Online, call (800) 827-6364, or (703) 448-8700.

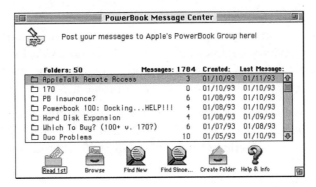

Figure 14.11 The PowerBook Message Center on AOL.

Publications

There are many publications and books covering Macintosh computers. Here are the publications that devote their pages exclusively to the Macintosh.

MacWEEK

MacWEEK is a weekly news magazine covering the Macintosh computer industry. A combination of news, technical reviews and market information, it is the most timely publication covering the Macintosh market. You cannot buy *MacWEEK* at the newsstand. Instead, *MacWEEK* offers annual subscription rates for national and international readers.

To qualify for a complimentary subscription, the publication requires a form be filled out, including questions on volume buying, and your role in influencing buying decisions in your company or otherwise. For subscription inquiries call (609) 461-2100, or write to:

MacWEEK Customer Service Department
c/o JCI
P.O. Box 1766
Riverton, NJ 08077.

MacUser

MacUser is a monthly magazine offering news, technical software and hardware reviews, commentaries, and help sections. *MacUser* has a section called Help Folder, where you can send in a problem or question. Help Folder might publish an answer to your problem.

MacUser is available on newsstands and in book stores. For more information on how to subscribe, call (800) 627-2247, or (303) 447-9330, or fax (international subscribers only) (303) 443-5080, or write to:

MacUser
P.O Box 56986
Boulder, CO 80322.

Macworld

Macworld magazine is *MacUser*'s competitor and offers similar content, including software and hardware reviews, tips and help columns, and a tips question and answer column, to which you can submit questions.

Macworld is available on newsstands and in bookstores. For more information on how to subscribe, call (800) 288-6848, or (303) 447-9330, or (415) 267-1743, or write to:

Macworld Subscriber Services
P.O. Box 54529
Boulder, CO 80322.

Conclusion

You may not need all the resources mentioned above, but knowing who your local authorized Apple dealer is and the technical support numbers of your favorite products will help you at some point. Appendix C lists a number of companies who offer software and hardware products and have technical support lines to answer your questions. Many will supply you with a catalog and advice, so don't hesitate to find out what resources are available to you.

If you are traveling abroad and need support overseas, you will not be able to access 800 phone numbers from outside the U.S. and Canada, so obtain a non-toll free number from the companies you might need to contact.

Glossary

-A-

accelerator   A card or chip you add to your computer to speed up processes such as calculations or a video display.

access privileges   The level of access a user has to a file server or shared volume on a network.

access time   The time it takes a computer to retrieve data stored on the device.

active window   The front window, recognizable by the horizontal stripes (called the title bar) at the top of the window. The active window is the window in which you are currently working. Dragging the horizontal bar at the top of the window enables you to move the window across the screen.

ADB   *See* Apple Desktop Bus.

Adobe   The company that created PostScript (a page description language), and other innovative publishing software applications.

Adobe Type Manager (ATM)   A system extension (INIT) that enables a Macintosh to scale Adobe fonts and Type 1 PostScript fonts to all sizes on the screen and the printed page.

Alarm Clock   A desk accessory under the Apple menu that enables the user to change the displayed computer time and date and to set an alarm.

alias   In System 7, a file that represents the real file found elsewhere (on another disk, network server, or other Macintosh volume). You create aliases in the Finder.

APDA   Apple Programmers and Developers Association; an organization designed to provide Macintosh developers with tools and information.

Apple Desktop Bus (ADB)   A port on the back of every Mac, used for connecting devices such as a mouse and keyboard.

Apple Events   A feature hidden from normal usage and designed to allow applications and system software to communicate with each other.

Apple File Exchange (AFE)   An application that comes with the Macintosh system software. It enables a Macintosh with a floppy disk drive to read PC disks and to transfer files between Macs and PCs.

Apple Menu   A menu available from within all applications; it appears on the very left end of the menu bar across the top of the Mac screen and is designated with an .

Apple Menu Items folder   A subfolder within the System folder when running System 7. Files placed in this folder appear in the Apple menu.

AppleShare file   An extension or INIT in the System folder (in the Extensions folder under System 7) that you select in the Chooser and enables you to access network file servers and shared volumes.

AppleShare File Server   A Macintosh running AppleShare file server software (sold by Apple), used to share files with users across an AppleTalk network.

AppleShare Print Server   A Macintosh running AppleShare print server software (sold by Apple), used to spool documents to send to the printer across an AppleTalk network.

AppleTalk   The network communication protocol used by Macs to communicate and share network services.

ASCII   American Standard Code for Information Interchange. A standard computer text format used when transferring text between different computer platforms or operating systems.

audio input port   A port found on the back of newer Macs for digitizing sound on the Macintosh. You can connect a microphone to it.

audio output port   A port on the back of the Macintosh for stereo (or mono on some Macs) headphones, speakers, and other audio output devices.

-B-

background printing   A feature that (when running System 7 or MultiFinder in System 6) enables a user to process printing jobs in the background while the user continues to work in an application. Works with the PrintMonitor (and other print spooling software).

Balloon Help   A help feature in System 7 and in applications that support Balloon Help. It is turned on from the Balloon Help menu in the right corner of the Macintosh menu bar; it then displays descriptions of application features and menu commands when you pass the mouse over the elements onscreen.

battery   There are two kinds of batteries: a small battery in all Macintosh computers that holds settings when the Macintosh is powered off; and PowerBook batteries that power the PowerBooks when the AC adapter is not plugged into an electrical outlet.

Battery desk accessory   On Macintosh PowerBooks, a desk accessory under the Apple menu that shows the amount of power remaining in the battery; this desk accessory also has a button that puts the PowerBook to sleep to conserve battery power.

BBS   *See* bulletin board system.

bit   The smallest unit of computer information; "bit" stands for "binary digit." A bit is either on or off (1 or 0); 8 bits make one byte of computer information.

bitmap   A way of representing a computer image with dots. Each dot is a pixel (picture element). Resizing a bitmap distorts the image.

Blessed System folder   A System folder with a valid System and Finder. The folder has a small Macintosh icon on it if it is "blessed." Removing the Finder "de-blesses" a System folder.

bridge (network)   A hardware device used to link network segments together or to divide a network into smaller segments while maintaining all communication between the segments.

bulletin board system (BBS)   An electronic data service accessed by means of phone lines, a modem, communications software, and a computer. Similar to an online service, on a smaller scale.

byte   A unit of measurement that describes the amount of computer information being stored. 8 bits equals 1 byte.

-C-

cache card   A card you add to a Macintosh to speed up computer operations. Fast RAM chips are on the cache card, which stores frequently used information for faster processing.

Cache Switch control panel   A control panel for the Macintosh Quadras that turns their built-in cache on or off. You achieve optimal performance when the cache is on.

Caps lock   A key on the Macintosh keyboard that sets all alphabet keys to uppercase. Can be off or on.

CD-ROM (Compact Disc-Read Only Memory)   A disk (that looks like an audio CD) that requires a CD-ROM drive attached to the Macintosh to read files from the disk. CD-ROM discs can hold about 600M of data.

cdev An acronym for Control panel device. Refers to the files that you use to control software settings. These files can be found in the Control Panels folder in the System 7 folder.

central processing unit (CPU) The main computer chip on the computer's logic board that controls all other computer functions. The Macintosh CPU is made by Motorola. The Macintosh Motorola chips include the 68000, 68020, 68030 and 68040. (Also, the term CPU is used to refer to the main unit of modular Macs—the unit that contains the processor.)

Chooser A desk accessory in the System folder used to connect to network services like printers and file servers. Accessed from the Apple menu.

Clipboard A space of memory (RAM) that holds the most recent information that you copied, which is then available to be pasted or viewed (if the application has an option to view the clipboard contents). The Finder's Show Clipboard option under the Edit menu displays the contents of the Clipboard. The Clipboard is lost when the Macintosh is turned off or restarted.

Clipboard file This is a file in the System folder that stores the contents of the Clipboard when the Clipboard has exceeded the memory space available to it in RAM.

CloseView A control panel that magnifies the screen image.

Color A control panel that enables you to change the highlight color (the color of highlighted text) and window accent colors on color monitors.

Command key The key next to the Spacebar that has a cloverleaf (⌘) and/or an Apple () symbol on it.

communications software Software that you use to exchange information with other computers over networks and telephone lines.

Compatibility Checker A HyperCard stack that comes with Apple's System 7 software upgrade kits that enables you to determine if your software is compatible with System 7.

Control panel devices (cdev) Files that are used to adjust software settings and add functionality to your Macintosh.

Control Panels folder A special folder in the System 7 folder for installing control panel devices.

CPU *See* central processing unit.

cursor keys Arrow keys on the keyboard that enable you to move the insertion point up, down, left, and right.

-D-

DA *See* desk accessory.

DAL *See* Data Access Language.

Data Access Language A language used to access databases on other computers. The DAL file is a System 7 system extension (formerly called CL/1).

Data fork The part of a Macintosh file that stores data created in an application.

DB-25 connector A serial connector used in early Macintosh models and still used as a serial connector on PCs.

Desk accessory An application that is accessible from the Apple menu. In System 7, any application, file, folder, or alias can be placed in the Apple Menu Items folder to make it available through the Apple menu.

Desktop Refers to the Finder's work area, with mounted disks, files, trash, and visible background space.

Desktop file An invisible file that the Finder uses to manage files, folders, applications, and icons.

dialog box A window used to communicate with the user; dialog boxes often offer options, settings, and data entry areas.

DIN A round connector with pins (such as the modem and printer ports).

Disk Operating System (DOS)   The operating software for PCs (IBM-compatibles). Also called MS-DOS (Microsoft DOS).

DOS   *See* Disk Operating System.

dots per inch.   A unit of measurement for resolution of images onscreen and in print.

double-click   To click twice with the mouse in quick succession. Double-clicking on an application or document icon usually opens the application or document.

download   To transfer (receive) a file from one computer to your own computer, usually over telephone lines.

dpi   *See* dots per inch.

-E-

Easy Access   A control panel that enables a Macintosh user to operate the computer one keystroke at a time, and without using the mouse.

electromagnetic interference   Interference from devices that create electromagnetic fields, such as fluorescent lights and power transformers. Electromagnetic interference can affect transmission of data across network cabling and network devices.

electronic mail (E-mail)   Files and messages exchanged over a network or telephone line.

E-mail   *See* electronic mail.

EPSF   *See* Encapsulated PostScript File.

Encapsulated PostScript File   A graphical file format used to store graphics and text for printing on a PostScript-based printer.

Ethernet   An industry standard wiring scheme. Commonly used and having a data transmission rate of 10 megabits per second (Mbps).

EtherTalk   Software that enables AppleTalk protocols to run over standard Ethernet cabling. EtherTalk files come with the Macintosh system software.

Extensions folder   A folder in the System 7 System folder where you install extensions (or INITs).

extensions   Under System 6, extensions were called INITs. Extensions are files that you install in the Extensions folder (found in the System folder) and that load into memory (RAM) at startup. Some extensions display an icon at the bottom of the screen when the Macintosh starts up.

-F-

FDHD   *See* Floppy Disk, High Density.

female connector   The element of a pair of connectors which has indentations or holes to accept the pins from the male connector.

file server   A computer dedicated to users on a network. File servers use software (such as AppleShare file server software) to share the files.

File Sharing   A System 7 feature that enables a Macintosh to share files across a network without a dedicated file server.

Finder   The application presents and manages the Macintosh desktop.

floating-point unit (FPU)   A computer processing chip (sometimes built into the CPU) that speeds up floating-point (or non-integer) calculations.

Floppy Disk, High Density (FDHD)   The old name for what is now called the SuperDrive. It is a floppy disk drive that formats, reads, and writes 1.4M high-density 3 1/2-inch disks (as well as older 800K and 400K disks).

Font/DA Mover   An application used with System 6 and earlier system versions to install desk accessories and fonts into the System file.

font   On the Macintosh, a font is a character typeface (examples are Helvetica and Courier). In the typesetting industry it actually means the reverse; a font is a particular style of a typeface (like Courier bold).

FPU   *See* floating-point unit.

fragmentation   In RAM and erasable disk storage (hard disks and removable disks), sometimes the stored information becomes scattered
across the memory space; units of information (such as files) are
broken up and stored among several different locations. This slows
down computer processing.

freeware   Software that computer users can obtain and use without
charge; freeware can be obtained from computer user groups and
online services.

Function keys   The keys on Apple Extended Keyboards, usually found
along the top of the keyboard, that have an F followed by a number
on the key.

fuse   A small component placed in a power line or an electrical device
that prevents surges of current from damaging the device. An open
or burned fuse indicates a device failure or a power surge.

-G-

General Controls   A control panel in the Control Panels folder. Settings
such as the date, time, and desktop pattern can be adjusted here; the
settings are then saved in PRAM.

Get Info   In the Finder, a command that enables you to view information
about a file. You can find Get Info under the File menu, or highlight
the file and press ⌘ - I.

gigabyte   About 1,000,000,000 bytes (one billion bytes); abbreviated
as G.

GUI   Pronounced "gooey." *See* graphical user interface

graphical user interface (GUI)   A visual way to represent computer
commands and objects on screen; graphical user interfaces are
designed to make computers easier to understand for novice users.

graphics tablet   An input device that translates a pen location into a
screen position.

grayscale   Shades of gray in an image or onscreen. Each pixel can vary in the intensity of gray it represents. Used for photorealistic images on-screen and in print.

-H-

hard disk   A magnetic storage device that stores large quantities of computer information; it attaches to the Macintosh internally (inside the Mac) or externally (via the SCSI port).

hard disk partition   A division of a single hard disk into two (or more) logically separate volumes.

highlight   To select an object such as text or an icon on the Desktop. The highlighted object is selected; that is, subsequent operations will be performed on that object.

HyperCard   An authoring environment (developed by Apple, taken over by Claris, and now returned to Apple) that supports the creation of applications and databases using a programming language called AppleTalk.

-I-J-

icon   A graphical image that represents elements such as disks, applications, folders, and files on the computer.

INIT   A program that is loaded when the Macintosh starts up that modifies or adds to the way the System software works. INITs are called extensions in System 7.

Installer   An application that installs software on the Macintosh; it automatically places the files on the disk in the correct configuration.

Interrupt switch   A button on the programmer's switch used for trouble-shooting (debugging) programming errors.

-K-

keyboard   A device used for inputting information into a computer. Not all keyboards have the same keys and some keyboards are used internationally and have different keys.

kilobyte   About 1,000 bytes (one thousand bytes); abbreviated as K.

-L-

Laser Prep file   A file used with System 6 printer drivers that processes print jobs. This file is no longer needed with System 7 because it was incorporated into the LaserWriter driver.

LaserWriter   An Apple printer that uses laser printing technology to print documents from computer applications. Most LaserWriters are PostScript printers and have built-in fonts.

LCD   Liquid crystal display. A low-power, flat screen display that uses reflective light and backlighting for contrasting screen images.

LocalTalk   A simple type of AppleTalk network wiring used to connect Macs and other network devices (printers) into small workgroups. LocalTalk connects via the Printer port on Macs, and has a maximum data transfer rate of 230.4 kilobits per second (Kbps).

logic board   Also referred to as the "motherboard." The main circuit board inside every computer that holds the CPU, RAM, ROM, and other main circuit components.

-M-

macro   A series of commands that you automate into one step by way of a saved file. Commonly uses the keyboard to enable the user to press one key combination to perform several repetitive tasks in a sequence.

MacroMaker   A keyboard macro program that came with the Macintosh System 6 software (not compatible with System 7).

male connector The element of a pair of connectors which has pins that fit into the holes or receptacles of the female connector.

Megabyte About 1,000,000 bytes (1 million bytes); abbreviated as M.

Megahertz A unit that measures frequency in cycles per second, used to rate the speed of computer chips (CPU).

memory Hardware on the computer that stores information and calculations. There are two types of memory; see RAM and ROM.

menu A list of commands. Menus are listed at the top of the screen (in the Menu bar); a menu is displayed by moving the mouse pointer to the title of the menu and holding the mouse button down.

Menu bar The white bar across the top of the screen that lists available menus.

microprocessor *See* CPU.

Microsoft Windows Software for PCs that creates a graphical interface.

modem A device used to link your computer by telephone lines to a network, information service, or bulletin board.

modifier key One of several keys on the Macintosh keyboard used to modify another key. Modifier keys include the Shift, Caps Lock, Command, Option, and Control keys.

monochrome A monitor that displays one color (usually white) against a black background.

motherboard *See* logic board.

mount When the Finder recognizes a disk and displays its icon and contents on the desktop.

mouse A hardware device for interacting with the computer screen with a pointer that moves and is used to select objects, tools, and text.

mouse pad A pad for the mouse to rest and roll over—usually made of plastic or rubber. A pad enables the mouse to roll smoothly, which translates into smooth movement of the pointer onscreen.

MS-DOS   *See* DOS.

MultiFinder   A feature of System 6 and earlier system software versions that enables two or more applications to be open simultaneously. System 7 offers the feature automatically; it cannot be turned off.

-N-

nanosecond   One billionth of a second in time (very fast). Used to measure computer hardware speed such as RAM speed.

network   A group of devices (such as computers and printers) that are wired together. Network connections also can be made by modem; see ARA.

Note Pad   A desk accessory under the Apple menu that can be used to type and save small pages of text. The text is saved in the Note Pad File in the System folder.

NuBus   A type of card slot standard used for video, network, and other add-in cards for the Macintosh.

num lock key   The key on the upper left corner of the keypad (on keyboards that have a numeric keypad). It is used with some applications to alternate between the standard use of the keypad (that is, to enter numbers), and another use, such as cursor control.

-O-

OCR   *See* optical character recognition.

Operating system   The basic software a computer needs to start up and perform basic tasks. The Macintosh operating system (usually called the System) is in both ROM and in the system software.

optical character recognition   Using a hardware device and software to convert text on paper to text in a computer document.

-P-

PMMU *See* Paged Memory Management Unit.

Paged Memory Management Unit (PMMU) A computer chip that enables a Macintosh to use memory features such as virtual memory.

Parameter RAM A battery-supported RAM area in the Macintosh used to store settings (such as the time and date) when the Macintosh is powered off.

Parity RAM Memory (RAM) that has an extra error-checking bit to ensure data integrity. Used primarily by PCs; some Macs are equipped with Parity RAM as well.

PDS *See* Processor Direct Slot.

peripheral A device that connects to the Mac by way of a SCSI, serial, video, or other port.

personal computer (PC) Generally refers to the IBM-compatible family of computers that run the DOS operating system. Sometimes refers to all personal computers.

PhoneNET An AppleTalk network connector system that connects Macintosh devices together in a network (by Farallon Computing).

pixel The smallest graphical element to display an image on the screen. A pixel can be black, white, gray, or a color in the monitor's display spectrum.

pointer The onscreen cursor controlled by the mouse.

PostScript A page description language created by Adobe Systems. It describes computer images mathematically and is used for printing smooth images and text on printers. PostScript is used in most laser printers.

PRAM *See* Parameter RAM.

PrintMonitor An application in the System folder that runs in the background to print documents while other applications are opened and being used. The PrintMonitor Documents folder in the System folder holds print jobs waiting to be printed.

Processor Direct Slot A slot standard in some Macs for adding cards to support video and accelerator add-ins. An alternative to the NuBus slot standard.

protocols A formal set of rules agreed upon and used for exchanging data between computers.

public domain software Software that is not copyrighted and may be used in any means desired (such as incorporated into a commercial program). Public domain software is less restricted than freeware, which is copyrighted.

-Q-

QuickDraw A set of routines (programs) that the Macintosh uses to display graphics on the screen. Also used for printing to QuickDraw printers.

QuickTime A system extension that enables applications to record and display time-based data such as video, animation, and sound.

-R-

RAM *See* Random Access Memory.

RAM cache RAM used to store frequently accessed data from the hard disk.

RAM disk A portion of RAM set aside to be used as a storage disk for files. Acts as a faster hard disk.

Random Access Memory Temporary memory that stores screen information, system software, application software, and data that is being used.

Read Only Memory A chip on the logic board that contains permanent information used by the computer. Usually contains some portion of the computer's operating system.

ResEdit An application used to modify resources in files.

Reset switch   A button on the programmer's switch that performs the same action as a restart.

resource   A part of an application that stores the code for items such as menus, dialog boxes, and more. Icons, fonts, and sounds are examples of resources (also referred to as resource files.)

resource fork   The part of a file that contains resources. The other type of fork is a data fork (not to be confused with a dinner fork).

RGB   Red, green and blue; the basic colors used to define more complex colors as displayed on a monitor.

RJ-11   A standard telephone jack, used to connect modems to a telephone cable or telephone wall jack. (Also used with PhoneNET cabling for networks.)

ROM   *See* Read Only Memory.

-S-

Scrapbook   A desk accessory under the Apple menu (stored in the Apple Menu Items folder) that stores pasted data such as text, sounds, and (most commonly) graphics.

SCSI   *See* Small Computer System Interface.

SCSI chain   A group of SCSI devices connected together with SCSI cables.

selecting   Marking text or an object with the mouse cursor so that an action can be performed on the object.

Shareware   Copyrighted software that is offered for a free trial period. The user is under the honor system to either pay for the software when it is kept and used, or to discard it.

Shut Down   The proper method to turn off the Macintosh. The Shut Down command is under the Special menu in the Finder.

SIMM   *See* Single In-line Memory Module.

Single In-line Memory Module (SIMM)   A small circuit board with RAM memory chips on it. Installed in computers and used for temporary memory (RAM).

Small Computer System Interface   A standard interface that enables you to connect hardware devices to the Macintosh, generally used to connect hard disks.

spooler   An application that stores documents so they can be sent to the printer.

startup disk   The disk that contains the System folder to start up (boot) the Macintosh. The System folder has a small Mac icon on it when it is the startup folder.

suitcase   A file that stores fonts or desk accessories.

SuperDrive   A high density disk drive in all recent Macintosh models and capable of reading high-density floppy disks (FDHD), as well as older (double-density) disks and PC-formatted disks.

surge   A sudden burst of voltage from a power source.

surge protector   A hardware device placed between the power cords of devices and the power outlet to protect devices from power surges.

-T-

terminating resistor   An electronic device that serves as an endpoint for a line of networked devices.

Token Ring   An industry standard network type, where network devices are arranged in rings. Has a speed of 4 or 16 megabits per second (Mbps).

TokenTalk   Software that enables Macintosh computers to communicate with AppleTalk over a Token Ring network.

Trash   The icon on the Finder's desktop where files are placed to be deleted. To delete the files in the trash, choose Empty Trash from the Special menu.

TrueType font   A font that can display or print characters at any size (also referred to as an "outline font"). TrueType fonts come with System 7; others can be purchased from third-party font makers.

-U-V-

user group   A group of enthusiasts who support other members and exchange information, tips, and software (such as shareware).

VGA   A standard monitor adapter used mostly with PC computers. They can be connected to Macintoshes with a special cable, and some Macs support VGA with the standard monitor cable. VGA is slightly lower in quality than the Macintosh monitors; however it is usually less expensive.

video card   The same as a monitor card. Used to connect monitors to Macs without built-in monitor support, or when the monitor requires its own video card.

virtual memory   Space on a hard disk designated for use as RAM.

virus   A small program designed to surreptitiously spread to many computers. Viruses often cause damage to the infected computers; programs exist that can screen for viruses to prevent them from spreading.

volume   A term used to describe a storage device that appears on the desktop. A volume may be an entire disk, part of a disk, or a network file server disk.

-W-Z-

WYSIWYG   "What You See Is What You Get," which means what you see on the screen will (or should) look exactly like the printout.

zone   A logical grouping of devices on an AppleTalk network. You select zones in the Chooser (under the Apple menu).

System Errors

When System errors occur, you will often receive a dialog box with a description of the error; however, you will often receive a less descriptive message, such as a bomb icon, a system error number, or a cryptic phrase. This appendix lists system errors, in numeric order.

Troubleshooting System Errors

The most likely causes of system errors are a software problem with the open application(s), a conflict between the open application and your system software; or in some cases a hardware problem.

Under System 6, a system error is more likely to be reported as a code (ID number), whereas in System 7, the error codes are translated into messages.

System errors may not always indicate what the real problem is, and understanding the error messages sometimes requires a knowledge of Macintosh programming. To make the most of a reported error, check the meaning of the error, and try some of these general troubleshooting tips:

✳ Make a note of the error ID, the text, and the version numbers of the application and system software you are using. Look up the meaning of the system error and see if you can make any sense out of it in order to isolate the probable cause.

✳ Check the amount of memory allocated to the application and increase it if you have enough RAM to do so.

✳ Check your disk to determine if you have enough available space to work with. You might have run out of disk space.

✳ Open other documents with the application. It may be just this document that is producing the error.

✳ Check for conflicts with your system extensions (INITs), control panels, desk accessories, and applications.

✳ Shut down and restart the Macintosh. Sometimes this clears the RAM of garbled data.

✳ Try to re-create the problem on your Mac or another Macintosh.

✳ Check for virus infections with a virus program.

✳ Reinstall the application by deleting it and installing a new copy. Then open the crashing document with the newly installed application.

✳ Reinstall the system software, especially the System and Finder files. See Chapter 4, "System Software," for more about reinstalling System software.

✳ Check the disk for file or other damage with a disk repair utility, and check out the hardware configuration.

System Errors and Some Explanations

Here are explanations of some of the more common System errors:

ID = 01 or Bus error

The Macintosh was told to access memory (RAM) that is not available or doesn't exist. Many times this is an error reflecting a software problem; however, it can mean there is a hardware problem.

ID = 02 or Address error

This is an error that occurs when reading information from or writing information into memory (RAM).

ID = 03 or Illegal Instruction

You will see this error if the Macintosh does not understand an instruction sent to it by an application.

ID = 04 or Zero Divide error

There is a programming error in the application.

ID = 05 or Range Check error

There is a programming error in the application.

ID = 06 or Overflow error

There is a programming error in the application.

ID = 07 or Privilege Violation

There is a programming error in the application.

ID = 08 or Trace Mode error

There is a programming error in the application.

ID = 09 and ID = 10 or Line 1010 and Line 1111 trap

This is a programming error in the application, or a conflict with another application, desk accessory, or extension (INIT) in the System folder.

ID = 12 or Unimplemented Core Routine

There is a programming error in the application.

ID = 13 or Uninstalled Interrupt

The Macintosh uses an "interrupt" to figure out when devices such as keyboards and disk drives need service. The programmer tells the Macintosh how to service these devices. This error message may appear when a disk driver or other software erroneously interacts with hardware.

ID=15 or Segment Loader error

Macintosh programs are broken into segments and each program has one or more segments that load into memory (RAM). This message indicates an error loading a segment of the program into RAM.

ID = 17 to ID = 24 or Packages 1 to 7 Are Not Present

The Macintosh uses packages, or small files, in the System file to carry out tasks. Examples of these packages include the International Utilities, Standard File Utilities, and Disk Initialization. If you receive this message, you probably have a damaged System file. Error ID 15, 16, 26, 27, 30, and 31 also indicate a damaged System file.

ID = 25 or Out of Memory

This error means you have run out of memory (RAM). It can be a faulty error report in a few cases when a previous action causes an error.

ID = 26 or Can't Launch File

The Macintosh cannot fully use the open application. Quit the application and try again. Otherwise, reinstall the application.

ID = 28 or Stack Has Moved into Application Heap

This is a problem similar to the ID = 25 out of memory error.

ID = 29

This is a system error under AppleShare. AppleShare reports all system errors as ID = 29. For example, system file errors on the AppleShare file server and problems with the AppleShare file server software will return an ID error of 29.

ID = -39 or End of File

The -39 error is an "End Of File" error, which usually indicates that an application encountered an "end of file" flag unexpectedly in a file it has open. The most likely cause of the error is a corrupt data file or preferences file. The fix may be to recover as much of the file as possible if it is a document with valuable data, or replace the file from a backup copy.

ID = -61 or Write Permissions error

The system is not allowing an application to write to a file (make a change). Check to see if any files are locked; otherwise, use a disk repair utility to check the disk for problems.

ID = -192 or Resource not found

This message is reported when a resource in a file is not present or corrupted. Files that have a resource fork, such as applications and system files, can become corrupted and report this message.

The System Error Table

Here is a table of the System error ID numbers and their translations. You also can find these translations in the System Error DA (desk accessory) included on the disk with this book.

DS Table

ID	Name	Description
1	dsBusError	bus error
2	dsAddressErr	address error
3	dsIllInstErr	illegal instruction error
4	dsZeroDivErr	zero divide error
5	dsChkErr	check trap error
6	dsOvflowErr	overflow trap error
7	dsPrivErr	privilege violation error
8	dsTraceErr	trace mode error
9	dsLineAErr	line 1010 trap error
10	dsLineFErr	line 1111 trap error
11	dsMiscErr	miscellaneous hardware exception error
12	dsCoreErr	unimplemented core routine error
13	dsIrqErr	uninstalled interrupt error

continues

DS Table Continued

ID	Name	Description
14	dsIOCoreErr	I/O Core error
15	dsLoadErr	segment loader error
16	dsFPErr	floating-point error
17	dsNoPackErr	package 0 not present [List Manager]
18	dsNoPk1	package 1 not present [reserved by Apple]
19	dsNoPk2	package 2 not present [Disk Initialization]
20	dsNoPk3	package 3 not present [Standard File]
21	dsNoPk4	package 4 not present [Floating-Point Arithmetic]
22	dsNoPk5	package 5 not present [Transcendental Functions]
23	dsNoPk6	package 6 not present [International Utilities]
24	dsNoPk7	package 7 not present [Binary/Decimal Conversion]
25	dsMemFullErr	out of memory!
26	dsBadLaunch	can't launch file
27	dsFSErr	file system map has been trashed
28	dsStknHeap	stack has moved into application heap
30	dsReinsert	request user to reinsert off-line volume
31	dsNotThe1	not the disk I wanted (obsolete)
33	negZcbFreeErr	ZcbFree has gone negative
40	dsGreeting	welcome to Macintosh greeting
41	dsFinderErr	can't load the Finder error
42	dsBadStartupDisk	unable to mount boot volume (obsolete)
43	dsSystemFileErr	can't find System file to open (obsolete)

ID	Name	Description
51	dsBadSlotInt	unserviceable slot interrupt
81	dsBadSANEopcode	bad opcode given to SANE Pack4
83	dsBadPatchHeader	SetTrapAddress saw the "come-from" header
84	menuPrgErr	happens when a menu is purged
85	dsMBarNFnd	SysErr—cannot find MBDF
86	dsHMenuFindErr	SysErr—recursively defined HMenus
87	dsWDEFnFnd	Could not load WDEF
88	dsCDEFnFnd	Could not load CDEF
89	dsMDEFnFnd	Could not load MDEF
90	dsNoFPU	FPU instruction executed, but machine has no FPU
98	dsNoPatch	Cannot patch for particular Model Mac
99	dsBadPatch	Cannot load patch resource
101	dsParityErr	memory parity error
102	dsOldSystem	System is too old for this ROM
103	ds32BitMode	booting in 32-bit on a 24-bit system
104	dsNeedToWrite BootBlocks	need to write new boot blocks
105	dsNotEnough RAMToBoot	need at least 1.5M of RAM to boot 7.0
20000	dsShutDown OrRestart	user choice between Shut Down and Restart
20001	dsSwitchOff OrRestart	user choice between Switch Off or or Restart
20002	dsForcedQuit	allow the user to ExitToShell, return if Cancel
32767	dsSysErr	general system error (catch-all used in DSAT)

General System (VBL Mgr., Queue, Etc.)

ID	Name	Description
0	noErr	0 for success
-1	qErr	queue element not found during deletion
-2	vTypErr	invalid queue element
-3	corErr	core routine number out of range
-4	unimpErr	unimplemented core routine
-5	SlpTypeErr	invalid queue element
-8	seNoDB	no debugger installed to handle debugger command

Color Manager

ID	Name	Description
-9	iTabPurgErr	from Color2Index/ITabMatch
-10	noColMatch	
-11	qAllocErr	from MakeITable
-12	tblAllocErr	
-13	overRun	
-14	noRoomErr	
-15	seOutOfRange	from SetEntry
-16	seProtErr	
-17	i2CRangeErr	
-18	gdBadDev	
-19	reRangeErr	
-20	seInvRequest	
-21	seNoMemErr	

I/O System

ID	Name	Description
-17	controlErr	driver cannot respond to Control call
-18	statusErr	driver cannot respond to Status call
-19	readErr	driver cannot respond to Read call
-20	writErr	driver cannot respond to Write call
-21	badUnitErr	driver ref num does not match unit table
-22	unitEmptyErr	driver ref num specifies NIL handle in unit table
-23	openErr	requested read/write permission does not match driver's open permission, or Attempt to open RAM SerD failed
-24	closErr	close failed
-25	dRemovErr	tried to remove an open driver
-26	dInstErr	drvrInstall could not find driver in resources
-27	abortErr	I/O call aborted by KillIO
-27	iIOAbortErr	I/O abort error (Printing Manager)
-28	notOpenErr	Could not rd/wr/ctl/sts because driver not opened
-29	unitTblFullErr	unit table has no more entries
-30	dceExtErr	dce extension error

File System

ID	Name	Description
-33	dirFulErr	directory full
-34	dskFulErr	disk full
-35	nsvErr	no such volume
-36	ioErr	I/O error (bummers)

continues

File System Continued

ID	Name	Description
-37	bdNamErr	there may be no bad names in the final system!
-38	fnOpnErr	file not open
-39	eofErr	end of file
-40	posErr	tried to position to before start of file (r/w)
-41	mFulErr	memory full (open) or file will not fit (load)
-42	tmfoErr	too many files open
-43	fnfErr	file not found
-44	wPrErr	diskette is write protected
-45	fLckdErr	file is locked
-46	vLckdErr	volume is locked
-47	fBsyErr	file is busy (delete)
-48	dupFNErr	duplicate filename (rename)
-49	opWrErr	file already open with write permission
-50	paramErr	error in user parameter list
-51	rfNumErr	refnum error
-52	gfpErr	get file position error
-53	volOffLinErr	volume not online error (was Ejected)
-54	permErr	permissions error (on file open)
-55	volOnLinErr	drive volume already online at MountVol
-56	nsDrvErr	no such drive (tried to mount a bad drive num)
-57	noMacDskErr	not a Mac diskette (sig bytes are wrong)
-58	extFSErr	volume in question belongs to an external fs
-59	fsRnErr	file system internal error: during rename the old entry was deleted but could not be restored

ID	Name	Description
-60	badMDBErr	bad master directory block
-61	wrPermErr	write permissions error

Font Manager

ID	Name	Description
-64	fontDecError	error during font declaration
-65	fontNotDeclared	font not declared
-66	fontSubErr	font substitution occured

Disk

ID	Name	Description
-64	lastDskErr	
-64	noDriveErr	drive not installed
-65	offLinErr	r/w requested for an off-line drive
-66	noNybErr	could not find 5 nybbles in 200 tries
-67	noAdrMkErr	could not find valid addr mark
-68	dataVerErr	read/verify compare failed
-69	badCksmErr	addr mark checksum did not check
-70	badBtSlpErr	bad addr mark bit slip nibbles
-71	noDtaMkErr	could not find a data mark header
-72	badDCksum	bad data mark checksum
-73	badDBtSlp	bad data mark bit slip nibbles
-74	wrUnderrun	write underrun occurred
-75	cantStepErr	step handshake failed
-76	tk0BadErr	track 0 detect does not change

continues

371

Disk Continued

ID	Name	Description
-77	initIWMErr	unable to initialize IWM
-78	twoSideErr	tried to read 2nd side on a one-sided drive
-79	spdAdjErr	unable to correctly adjust disk speed
-80	seekErr	track number wrong on address mark
-81	sectNFErr	sector number never found on a track
-82	fmt1Err	cannot find sector 0 after track format
-83	fmt2Err	cannot get enough sync
-84	verErr	track failed to verify
-84	firstDskErr	

Serial Ports, PRAM/Clock

ID	Name	Description
-85	clkRdErr	unable to read same clock value twice
-86	clkWrErr	time written did not verify
-87	prWrErr	parameter ram written did not read-verify
-88	prInitErr	InitUtil found the parameter ram uninitialized
-89	rcvrErr	SCC receiver error (framing, parity, OR)
-90	breakRecd	break received (SCC)

AppleTalk

ID	Name	Description
-91	ddpSktErr	error in socket number
-92	ddpLenErr	data length too big
-93	noBridgeErr	no network bridge for non-local send

ID	Name	Description
-94	lapProtErr	error in attaching/detaching protocol
-95	excessCollsns	excessive collisions on write
-97	portInUse	driver Open error code (port is in use)
-98	portNotCf	driver Open error code (parameter RAM not configured for this connection)

Memory Manager

ID	Name	Description
-99	memROZErr	hard error in ROZ
-99	memROZError	hard error in ROZ
-99	memROZWarn	soft error in ROZ

Scrap Manager

ID	Name	Description
-100	noScrapErr	no scrap exists error
-102	noTypeErr	no object of that type in scrap

Memory Manager

ID	Name	Description
-108	memFullErr	not enough room in heap zone
-109	nilHandleErr	Handle was NIL in HandleZone or other
-110	memAdrErr	address was odd, or out of range
-111	memWZErr	WhichZone failed (applied to free block)
-112	memPurErr	trying to purge a locked or non-purgeable block

continues

Memory Manager Continued

ID	Name	Description
-113	memAZErr	Address in zone check failed
-114	memPCErr	pointer check failed
-115	memBCErr	block check failed
-116	memSCErr	size check failed
-117	memLockedErr	trying to move a locked block (MoveHHi)

HFS

ID	Name	Description
-120	dirNFErr	directory not found
-121	tmwdoErr	no free WDCB available
-122	badMovErr	move into offspring error
-123	wrgVolTypErr	wrong volume type error: not supported for MFS
-124	volGoneErr	server volume has been disconnected
-125	updPixMemErr	insufficient memory to update a pixmap
-127	fsDSIntErr	internal file system error

Menu Manager

ID	Name	Description
-126	dsMBarNFnd	system error code for MBDF not found
-127	dsHMenuFindErr	could not find HMenu's parent in MenuKey
-128	userCanceledErr	user canceled the operation status

HFS FileID

ID	Name	Description
-130	fidNotFound	no file thread exists
-131	fidNotAFile	directory specified
-132	fidExists	file id already exists

Color Quickdraw & Color Manager

ID	Name	Description
-145	noMemForPict PlaybackErr	
-147	rgnTooBigError	region accumulation failed; rgn may be corrupt
-148	pixMapTooBigErr	passed pixelmap is too large
-149	nsStackErr	not enough stack space for the necessary buffers
-150	cMatchErr	Color2Index failed to find an index
-151	cTempMemErr	failed to allocate memory for temporary structures
-152	cNoMemErr	failed to allocate memory for structure
-153	cRangeErr	range error on colorTable request
-154	cProtectErr	colorTable entry protection violation
-155	cDevErr	invalid type of graphics device
-156	cResErr	invalid resolution for MakeITable
-157	cDepthErr	invalid pixel depth
-158	cParmErr	invalid parameter

B

Resource Manager

ID	Name	Description
-185	badExtResource	extended resource has a bad format
-186	CantDecompress	resource bent ("the bends") cannot decompress a compressed resource
-192	resNotFound	resource not found
-193	resFNotFound	resource file not found
-194	addResFailed	AddResource failed
-195	addRefFailed	AddReference failed
-196	rmvResFailed	RmveResource failed
-197	rmvRefFailed	RmveReference failed
-198	resAttrErr	attribute inconsistent with operation
-199	mapReadErr	map inconsistent with operation

Sound Manager

ID	Name	Description
-200	noHardware	no hardware support for the specified synthesizer
-201	notEnoughHardware	no more channels for the specified synthesizer
-203	queueFull	no more room in queue
-204	resProblem	problem loading resource
-205	badChannel	invalid channel queue length
-206	badFormat	handle to 'snd' resource was invalid
-207	notEnoughBufferSpace	could not allocate enough memory
-208	badFileFormat	was not type AIFF or was of bad format, corrupt
-209	channelBusy	the Channel is being used for a PFD already

ID	Name	Description
-210	buffersTooSmall	cannot operate in the memory allowed
-211	channelNotBusy	
-212	noMoreRealTime	not enought CPU cycles left to add another task
-220	siNoSoundInHardware	
-221	siBadSoundInDevice	invalid index, SoundInGetIndexedDevice
-222	siNoBufferSpecified	nil buffer passed to synchronous SPBRecord
-223	siInvalidCompression	invalid compression type
-224	siHardDriveTooSlow	hard drive too slow to record to disk
-225	siInvalidSampleRate	invalid sample rate
-226	siInvalidSampleSize	invalid sample size
-227	siDeviceBusyErr	input device already in use
-228	siBadDeviceName	input device could not be opened
-229	siBadRefNum	invalid input device reference number
-230	siInputDeviceErr	input device hardware failure
-231	siUnknownInfoType	driver returned invalid info type selector
-232	siUnknownQuality	invalid quality selector returned by driver

MIDI Manager

ID	Name	Description
-250	midiNoClientErr	no client with that ID found
-251	midiNoPortErr	no port with that ID found

continues

MIDI Manager

ID	Name	Description
-252	midiTooManyPortsErr	too many ports already installed in system
-253	midiTooManyConsErr	too many connections made
-254	midiVConnectErr	pending virtual connection created
-255	midiVConnectMade	pending virtual connection resolved
-256	midiVConnectRmvd	pending virtual connection removed
-257	midiNoConErr	no connection exists between specified ports
-258	midiWriteErr	could not write to all connected ports
-259	midiNameLenErr	name supplied is longer than 31 characters
-260	midiDupIDErr	duplicate client ID
-261	midiInvalidCmdErr	command not supported for port type

Notification Manager

ID	Name	Description
-299	nmTypErr	wrong queue type

Start Manager

ID	Name	Description
-290	smSDMInitErr	SDM could not be initialized
-291	smSRTInitErr	Slot Resource Table could not be initialized
-292	smPRAMInitErr	Slot Resource Table could not be initialized
-293	smPriInitErr	cards could not be initialized

ID	Name	Description
-300	smEmptySlot	no card in slot
-301	smCRCFail	CRC check failed for declaration data
-302	smFormatErr	FHeader format is not Apple's
-303	smRevisionErr	wrong revison level
-304	smNoDir	directory offset is Nil
-305	smDisabledSlot	this slot is disabled
-306	smNosInfoArray	no sInfoArray; Memory Mgr error
-307	smResrvErr	fatal reserved error; reserved field <> 0
-308	smUnExBusErr	unexpected BusError
-309	smBLFieldBad	ByteLanes field was bad.
-310	smFHBlockRdErr	error occured during _sGetFHeader
-311	smFHBlkDispErr	error occured during _sDisposePtr (dispose of FHeader block)
-312	smDisposePErr	_DisposePointer error
-313	smNoBoardsRsrc	no Board sResource
-314	smGetPRErr	error occured during _sGetPRAMRec (See SIMStatus)
-315	smNoBoardId	no Board Id
-316	smIntStatVErr	the InitStatusV field was negative after primary or secondary init
-317	smIntTblVErr	an error occured while trying to initialize the Slot Resource Table
-318	smNoJmpTbl	SDM jump table could not be created
-319	smBadBoardId	BoardId was wrong, re-init the PRAM record
-320	smBusErrTO	BusError time-out
-330	smBadRefId	reference Id not found in list

continues

Start Manager Continued

ID	Name	Description
-331	smBadsList	bad sList: Id1<Id2<Id3...format is not followed
-332	smReservedErr	reserved field not zero
-333	smCodeRevErr	code revision is wrong
-334	smCPUErr	code revision is wrong
-335	smsPointerNil	LPointer is nil from sOffsetData (if this error occurs, check sInfo rec for more information)
-336	smNilsBlockErr	Nil sBlock error (don't allocate and try to use a nil sBlock)
-337	smSlotOOBErr	slot out-of-bounds error
-338	smSelOOBErr	selector out-of-bounds error
-339	smNewPErr	_NewPtr error
-340	smBlkMoveErr	_BlockMove error
-341	smCkStatusErr	status of slot = fail
-342	smGetDrvrNamErr	error occured during _sGetDrvrName
-343	smDisDrvrNamErr	error occured during _sDisDrvrName
-344	smNoMoresRsrcs	no more sResources
-345	smsGetDrvrErr	error occurred during _sGetDriver
-346	smBadsPtrErr	bad pointer was passed to sCalcsPointer
-347	smByteLanesErr	NumByteLanes was determined to be zero
-348	smOffsetErr	offset was too big (temporary, should be fixed)
-349	smNoGoodOpens	no opens were successfull in the loop
-350	smSRTOvrFlErr	SRT over flow
-351	smRecNotFnd	record not found in the SRT

Device Manager Slot Support

ID	Name	Description
-360	slotNumErr	invalid slot # error
-400	gcrOnMFMErr	gcr format on high-density media error

Edition Manager

ID	Name	Description
-450	editionMgrInitErr	edition manager not inited by this app
-451	badSectionErr	not a valid SectionRecord
-452	notRegisteredSectionErr	not a registered SectionRecord
-453	badEditionFileErr	edition file is corrupt
-454	badSubPartErr	cannot use sub parts in this release
-460	multiplePublisherWrn	Pub already registered for container
-461	containerNotFoundWrn	could not find editionContainer
-462	containerAlreadyOpenWrn	container is open by this section
-463	notThePublisherWrn	different pub last wrote that container

SCSI Manager

ID	Name	Description
-470	scsiBadPBErr	invalid field(s) in the parameter block
-471	scsiOverrunErr	attempted to transfer too many bytes
-472	scsiTransferErr	write flag conflicts with data transfer phase
-473	scsiBusTOErr	Bus Error during transfer

continues

SCSI Manager

ID	Name	Description
-474	scsiSelectTOErr	scsiSelTO exceeded (selection failed)
-475	scsiTimeOutErr	scsiReqTO exceeded
-476	scsiBusResetErr	the bus was reset, so your request was aborted
-477	scsiBadStatus	non-zero (not "good") status returned
-478	scsiNoStatusErr	device did not go through a status phase
-479	scsiLinkFailErr	linked command never executed
-489	scsiUnimpVctErr	unimplemented routine was called

SysErrs used instead of inline $A9FF & $ABFF

ID	Name	Description
-490	userBreak	user debugger break
-491	strUserBreak	user debugger break—display string on stack
-492	exUserBreak	user debugger break—execute commands on stack

QuickDraw

ID	Name	Description
-500	rgnTooBigErr	region too big error

Text Edit

ID	Name	Description
-501	teScrapSizeErr	scrap item too big for text edit record

O/S

ID	Name	Description
-502	hwParamrErr	bad selector for _HWPriv

Process Manager

ID	Name	Description
-600	procNotFound	no eligible process with specified descriptor
-601	memFragErr	not enough room to launch application w/special requirements
-602	appModeErr	memory mode is 32-bit, but application not 32-bit clean
-603	protocolErr	application made module calls in improper order
-604	hardwareConfigErr	hardware configuration not correct for call
-605	appMemFullErr	application SIZE not big enough for launch
-606	appIsDaemon	application is BG-only, and launch flags disallow this

Memory Dispatch

ID	Name	Description
-620	notEnoughMemoryErr	insufficient physical memory
-621	notHeldErr	specified range of memory is not held
-622	cannotMakeContiguousErr	cannot make specified range contiguous
-623	notLockedErr	specified range of memory is not locked

continues

Memory Dispatch Continued

ID	Name	Description
-624	interruptsMaskedErr	don't call with interrupts masked
-625	cannotDeferErr	unable to defer additional functions

DatabaseAccess (Pack 13)

ID	Name	Description
-800	rcDBNull	
-801	rcDBValue	
-802	rcDBError	
-803	rcDBBadType	
-804	rcDBBadCol	
-805	rcDBBreak	
-806	rcDBExec	
-807	rcDBBadSessID	
-808	rcDBBadSessNum	
-809	rcDBBadDDEV	
-810	rcDBCancel	
-811	rcDBAsyncNotSupp	
-812	rcDBBadAsyncPB	
-813	rcDBNoHandler	
-814	rcDBWrongVersion	
-815	rcDBPackNotInited	
-816	rcDBStatusCancel	

Help Manager

ID	Name	Description
-850	hmHelpDisabled	Show Balloons mode off, call to routine ignored
-851	hmResNotFound	
-852	hmMemFullErr	
-853	hmBalloonAborted	mouse was moving/wasn't in window port rect
-854	hmBadHelpData	HMShowMenuBalloon menu and item same as last time
-855	hmHelpManagerNotInited	HMGetHelpMenuHandle help menu not setup
-856	hmBadSelector	
-857	hmSkippedBalloon	Helpmsg specified a skip balloon
-858	hmWrongVersion	Help mgr resource was the wrong version
-859	hmUnknownHelpType	Help msg record contained a bad type
-860	hmCouldNotLoadPackage	
-861	hmOperationUnsupported	bad method passed to HMShowBalloon
-862	hmNoBalloonUp	no balloon visible when HMRemoveBalloon called
-863	hmCloseViewActive	CloseView active when HMRemoveBalloon called

PPC Toolbox

ID	Name	Description
-900	notInitErr	PPCToolBox not initialized
-902	nameTypeErr	invalid locationKindSelector in locationName

continues

PPC Toolbox Continued

ID	Name	Description
-903	noPortErr	unable to open port or bad portRefNum
-904	noGlobalsErr	the system is hosed, better reboot
-905	localOnlyErr	network activity is currently disabled
-906	destPortErr	port does not exist at destination
-907	sessTableErr	out of session tables, try again later
-908	noSessionErr	invalid session reference number
-909	badReqErr	bad parameter or invalid state for operation
-910	portNameExistsErr	port is already open (perhaps another application)
-911	noUserNameErr	user name unknown on destination machine
-912	userRejectErr	destination rejected the session request
-913	noMachineNameErr	user has not named his Macintosh
-914	noToolboxNameErr	a system resource is missing, not too likely
-915	noResponseErr	unable to contact destination
-916	portClosedErr	port was closed
-917	sessClosedErr	session was closed
-919	badPortNameErr	PPCPortRec malformed
-922	noDefaultUserErr	user has not typed in owner's name
-923	notLoggedInErr	the default userRefNum does not yet exist
-924	oUserRefErr	unable to create a new userRefNum
-925	networkErr	an error has occured in the network, not too likely

ID	Name	Description
-926	noInformErr	PPCStart failed: test did not have inform pending
-927	authFailErr	unable to authenticate user at destination
-928	noUserRecErr	invalid user reference number
-930	badServiceMethodErr	illegal service type, or not supported
-931	badLocNameErr	location name malformed
-932	guestNotAllowedErr	destination port requires authentication

AppleTalk—NBP

ID	Name	Description
-1024	nbpBuffOvr	buffer overflow in LookupName
-1025	nbpNoConfirm	name not confirmed on ConfirmName
-1026	nbpConfDiff	name confirmed at different socket
-1027	nbpDuplicate	duplicate name exists already
-1028	nbpNotFound	name not found on remove
-1029	nbpNISErr	error trying to open the NIS

AppleTalk—ASP (XPP driver)

ID	Name	Description
-1066	aspBadVersNum	server cannot support this ASP version
-1067	aspBufTooSmall	buffer too small
-1068	aspNoMoreSess	no more sessions on server
-1069	aspNoServers	no servers at that address
-1070	aspParamErr	parameter error

continues

AppleTalk—ASP (XPP driver) Continued

ID	Name	Description
-1071	aspServerBusy	server cannot open another session
-1072	aspSessClosed	session closed
-1073	aspSizeErr	command block too big
-1074	aspTooMany	too many clients (server error)
-1075	aspNoAckn	No acknowledgement on attention request (server error)

AppleTalk—ATP

ID	Name	Description
-1096	reqFailed	SendRequest failed: retry count exceeded
-1097	tooManyReqs	too many concurrent requests
-1098	tooManySkts	too many concurrent responding sockets
-1099	badATPSkt	bad ATP-responding socket
-1100	badBuffNum	bad response buffer number specified
-1101	noRelErr	no release received
-1102	cbNotFound	Control Block (TCB or RspCB) not found
-1103	noSendResp	AddResponse issued without SendResponse
-1104	noDataArea	no data area for request to MPP
-1105	reqAborted	SendRequest aborted by RelTCB

Data Stream Protocol—DSP driver

ID	Name	Description
-1273	errOpenDenied	open connection request was denied
-1274	errDSPQueueSize	send or receive queue is too small
-1275	errFwdReset	read terminated by forward reset
-1276	errAttention	attention message too long
-1277	errOpening	open connection request was denied
-1278	errState	bad connection state for this operation
-1279	errAborted	control call was aborted
-1280	errRefNum	bad connection refNum

HFS

ID	Name	Description
-1300	fidNotFound	no file thread exists
-1301	fidExists	file id already exists
-1302	notAFileErr	directory specified
-1303	diffVolErr	files on different volumes
-1304	catChangedErr	catalog has been modified
-1305	desktopDamagedErr	desktop database files are corrupted
-1306	sameFileErr	cannot exchange a file with itself
-1307	badFidErr	file id is dangling or does not match file number
-1308	notARemountErr	if _Mount allows only remounts and doesn't get 1

AppleTalk—ATP

ID	Name	Description
-3101	buf2SmallErr	buffer too small error
-3102	noMPPErr	no MPP error
-3103	ckSumErr	check sum error
-3104	extractErr	extraction error
-3105	readQErr	read queue error
-3106	atpLenErr	ATP length error
-3107	atpBadRsp	ATP bad response error
-3108	recNotFnd	record not found
-3109	sktClosedErr	socket closed error

Print Manager with LaserWriter

ID	Name	Description
-4096	???	no free Connect Control Blocks available
-4097	???	bad connection reference number
-4098	???	request already active
-4099	???	write request too big
-4100	???	connection just closed
-4101	???	printer not found, or closed

File Manager Extensions

ID	Name	Description
-5000	accessDenied	Incorrect access for this file/folder
-5006	DenyConflict	Permission/Deny mode conflicts with the current mode in which this fork is already open

ID	Name	Description
-5015	NoMoreLocks	Byte range locking failure from Server
-5020	RangeNotLocked	Attempt to unlock an already unlocked range
-5021	RangeOverlap	Attempt to lock some of an already locked range

AppleTalk—AFP (XPP driver)

ID	Name	Description
-5000	afpAccessDenied	AFP access denied
-5001	afpAuthContinue	AFP authorization continue
-5002	afpBadUAM	AFP bad UAM
-5003	afpBadVersNum	AFP bad version number
-5004	afpBitmapErr	AFP bitmap error
-5005	afpCantMove	AFP cannot move error
-5006	afpDenyConflict	AFP deny conflict
-5007	afpDirNotEmpty	AFP directory not empty
-5008	afpDiskFull	AFP disk full
-5009	fpEofError	AFP end-of-file error
-5010	afpFileBusy	AFP file busy
-5011	afpFlatVo	AFP flat volume
-5012	afpItemNotFound	AFP item not found
-5013	afpLockErr	AFP lock error
-5014	afpMiscErr	AFP misc error
-5015	afpNoMoreLocks	AFP no more locks
-5016	afpNoServer	AFP no server
-5017	afpObjectExists	AFP object already exists

continues

AppleTalk—AFP (XPP driver) Continued

ID	Name	Description
-5018	afpObjectNotFound	AFP object not found
-5019	afpParmErr	AFP parm error
-5020	afpRangeNotLocked	AFP range not locked
-5021	afpRangeOverlap	AFP range overlap
-5022	afpSessClosed	AFP session closed
-5023	afpUserNotAuth	AFP user not authorized
-5024	afpCallNotSupported	AFP call not supported
-5025	afpObjectTypeErr	AFP object-type error
-5026	afpTooManyFilesOpen	AFP too many files open
-5027	afpServerGoingDown	AFP server going down
-5028	afpCantRename	AFP cannot rename
-5029	afpDirNotFound	AFP directory not found
-5030	afpIconTypeError	AFP icon-type error
-5031	afpVolLocked	volume is read only
-5032	afpObjectLocked	object is M/R/D/W inhibited
-5033	afpContainsSharedErr	folder being shared has a shared folder
-5034	afpIDNotFound	
-5035	afpIDExists	
-5036	afpDiffVolErr	
-5037	afpCatalogChanged	
-5038	afpSameObjectErr	
-5039	afpBadIDErr	
-5040	afpPwdSameErr	same password on a mantadory password change

ID	Name	Description
-5041	afpPwdTooShortErr	password being set is too short
-5042	afpPwdExpiredErr	password being used is too old
-5043	afpInsideSharedErr	folder being shared is in a shared folder
-5044	afpInsideTrashErr	folder being shared is in the trash folder

SysEnvirons

ID	Name	Description
-5500	envNotPresent	SysEnvirons trap not present—returned by glue
-5501	envBadVers	version nonpositive
-5502	envVersTooBig	version bigger than call can handle

Gestalt

ID	Name	Description
-5550	gestaltUnknownErr	Gestalt does not know the answer
-5551	gestaltUndefSelectorErr	undefined code was passed to Gestalt
-5552	gestaltDupSelectorErr	tried to add entry that already existed
-5553	gestaltLocationErr	Gestalt function ptr was not in sysheap

LaserWriter Driver

ID	Name	Description
-8132	????	manual feed time-out
-8133	????	general PostScript error
-8150	????	no LaserWriter chosen
-8151	????	version mismatch between LaserPrep dictionaries
-8150	????	no LaserPrep dictionary installed
-8160	????	zoom scale factor out of range

Picture Utilities

ID	Name	Description
-11000	pictInfoVersionErr	wrong version of the PictInfo structure
-11001	pictInfoIDErr	internal consistancy check is wrong
-11002	pictInfoVerbErr	the passed verb was invalid
-11003	cantLoadPickMethodErr	unable to load the custom pick procedure
-11004	colorsRequestedErr	the number of colors requested was illegal
-11005	pictureDataErr	the picture data was invalid

Power Manager

ID	Name	Description
-13000	pmBusyErr	Power Manager never ready to start handshake
-13001	pmReplyTOErr	timed-out waiting for reply
-13002	pmSendStartErr	during send, Power Manager did not start hs

ID	Name	Description
-13003	pmSendEndErr	during send, pmgr did not finish hs
-13004	pmRecvStartErr	during receive, pmgr did not start hs
-13005	pmRecvEndErr	during receive, pmgr did not finish hs

Mac TCP

ID	Name	Description
-23000	ipBadLapErr	bad network configuration
-23001	ipBadCnfgErr	bad IP configuration error
-23002	ipNoCnfgErr	missing IP or LAP configuration error
-23003	ipLoadErr	error in MacTCP load
-23004	ipBadAddr	error in getting address
-23005	connectionClosing	connection in closing
-23006	invalidLength	
-23007	connectionExists	request conflicts with existing connection
-23008	connectionDoesntExist	connection does not exist
-23009	insufficientResources	insufficient resourecs to perform request
-23010	invalidStreamPtr	
-23011	streamAlreadyOpen	
-23012	connectionTerminated	
-23013	invalidBufPtr	
-23014	invalidRDS	
-23014	invalidWDS	
-23015	openFailed	
-23016	commandTimeout	
-23017	duplicateSocket	

continues

B

Mac TCP Continued

ID	Name	Description
-23030	ipOpenProtErr	cannot open new protocol, table full
-23031	ipCloseProtErr	cannot find protocol to close
-23032	ipDontFragErr	packet too large to send without fragmenting
-23033	ipDestDeadErr	destination not responding
-23034	ipBadWDSErr	error in WDS format
-23035	icmpEchoTimeoutErr	ICMP echo timed-out
-23036	ipNoFragMemErr	no memory to send fragmented packet
-23037	ipRouteErr	cannot route packet off-net
-23041	nameSyntaxErr	
-23042	cacheFault	
-23043	noResultProc	
-23044	noNameServer	
-23045	authNameErr	
-23046	noAnsErr	
-23047	dnrErr	
-23048	outOfMemory	

Font Manager

ID	Name	Description
-32615	fontNotOutlineErr	bitmap passed, routine does outlines only

Primary or Secondary Init Code

ID	Name	Description
-32768	svTempDisable	temporarily disable card but run primary INIT
-32640	svDisabled	reserve -32640 to -32768 for Apple temporary disables

Primary or Secondary Messages

Internal File System

ID	Name	Description
1	chNoBuf	no free cache buffers (all in use)
2	chInUse	requested block in use
3	chnotfound	requested block not found
4	chNotInUse	block being released was not in use
16	fxRangeErr	file position beyond mapped range
17	fxOvFlErr	extents file overflow
32	btnotfound	record not found
33	btexists	record already exists
34	btnospace	no available space
35	btnoFit	record doesn't fit in node
36	btbadNode	bad node detected
37	btbadHdr	bad BTree header record detected
48	cmnotfound	CNode not found
49	cmexists	CNode already exists
50	cmnotempty	directory CNode not empty (valence = 0)
51	cmRootCN	invalid reference to root CNode

continues

Internal File System Continued

ID	Name	Description
52	cmbadnews	detected bad catalog structure
53	cmFThdDirErr	thread belongs to a directory not a file
54	cmFThdGone	file thread doesn't exist
64	dsBadRotate	bad BTree rotate

Slot Declaration ROM Manager

ID	Name	Description
1	siInitSDTblErr	slot int dispatch table could not be initialized
2	siInitVBLQsErr	VBLqueues for all slots could not be initialized
3	siInitSPTblErr	slot priority table could not be initialized
10	sdmJTInitErr	SDM Jump Table could not be initialized
11	sdmInitErr	SDM could not be initialized
12	sdmSRTInitErr	slot Resource Table could not be initialized
13	sdmPRAMInitErr	slot PRAM could not be initialized
14	sdmPriInitErr	cards could not be initialized

HD20 Driver

ID	Name	Description
16	wrtHsLw	HSHK low before starting
17	wrtHSLwTO	time-out waiting for HSHK to go low
19	wrtHSHighTO	time-out waiting for HSHK to go high
32	rdHsHi	HSHK high before starting
33	rdSyncTO	time-out waiting for sync ($AA) bye

ID	Name	Description
34	rdGroupTO	time-out waiting for group
36	rdHoffSyncTO	time-out waiting for sync after holdoff
37	rdHsHiTO	time-out waiting for HSHK high
38	rdChksumErr	Checksum error on response packet
48	invalidResp	first byte in response packet was wrong
49	sqncNumErr	sequence number in response packet was wrong
50	dNumberErr	drive number in response packet was wrong
64	noResp	no response packet ever received

SCSI Manager

ID	Name	Description
2	scCommErr	communications error (operations time-out)
3	scArbNBErr	arbitration failed during SCSIGet—bus busy
4	scBadparmsErr	bad parameter or TIB opcode
5	scPhaseErr	SCSI bus not in correct phase for operation
6	scCompareErr	SCSI Manager busy with another operation when SCSIGet was called
7	scMgrBusyErr	SCSI Manager busy with another operation when SCSIGet was called
8	scSequenceErr	attempted operation is out of sequence—e.g., calling SCSISelect before doing SCSIGet
9	scBusTOErr	bus time-out before data ready on SCSIRBlind and SCSIWBlind
10	scComplPhaseErr	SCSIComplete failed—bus not in Status phase

Connection Manager

ID	Name	Description
0	cmNoErr	
1	cmRejected	
2	cmFailed	
3	cmTimeOut	
4	cmNotOpen	
5	cmNotClosed	
6	cmNoRequestPending	
7	cmNotSupported	
8	cmNoTools	
9	cmUserCancel	
11	cmUnknownError	
-1	cmGenericError	

File Transfer Manager

ID	Name	Description
0	ftNoErr	
1	ftRejected	
2	ftFailed	
3	ftTimeOut	
4	ftTooManyRetry	
5	ftNotEnoughDSpace	
6	ftRemoteCancel	
7	ftWrongFormat	

ID	Name	Description
8	ftNoTools	
9	ftUserCancel	
10	ftNotSupported	
11	ftUnknownError	
-1	ftGenericError	

Terminal Manager

ID	Name	Description
0	tmNoErr	
1	tmNotSent	
2	tmEnvironsChanged	
7	tmNotSupported	
8	tmNoTools	
11	tmUnknownError	
-1	tmGenericError	

Product Information

The products listed below can assist you in troubleshooting your Macintosh. They are listed by category; the level of Macintosh technical knowledge needed to use the product (Basic, Intermediate, or Advanced) is given as well.

You can purchase most products from a mail order company or dealer, as well as from the manufacturer; often you'll pay less when you order from a mail order company. You can obtain products made by Apple from the Apple Catalog, a computer dealer, a software/hardware distributor, or a mail order company.

Mac/PC Exchange Utilities

AccessPC

Insignia Solutions
526 Clyde Avenue
Mountain View, CA 94943
(415) 694-7600

Description: A system extension that automatically mounts PC-formatted disks on the Macintosh desktop, as well as PC removable disks and cartridges.

Level: Basic

AG Group

2540 Camino Diablo
Walnut Creek, CA 94596
(510) 937-7900

Description: Offers network-protocol analyzer software for LocalTalk, Ethernet, and Token Ring networks.

Apple File Exchange

Apple Computer, Inc.
20525 Mariani Avenue
Cupertino, CA 95014
(800) 776-2333
(408) 996-1010

Description: Mac-to-Mac and Mac-to-PC and back. Comes with Macintosh system software.

Level: Basic

AppleShare File Server

Apple Computer, Inc.
20525 Mariani Avenue
Cupertino, CA 95014
(800) 776-2333
(408) 996-1010

Description: File server software that runs on Macintosh computers on an AppleTalk network.

Level: Advanced

Cabletron Systems, Inc.

35 Industrial Way
P.O. Box 6257
Rochester, NH 03867
(603) 332-9400

Description: Offers network devices, cards, and utilities for various types of networks.

Cayman Systems

26 Landsdowne Street
Cambridge, MA 02139
(617) 494-1999

Description: Offers network devices for routing and exchange between various network types.

Compatible Systems Corporation

Description: Offers network cards, routers, and other network devices.

Dayna Communications

Dayna Communications, Inc.
50 S. Main Street
Salt Lake City, UT 84144
(801) 531-0600

Description: Offers network devices, cards, and data exchange solutions.

DaynaFile II

Dayna Communications
50 South Main Street
Salt Lake City, UT 84144
(801) 531-0600

Description: A drive that reads 3 1/2-inch and 5 1/4-inch DOS-formatted
floppy disks (dual drive configuration). Also supports Mac high-density
disks and all PC formats. Uses a system extension called DOS Mounter
to mount PC disks on the desktop. Requires a Mac Plus or later model.

Level: Basic

DOS Mounter

Dayna Communications, Inc.
50 South Main Street
Salt Lake City, UT 84144
(801) 531-0600

Description: A system extension that enables the Finder to mount
PC-formatted disks.

Level: Basic

Farallon Computing, Inc.

2470 Mariner Square Loop
Alameda, CA 94501
(510) 814-5000

Description: Offers a complete collection of networking tools and hardware, including PhoneNET connectors, accompanying utilities, and
LocalTalk boards for PCs.

GraceLAN

Technology Works, Inc.
4030 Braker Lane W
Austin, TX 78759
(800) 926-3148

Description: Network management software for collecting detailed information about Macs on a network. Also scans DOS-based computers on the network, and can update and copy files to Macs.

Level: Advanced

Grappler Connectors

Orange Micro, Inc.
1400 North Lakeview Avenue
Anaheim, CA 92807
(714) 779-2772

Description: A line of dot-matrix interface boxes for several types of printers.

Level: Intermediate

Inter•Poll

Apple Computer, Inc.
20525 Naruabu Avenue
Cupertino, CA 95014
(800) 776-2333
(408) 996-1010

Description: Simple network administration software for LocalTalk networks.

Level: Advanced

LapLink Mac III

Traveling Software, Inc.
18702 North Creek Parkway
Bothell, WA 98011
(800) 343-8080
(206) 483-8088

Description: Mac-to-PC and Mac-to-Mac file transfer program, and serial cable.

Level: Basic

MacLinkPlus/PC

DataViz, Inc.
55 Corporate Drive
Trumbell, CT 06611
(800) 733-0030
(203) 268-0030

Description: File translation between Mac and PC file formats and a Mac-to-PC serial cable. Translators also work with Apple File Exchange.

Level: Basic

MacLinkPlus/Translators

DataViz, Inc.
55 Corporate Drive
Trumbell, CT 06611
(800) 733-0030
(203) 268-0030

Description: File translation package offering a variety (over 350) of file translators for Mac and PC files, including graphic file formats. Also works with Apple File Exchange.

Level: Basic

MacPrint

Insight Development Corporation
2200 Powell Street
Emeryville, CA 94608
(510) 652-4115

Description: A printer driver for the Macintosh that enables the Mac to print to non-PostScript, Hewlett-Packard compatible printers. Comes with screen fonts for printer font cartridges and a printer serial cable.

Level: Basic

Neon Software, Inc.

1009 Oak Hill Road, Suite 203
Lafayette, CA 94549
(510) 283-9771

Description: Offers network-protocol analyzer software for LocalTalk, EtherNet, and Token Ring networks.

Level: Advanced

NetOctopus

MacVONK, Inc.
940 Sixth Avenue S.W., Suite 1100
Calgary, Alberta T2P3T1 Canada
(403) 232-6545

Description: Network management software for collecting information about Macs on networks. Can update and distribute files to networked Macs.

Level: Advanced

PowerBook/DOS Companion

Apple Computer Inc.
20525 Mariani Avenue
Cupertino, CA 95014
(800) 776-2333
(408) 996-1010

Description: Includes MacLinkPlus/PC software, Mac PC Exchange,
MacVGA Video Adapter, and PowerPrint for serial to parallel port
cable connections.

Level: Intermediate

PowerPrint

GDT Softworks, Inc.
4664 Lougheed Hwy., Suite 188
Burnaby, British Columbia V5C 6B7 Canada
(800) 663-6222
(604) 291-9121

Description: PowerPrint is a set of custom print drivers for dot-matrix,
inkjet, and non-PostScript laser printers. Includes a serial-to-parallel
converter cable and offers many features, such as background printing
and print job spooling.

Level: Intermediate

Shiva Corporation

One Cambridge Center
Cambridge, MA 02142
(800) 458-3550
(617) 864-8500

Description: Offers network devices for routing, bridging, and modem
communications.

SoftPC

Insignia Solutions
526 Clyde Avenue
Mountain View, CA 94043
(415) 694-7600

Description: Software that enables a Macintosh to emulate a PC. Various types of PC emulation are available, from AT to 386-based PCs. Has specific software and RAM requirements. Allows PC software to be run on the Macintosh.

Level: Intermediate

Software Bridge/Mac

Systems Compatibility, Inc.
401 North Wabash, Suite 600
Chicago, IL 60611
(800) 333-1395

Description: Collection of file translators for PC-to-Mac file translation; software works with Apple File Exchange as well. Provides Mac word processor and over 20 PC word processor file formats.

Level: Basic

Status*Mac

ON Technology, Inc.
155 Second Street
Cambridge, MA 02141
(617) 876-0900

Description: Network management software for collecting detailed information about Macs on networks.

Level: Advanced

Timbuktu

Farallon Computing, Inc.
2470 Mariner Square Loop
Alameda, CA 94501
(510) 814-5000

Description: Software for communications and file exchange across networks or via modem. Available for Macintosh and Windows systems.

Level: Intermediate

Word for Word/Mac

Software ToolWorks
60 Leveroni Court
Novato, CA 94949
(800) 234-3088
(415) 883-3000

Description: Stand-alone Mac-to-DOS file translation program; also supports DOS-to-DOS and various graphics formats.

Level: Basic

Font Utilities

Adobe Type Manager (ATM)

Adobe Systems
1585 Charleston Road
P.O. Box 7900
Mountain View, CA 94039
(800) 344-8335
(415) 961-4400

Description: Utility (system extension and control panel) for creating smooth screen display and printout of PostScript fonts at any size.

Level: Basic

Apple LaserWriter Utility

Apple Computer, Inc.
20525 Mariani Avenue
Cupertino, CA 95014
(800) 776-2333
(408) 996-1010

Description: Laser printer utility for downloading fonts and PostScript code to a printer; also controls other printer features. Comes with Macintosh printer software.

Level: Intermediate

The Namer

Apple Computer, Inc.
20525 Mariani Avenue
Cupertino, CA 95014
(800) 776-2333
(408) 996-1010

Description: Printer utility for naming printers. Comes with the Macintosh printer software.

Level: Basic

Disk Formatting Utilities

Apple HD SC Setup

Apple Computer, Inc.
20525 Mariani Avenue
Cupertino, CA 95014
(800) 776-2333
(408) 996-1010

Description: Included on the Disk Tools disk of the Macintosh system software. Formats and updates Apple hard disks. Included with the Macintosh system software.

Level: Basic

Disk Café

Bering Industries
246 E. Hacienda Avenue
Campbell, CA 95008
(800) 237-4641
(408) 364-2233

Description: Utility for optimizing SCSI drives. Also comes with diagnostic tools.

Level: Advanced

DiskExpress II

ALSoft, Inc.
P.O. Box 927
Spring, TX 77383
(713) 353-4090

Description: A software hard disk optimizer that defragments files and can run in the background.

Level: Intermediate

DiskCopy

Apple Computer, Inc.
20525 Mariani Avenue
Cupertino, CA 95014
(800) 776-2333
(408) 996-1010

Description: Floppy disk formatting utility that reads a master floppy disk and then formats and copies the information to other floppy disks.

Level: Intermediate

Drive7

Casa Blanca Works, Inc.
148 Bon Air Center
Greenbrae, CA 94904
(415) 461-2227

Description: System 7 utility for updating disk drivers to be System 7-compatible. Works with most fixed and removable drives.

Level: Intermediate

Drive7rem

Casa Blanca Works, Inc.
148 Bon Air Center
Greenbrae, CA 94904
(415) 461-2227

Description: Control panel (also included with Drive7 product) for mounting hard drives, cartridges, and floppy disks, regardless of the original formatting utility used to format the disks.

Level: Basic

Hard Disk ToolKit

FWB, Inc.
2040 Polk Street, Suite 215
San Francisco, CA 94109
(415) 474-8055

Description: Set of hard disk tools for formatting, partitioning, optimizing, and analyzing disks. Works with removable drives as well.

Level: Intermediate

Hard Disk ToolKit Personal Edition

FWB, Inc.
2040 Polk Street, Suite 215
San Francisco, CA 94109
(415) 474-8055

Description: A slimmed-down, lower-priced version of FWB Inc.'s Hard Disk ToolKit. Offers formatting, partitioning, password-protection, and diagnostic options. Supports removable drives.

Level: Basic

MultiDisk

ALSoft, Inc.
P.O. Box 927
Spring, TX 77383
(713) 353-4090

Description: Hard disk software for partitioning hard disks. Partitions can be resized, password-protected, and encrypted.

Level: Intermediate

Norton Floppier

Symantec Corporation
10201 Torre Avenue
Cupertino, CA 95014
(800) 441-7234
(408) 253-9600

Description: Comes with Norton Utilities for the Macintosh. Like DiskCopy, it formats disks and copies information to them in series.

Level: Intermediate

SCSIProbe

Freeware by Robert Polic

Included with this book and available from online services and user groups

Description: A control panel and extension for identifying and mounting SCSI devices. You can determine the device type, vendor, product, and version for every connected SCSI device.

Level: Basic

Silverlining

La Cie Ltd.
8700 S.W. Creekside Place
Beaverton, OR 97005
(800) 999-143
(503) 520-9000

Description: An advanced set of hard disk utilities and disk partitioning software; works with most hard drives. Optimizing, some diagnostic and performance testing.

Level: Advanced

Disk Repair and File Recovery Utilities

CanOpener

Abbott Systems
62 Mountain Road
Pleasantivlle, NY 10570
(800) 552-9157
(914) 747-4171

Description: A handy application for finding, reading, and recovering all or part of a file. It can display and save text and graphic formats such as TIFF, EPS, PICT and others.

Level: Basic

Complete Undelete

DataWatch (formerly Microcom Utilities)
(919) 490-1277

Description: A file-recovery program for recovering deleted files, and fragments of partially overwritten files.

Level: Basic

CleanPath Computer Controlled Maintenance

Discwasher, Inc.
2950 Lake Enna Road
Lake Mary, FL 32746
(800) 325-0573
(407)333-8900

Description: A collection of cleaning tools for your Macintosh floppy drive, keyboard, screen, and (dot-matrix) printer. Software instructions are included.

Level: Basic

DiskCheck

ALSoft, Inc.
P.O. Box 927
Spring, TX 77383
(713) 353-4090

Description: Program scans the disk for directory damage and diagnoses problems.

Level: Basic

Disk First Aid

Apple Computer, Inc.
20525 Mariani Avenue
Cupertino, CA 95014
(800) 776-2333
(408) 996-1010

Description: Apple's simple diagnostic tool for floppy and hard disks. Can repair disks or warn of problems. Included with the Macintosh system software.

Level: Basic

MacTools

Central Point Software, Inc.
15220 N.W. Greenbrier Pkwy.
Beaverton, OR 97006
(800) 445-4208
(503) 690-8088

Description: Collection of data recover and disk repair utilities; also including virus protection, backup software, an undelete file tool, and disk optimization software.

Level: Basic

Norton Utilities for the Macintosh

Symantec Corporation
10201 Torre Avenue
Cupertino, CA 95014
(800) 441-7234
(408) 253-9600

Description: Collection of tools for protecting, repairing, and restoring files on hard disks (works on floppy disks as well). Optimization, backup software, partitioning, and password security are other features included in the package. Some advanced features.

Level: Basic

Public Utilities for the Macintosh

Fifth Generation Systems
100049 N. Reiger Rd.
Baton Rouge, LA 70809
(800) 873-4384

Description: A data recovery and disk repair utility for protection and emergency recovery. Undeletes files, repairs files, repairs a disk's directory, and has an expert mode. Friendly interface and easy to use.

Level: Basic

File Management Utilities

At Ease

Apple Computer, Inc.
20525 Mariani Avenue
Cupertino, CA 95014
(800) 776-2333
(408) 996-1010

Description: A Finder replacement for novice users. Password protection and no Trash Can; uses a file launching pad.

Level: Basic

AutoSave II

Magic Software, Inc.
2239 Franklin St.
Bellevue, NE 68005
(402) 291-0670

Description: Saves your work automatically at intervals from 1 to 99 minutes.

Level: Basic

Disktop

CE Software, Inc.
1801 Industrial Circle
P.O. Box 65580
West Des Moines, IA 50265
(800) 523-7638

Description: Handy utility for all disks on the desktop. It launches applications, performs batch copies, and moves files. Pseudo-Finder replacement.

Level: Basic

Shredder

DLM Software, Inc.
3525 Del Mar Heights Road
San Diego, CA 92130
(619) 283-2343

Description: Utility for deleting files, so they cannot be recovered—even with a file recovery utility. Includes Scrubber, a utility that erases unused space on a disk.

Level: Intermediate

System Utilities

Blesser

Freeware
Available from online services and user groups

Description: Enables you to switch between two or more System folders to be designated as the startup folder. Old version for use with System 6—it may not be compatible with some System 7 Macs.

Level: Basic

Conflict Catcher

Casady & Greene, Inc.
22734 Portola Drive
Salinas, CA 93908
(408) 484-9228

Description: An extension and control panel for managing startup files; can identify sources of crashes and conflicts.

Level: Basic

Extensions Manager

Apple Computer, Inc. (by Ricardo Batista)
20525 Mariani Avenue
Cupertino, CA 95014
(800) 776-2333
(408) 996-1010

Available from online services and user groups as well.

Description: Manages system extensions and control panels by allowing them to be turned on and off in a control panel file. Can design sets of extensions to load at startup. A scrollable list of all extensions and control panels can be selected and deselected.

Level: Basic

INIT-cdev

Freeware by John Rotenstein
Available from user groups and online services

Description: A simple extension (INIT) manager

Level: Basic

INITPicker

Inline Design
308 Main Street
Lakeville, CT 06039
(800) 453-7671
(203) 435-4995

Description: A control panel for turning system extensions (INITs) on and off. A keystroke at startup turns off all extensions; INITPicker can create different sets of extensions for loading.

Level: Basic

MasterJuggler

ALSoft, Inc.
P.O. Box 927
Spring, TX 77383
(713) 353-4090

Description: A resource management utility that manages (suitcases) fonts, DAs, sounds, and more.

Level: Intermediate

MugShot

Mi Concepts; Freeware
Available from online services and user groups

Description: Analyzes and informs you of your Mac's system and hardware settings.

Level: Basic

QuickTime Starter Kit

Apple Computer, Inc.
20525 Mariani Avenue M/S 33-G
Cupertino, CA 95014
(800) 776-2333
(408) 996-1010

Description: This kit includes a CD-ROM disc with over 400M of digital video, animation, and still images; tools to build QuickTime movies; and the QuickTime extension.

Level: Basic

ResEdit

APDA
Apple Computer, Inc.
20525 Mariani Avenue M/S 33-G
Cupertino, CA 95014
(800) 282-2737 USA
(800) 637-0029 Canada
(408) 562-3910 International

Description: Programming utility used to create and edit application resources.

Level: Advanced

Suitcase II

Fifth Generation Systems
100049 N. Reiger Rd.
Baton Rouge, LA 70809
(800) 873-4384

Description: A system extension for managing resources—suitcases of fonts, DAs, sounds, and more. Includes Font Harmony (an application designed to resolve font ID conflicts), and the Font & Sound Valet application for compressing fonts and sounds.

Level: Intermediate

System 7 Upgrade Kit

Apple Computer, Inc.
20525 Mariani Avenue
Cupertino, CA 95014
(800) 776-2333
(408) 996-1010

Description: System 7 software upgrade.

Level: Basic

System 7 Group Upgrade Kit

Apple Computer, Inc.
20525 Mariani Avenue
Cupertino, CA 95014
(800) 776-2333
(408) 996-1010

Description: System 7 upgrade kit—including help for upgrading both workstations and networks to System 7.

Level: Basic

System Picker

Freeware by Kevin Aitken
Included with this book and available from online services and user groups

Description: Lets you switch easily between different System folders. It can help ease the transition to System 7.0 by enabling you to keep System 6.0x and System 7.0 in the same volume.

Level: Basic

TattleTale

Freeware by John Mancino
Included with this book and available from online services and user groups

Description: TattleTale is available as a desk accessory or an application; it provides information about your Macintosh hardware and its system-related software.

Level: Basic

Memory Utilities

Maxima

Connectix Corporation
2655 Campus Drive
San Mateo, CA 94403
(800) 950-5880
(415) 571-5100

Description: A software memory extension utility for recognizing up to 14M of installed RAM. Also has a RAM disk feature that survives shut-downs, restarts, and crashes. Works with System 6 and 7, and requires more than 8M of RAM installed in your Mac.

Level: Intermediate

MODE32

Free from Apple Computer Inc. and Connectix Corporation
Also available from online services and user groups

Description: Software that enables the use of System 7 32-bit addressing on a Mac II, IIx, IIcx, or SE/30.

Level: Basic

NanoDISK

Technology Works, Inc.
4030 Braker Lane W.
Austin, TX 78759
(800) 926-3148

Description: A utility that allows Mac SE and II to recognize more than 8M
of RAM.

Level: Intermediate

Optima

Connectix Corporation
2655 Campus Drive
San Mateo, CA 94403
(800-950-5880)
(415) 571-5100

Description: Software that adds the 32-bit addressing feature for Mac II
models running System 6. Enables up to 32M of RAM to be recognized
when installed. Connectix also offers Optima/128, which is the same
except that it recognizes 128M of installed RAM.

Level: Intermediate

Virtual

Connectix Corporation
2655 Campus Drive
San Mateo, CA 94403
(800) 950-5880
(415) 571-5100

Description: A program that enables a Macintosh to use part of its hard
disk as virtual memory. Supports up to 15M of total RAM and works with
both System 6 and System 7.

Level: Intermediate

Backup Software

Backmatic

Magic Software, Inc.
2239 Franklin St
Bellevue, NE 68005
(402) 291-0670

Description: Simple tool that automates the task of backing up hard disks. Does not compress files or back up to tape drives, but reminds you to back up your Mac.

Level: Basic

DiskFit Pro

Dantz Development Corporation
1400 Shattuck Avenue
Berkeley, CA 94709
(510) 849-0293

Description: Easy-to-use backup program that offers several features not in the lower-end DiskFit Direct, including backup to and from network volumes, shared volumes, and auto-launching for unattended backups. Works with many disks and removable cartridges.

Level: Basic

DiskFit Direct

Dantz Development Corporation
1400 Shattuck Avenue
Berkeley, CA 94709
(510) 849-0293

Description: Easy-to-use backup program for creating exact copies of a hard disk, and then adding to the backup. Works with many disks and removable cartridges.

Level: Basic

FastBack Plus

Fifth Generation Systems
100049 N. Reiger Rd.
Baton Rouge, LA 70809
(800) 873-4384

Description: A backup utility that supports incremental, partial, and full backups.

Level: Basic

HFS Backup

Personal Computer Peripherals Corporation (PCPC)
4 Daniels Farm Road
Trumbull, CT 06611
(800) 622-2888
(203) 459-8305

Description: Personal backup software for floppy disks, hard disks, and other removable disks and tape drives. Features data encryption and password protection, and can be used with file servers.

Level: Basic

Redux

Inline Design
308 Main Street
Lakeville, CT 06039
(800) 453-7671
(203) 435-4995

Description: Backup program offering full and incremental backups and scripting.

Level: Basic

NetStream

Personal Computer Peripherals Corporation (PCPC)
4 Daniels Farm Road
Trumbull, CT 06611
(800) 622-2888
(203) 459-8305

Description: Network backup software for workstations and servers.

Level: Intermediate

NightShift

Transitional Technology (TTI)
5401 East La Palma Ave.
Anaheim, CA 92807
(714) 693-7707

Description: Network backup software for workstations and servers.

Level: Basic

Retrospect

Dantz Development Corporation
1400 Shattuck Avenue
Berkeley, CA 94709
(510) 849-0293

Description: Full-featured backup software that supports many types of storage devices.

Level: Intermediate to Advanced

Retrospect Remote

Dantz Development Corporation
1400 Shattuck Avenue
Berkeley, CA 94709
(510) 849-0293

Description: Network backup software for workstations and Macintosh servers across AppleTalk networks.

Level: Advanced

Virus Utilities

Disinfectant

Freeware
Included with this book and available from online services and user groups

Description: Virus software with a protection extension and eradication software. Removes known viruses.

Level: Basic

Gatekeeper

Freeware by Chris Johnson
Available from online services and user groups

Description: Virus software extension that is configured through a control panel; protects against infection.

Level: Basic

Rival

Inline Design
308 Main Street
Lakeville, CT 06039
(800) 453-7671
(203) 435-4995

Description: A system extension that inspects files for known viruses, scans files, and repairs some files.

Level: Basic

SAM (Symantec AntiVirus For Macintosh)

Symantec Corporation
10201 Torre Avenue
Cupertino, CA 95014
(800) 441-7234
(408 253-9600

Description: Full-featured extension for virus removal as well as virus protection. Continued subscription offers a 24-hour virus hotline. Extensive tracking of any file intrusion, including changes made to any resource.

Level: Intermediate

Virex

DataWatch (formerly Microcom Utilities)
(919) 490-1277

Description: Virus software for preventing, detecting, and removing viruses.

Level: Basic

Hardware and Software Troubleshooting Utilities

Crash Barrier

Casady & Greene, Inc.
22734 Portola Drive
Salinas, CA 93908
(408) 484-9228

Description: A control panel that enables you to recover from various types of crashes; sometimes enables you to save or just quit the application. It replaces the Mac's bomb dialogs with a dialog box that offers possible recovery actions.

Level: Basic

Help!

Teknosys, Inc.
3923 Coconut Palm Drive
Tampa, FL 33619
(800) 873-3494

Description: A program that analyzes your Mac and highlights potential
software and hardware problems, outdated software, and extension
conflicts.

Level: Basic

Mac EKG

MicroMat Computer Systems
7075 Redwood Boulevard
Novato, CA 94945
(800) 829-6227 US Sales & Service
(415) 898-6227 International Sales & Service
(415) 898-2935 Technical Support

Description: A utility for power users that diagnoses and troubleshoots
hardware problems; complete set of diagnostic sequences.

Level: Advanced

MicroRX SE1

MicroMat Computer Systems
7075 Redwood Boulevard
Novato, CA 94945
(800) 829-6227 US Sales & Service
(415) 898-6227 International Sales & Service
(415) 898-2935 Technical Support

Description: A HyperCard stack that diagnoses Mac SE problems. The
details are technical and good for service technicians.

Level: Advanced

Snooper

Maxa Corporation
116 N. Maryland Avenue, Suite 100
Glendale, CA 91206
(800) 788-6292

Description: Software for testing and diagnostic information on the video, drive, audio, and logic boards of your Macintosh. Also includes benchmark testing and an optional NuBus hardware testing board.

Level: Intermediate

File Compression Utilities

AutoDoubler

Fifth Generation Systems
100049 N. Reiger Rd.
Baton Rouge, LA 70809
(800) 873-4384

Description: Automatic and transparent file compression and decompression from storage devices. Exclusion and inclusion of files and memory management.

Level: Basic

Compact Pro

Cyclos Software
P.O. Box 31417
San Francisco, CA 94131
(415) 821-1448
Also available from online services and user groups

Description: Shareware file compression utility that quickly compresses files and can create self-extracting archives.

Level: Basic

DiskDoubler

Fifth Generation Systems
100049 N. Reiger Rd.
Baton Rouge, LA 70809
(800) 873-4384

Description: A combination of an extension and a program for file compression and expansion. Adds a pull-down menu for Finder and application access.

Level: Basic

Stacker for Macintosh

STAC Electronics
5993 Avenida Encinas
Carlsbad, CA 92008
(800) 522-STAC
(619) 431-7474

Description: Software that compresses your entire disk, essentially doubling the size of your hard disk. Compresses all data and works on the fly. Also works with file recovery software.

Level: Basic

StuffIt Deluxe

Aladdin Systems Inc.
165 Westridge Drive
Watsonville, CA 95076
(408) 761-6200

Description: The commercial version of the shareware program StuffIt Classic; it is a full-featured compression utility for compressing and archiving individual files. Includes security features and a control panel called SpaceSaver that automatically compresses files with optional compression speeds.

Level: Basic

StuffIt Lite

Aladdin Systems Inc.
165 Westridge Drive
Watsonville, CA 95076
(408) 761-6200

Description: Compresses files for transfer and storage. Shareware version of
the full-featured commercial program StuffIt Deluxe.

Level: Basic

SuperDisk!

Alysis Software Corporation
1231 31st Avenue
San Francisco, CA 94122
(415) 566-2263

Description: Fast and easy-to-use file compression program; however,
program doesn't combine files into one archive as StuffIt and Compactor do.

Level: Basic

Screen Savers

After Dark

Berkeley Systems, Inc.
2095 Rose Street
Berkeley, CA 94709
(510) 540-5535

Description: A screen saver that is a system extension. Offers many different screen savers—including the Flying Toasters (with the sound of
flapping wings) and the Fish Aquarium.

Level: Basic

Intermission

ICOM Simulations, Inc.
648 S. Wheeling Road
Wheeling, IL 60090
(800) 877-4266
(708) 520-4440

Description: Another screen saver with modules for varying pictures on the screen and sound effects too.

Level: Basic

QuickLock

Kent Marsh Ltd.
3260 Sul Ross Street
Houston, TX 77098
(800) 325-3587
(713) 522-5625

Description: Screen saver with password protection.

Level: Basic

Security Utilities

A.M.E. (Access Managed Environment)

Casady & Greene, Inc.
22734 Portola Drive
Salinas, CA 93908
(408) 484-9228

Description: Security system software for high-level users and administrators. Password protection and encryption.

Level: Advanced

CaseLock/DriveLock

Kent Marsh Ltd.
3260 Sul Ross Street
Houston, TX 77098
(800) 325-3587
(713) 522-5625

Description: Physical hardware locks for the Macintosh case and disk drive.

Level: Intermediate

DiskLock

Fifth Generation Systems
100049 N. Reiger Rd.
Baton Rouge, LA 70809
(800) 873-4384

Description: Easy and straightforward security program that protects drive contents with file locking, encryption, privileges, and password protection.

Level: Basic

Empower II

Magna
332 Commercial Street
San Jose, CA 95112
(408) 282-0900

Description: A control panel for setting up access privileges for File Sharing, as well as file encryption.

Level: Intermediate

FileGuard

ASD Software, Inc.
4650 Arrow Hwy.
Montclair, CA 91763
(714) 624-2594

Description: Security package that operates in the background to protect folders, applications, and files with access privileges.

Level: Intermediate

FolderBolt

Kent Marsh Ltd.
3260 Sul Ross Street
Houston, TX 77098
(800) 325-3587
(713) 522-5625

Description: A security program for folder security. Creates read-only, one-way drop folders, and locks system files and the Trash.

Level: Basic

KeyLock

VikingTech
533 1/2 Via De La Valle, Suite E
Solana Beach, CA 92075
(619) 792-1375

Description: Security software and hardware with a hardware key inserted into the floppy disk slot, an extension, and a desk accessory with password protection.

Level: Intermediate

MacSafe II

Kent Marsh Ltd.
3260 Sul Ross Street
Houston, TX 77098
(800) 325-3587
(713) 522-5625

Description: Security program for files and networks. Uses a "safe" to place files; also offers encryption.

Level: Intermediate

NightWatch II

Kent Marsh Ltd.
3260 Sul Ross Street
Houston, TX 77098
(800) 325-3587
(713) 522-5625

Description: Locks the hard drive, using a floppy disk as a key. Password protected. Can be used diskless, with a disk key or a token (Mac Classic).

Level: Intermediate

PowerKey

Sophisticated Circuits
19017-120 Avenue NE
Bothell, WA 98011
(206) 485-7979

Description: Hardware device that goes between your computer (and peripherals) and the wall outlet. Works with a control panel to enable you to turn your entire Mac setup on and off from the Power-On key on the keyboard.

Level: Basic

Online Services

America Online

America Online, Inc.
8619 Westwood Enter Drive
Vienna, VA 22182
(800) 827-6364
(703) 448-8700

Description: An online service with software, clubs, and support forums. Requires their custom software.

AppleLink

Apple Computer, Inc.
20525 Mariani Avenue
Cupertino, CA 95014
(800) 776-2333
(408) 996-1010

Description: Apple's online service, offers product information, software libraries, training information, discussion forums, and technical support. Requires Apple's AppleLink software.

AppleLink CD

Apple Computer, Inc.
20525 Mariani Avenue
Cupertino, CA 95014
(800) 776-2333
(408) 996-1010

Description: Annual subscription fee for a CD-ROM that contains all the information accessible on Apple's AppleLink online service.

CompuServe Information Service

5000 Arlington Centre Blvd.
Columbus, OH 43220
(614) 457-8600

Description: Online service with a vast amount of interest categories, software, clubs, and forums.

ZiffNet Information Service

ZiffNet/Mac (Zmac)
25 First Street
Cambridge, MA 02141
(800) 666-0330
(800) 635-6225 (to find your local ZiffNet number)

Description: Online service containing magazine product reviews, forums, support and software. Covers information from Ziff-Davis publications like *MacWEEK*, *MacUser* and *PC Magazine*.

Other Resources

American Power Conversion Corp.

132 Fairgrounds Road
P.O. Box 278
West Kingston, RI 02892
(401) 789-5735
(800) 788-2208

Description: Offers a line of UPS (uninterrupted power supply) devices for Macintosh devices.

Apple Catalog

Apple Computer, Inc.
One Apple Plaza
P.O. Box 9001
Clearwater, FL 34618
(800) 795-1000

Description: Mail order catalog directly from Apple Computer, Inc.

Black Box Catalog

Black Box Corporation
1000 Park Drive
Lawrence PA 15055
(412) 746-5500

Description: A network mail order catalog that offers a vast array of cabling, printing, and other computer network and electrical supplies.

CompUSA

15160 Marsh Lane
Dallas, TX 75234
(800) 451-7638

Description: A computer superstore and mail order company with competitive pricing, on-site service, training, government sales, and corporate support. Locations include Massachusetts, New York, Pennsylvania, Rhode Island, and Washington, DC.

Curtis Manufacturing Company, Inc.

30 Fitzgerald Drive
Jaffrey, NH 03452
(603) 532-4123
(800) 548-4900

Description: Offers a variety of power devices for the Macintosh, including power strips and UPS devices.

DriveSavers

30-D Pamaron Way
Novato, CA 94949
(415) 883-4232

Description: A company offering data recovery and drive repair service. Different levels of service turnover—including 24-hour express service. Also deals with removable drives, optical cartridges, and floppy disks.

Focus Enhancements, Inc.

800 West Cummings Park
Woburn, MA 01801
(800) 538-8866
(617) 938-8088

Description: Offers a variety of Macintosh hardware products, including network connectors (TurboStar), hard disks, optical drives, and removable storage.

GE Rental/Lease

P.O. Box 105625
Atlanta, GA 30348
(800) GE-RENTS for anywhere in the U.S.

Description: Rents and leases a complete line of Macs, PCs, monitors, printers, and more.

MacConnection

14 Mill Street
Marlow, NH 03456
(800) 800-2222

Description: One of the many mail order companies selling Macintosh software and hardware.

MacGlare/Guard Series

Optical Coating Laboratory, Inc.
Santa Rosa, CA 95407
(800) 545-6254

Description: Manufactures a complete line of anti-glare filters to fit Apple's Macintosh monitors and others.

MacWarehouse

1720 Oak Street
P.O. Box 3031
Lakewood, NJ 08701
(800) 255-6227

Description: Macintosh mail order company.

Mac Zone

18005 NE 68th Street, Suite A-110
Redmond, WA 98052
(800) 883-0800

Description: Macintosh mail order company.

MicroMat Computer Systems

7075 Redwood Boulevard
Novato, CA 4945
(800) 829-6227 US Sales & Service
(415) 898-6227 International Sales & Service
(415) 898-2935 Technical Support

Description: Develops diagnostic and repair-reference software for
Macintosh and compatible equipment; serves Macintosh technicians,
consultants, and end users in need of repair software, components, tools,
information, or service. Also offers repair services, replacement components, assemblies, and parts.

Paper Direct

205 Chubb Avenue
Lyndhurst, NJ 07071
(800) A-Papers
(800) 272-7377

Description: Offers wide variety of paper for laser and dot-matrix printers:
colored paper, envelopes, recycled paper, business cards, and more. They
sell a sample paper kit and apply the money paid toward an order.

Radio Shack

Nationwide electronics store chain

Description: They sell computer accessories as well as electronics accessories like power adapters, wiring, and cables.

TechWorks

4030 Braker Lane West, Suite 350
Austin, TX 78759
(800) 765-9864 Order number
(800) 933-6113 Technical support number
(512) 794-8533 Direct

Description: Mail order company with a full line of Macintosh RAM and
other upgrades. Instructions and toll-free technical support are offered
with every purchase.

UltraGlass Shields

NoRad Corporation
1549 11th Street
Santa Monica, CA 90401
(310) 395-0800

Description: Carries a full line of glass anti-glare screens for monitors.

Upsonic Inc.

1392 Industrial Drive
Tustin, CA 92680
(714) 258-0808
(800) 877-6642

Description: Offers UPS devices for the Macintosh.

Index

S

Sad Macintosh icon, 173, 305-306
SAM (Symantec AntiVirus For
  Macintosh) system extension,
  124, 432
saving
    control panels, unable to, 299-300
    files, insufficient memory for, 324
scalable fonts, 94
scanners, 271-273
Scrap Manager System errors, 373
Scrapbook desk accessory, 358
screen dumps, printing to laser
  printers, 269
screen savers, 36
    password protection, 32
    software, 436-437
screen shots, 321
screens
    anti-glare, 196
    cleaning, 36
    color settings, 84-86
    distorted images, 198-199
    flicker, 196-197
    frozen, 60-61
    ghost images, 200
    resolution affecting images, 195
    rotated, 197
    warped, 196
screwdrivers
    #15 Torx, 136
    flat-blade, 137
SCSI (Small Computer System Interface), 359
    bus, 214-215
    cables, 215-216, 221
    chains, 215, 358

connectors, 215-216
devices
    troubleshooting, 222-223
    turning on, 318-319
drivers, 226-227
ID numbers, 214, 220
ports, 130, 213-214
power, 220
terminators, 216-222
SCSI Manager System errors,
  381-382, 399
SCSI Peripheral Interface Cable, 215
SCSIProbe control panel, 6, 44,
  222-223, 417
SCSI System Cable, 215
searching
    for disappearing files, 71-72
    for Finder settings in System 7,
      62-63
security
    encrypting files, 34
    Finder-level, utilities for, 33-34
    hardware locking, 34
    hiding files, 35
    password protection, 32
    shredding files, 34-35
    software for, 437-440
security slots, 133
selecting, 358
Serial Ports System errors, 372
servers
    file, 279-280, 350
        appearing in Chooser, 78-79
        AppleShare File Server, 344, 405
        eradicating viruses, 125
        logging on, 90
        selecting, 278
        shutting down, 91

Your one-stop resource to technical-everything help.

BMUG

The world's largest Macintosh User Group

With over 12,000 members, BMUG is the world's largest non-profit Macintosh User Group. We offer a huge Shareware Disk Library, a tremendous 17-line GUI BBS, and a volunteer-based technical Helpline for any Mac emergency.

Individual membership to BMUG includes two advertising-free 400-page BMUG Newsletters and a year's access to both our BBS and our Helpline.

We have packs of Shareware to meet your needs, from a three disk set of System 7 Utilities to a ten disk set of Color Games. Write for a free listing!

One Year Memberships

Individual: $40
2 BMUG Newsletters
Helpline access
1 BBS Account

Family: $70
2 BMUG Newsletters
Helpline access for 4 people
up to 3 BBS Accounts

Company: $120
2 BMUG Newsletters, 2 copies each
Helpline access for 10 people
up to 5 BBS Accounts

**For more information
write, call, or fax
800-776-BMUG**

BMUG, Inc.
(510) 549-2684
fax (510) 849-9026
1442A Walnut Street #62
Berkeley, CA 94709

What's On The Disk

The disk with this book has five freeware utilities that will help you trouble-shoot and solve Macintosh problems. All the utilities (except for the System Error DA) come with documentation in the form of a read-me text file or help within the utility.

All the utilities are compatible with both Systems 6 and 7. Each description includes instructions for how to install the utility.

TIP: Make a backup of every file on this disk and store the disk as a safe copy. Before using the disk, lock it by sliding the write-protect tab so that the hole is open.

Disinfectant

Disinfectant is a virus protection program with an accompanying protection extension, created by John Norstad at the Academic Computing and Network Services department at Northwestern University. An INIT (referred to in System 7 as an extension) is a system software file that you place in the System folder; it loads into memory during startup.

Disinfectant is reliable and non-intrusive. Disinfectant releases updates to the program when new viruses are discovered.

A help manual comes with Disinfectant. (The manual is recommended reading, even if you don't use Disinfectant.) The manual includes an explanation of the techniques for virus protection and eradication, and a list of known viruses. Figure 1 shows how to access the help manual after opening Disinfectant.

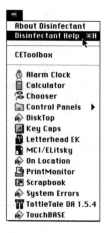

Figure 1   Disinfectant's Help Manual.

The Disinfectant help manual is easily viewable through the program, and can be saved as a text file and printed. Figure 2 shows help information about the WDEF virus.

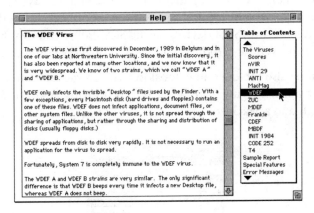

Figure 2   Disinfectant's WDEF Help.

Installing Disinfectant

Disinfectant consists of two parts: an application and a System extension. To install the application, drag the Disinfectant 2.9 folder to the disk where you want it to reside—or, over a particular folder if you want it to reside within a folder on the disk.

To launch Disinfectant, double-click on its folder; then double-click on the "Disinfectant" icon.

Installing Disinfectant's Virus Protection INIT

The second part of Disinfectant is a System extension (INIT). To use the protection feature, you need to install the Disinfectant INIT. When properly installed, it protects a "clean" system against infection by known non-HyperCard Macintosh viruses. To install the INIT, launch Disinfectant (as described above), choose Install Protection INIT from the Protect menu, and restart your Macintosh.

SCSIProbe

SCSIProbe is a Control Panel device (a cdev, pronounced "see-dev") created by Robert Polic. A control panel is a file placed in the System folder, used to adjust system and applications settings. SCSIProbe is handy for identifying and mounting SCSI devices. Using SCSIProbe, you can determine the device type, vendor, product, and version of every connected SCSI device.

SCSIProbe also includes an extension that can mount volumes automatically at startup. Figure 3 shows SCSIProbe looking at all the SCSI devices connected to a Macintosh.

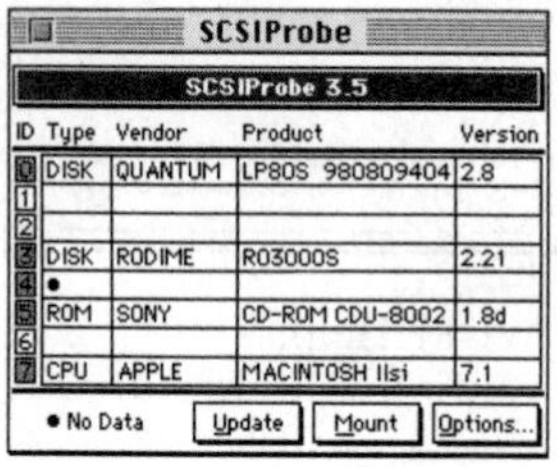

Figure 3   SCSIProbe's window.

SCSIProbe is especially useful when you troubleshoot a Macintosh volume (hard disk or other disk type) that does not appear on the Desktop.

Installing SCSIProbe

To install SCSIProbe, double-click on the SCSI Probe 3.5 folder to open it. Drag the file named "SCSIProbe" onto your System folder. Under System 7, you will be asked if you want to place the file in the Control Panels folder. Click OK; this is where it belongs. Restart the Macintosh.

To access SCSIProbe under System 6, select Control Panel from the Apple (🍎) menu and then click the SCSIProbe icon.

Under System 7, select Control Panels from the Apple (🍎) menu and double-click the SCSIProbe icon.

Installing the SCSIProbe INIT

Once SCSIProbe is open, click the Options... button to bring up a dialog box. This dialog box enables you to install the SCSIProbe INIT. The INIT can mount volumes without having to access the control panel, close device drivers when ejecting removable media, and mount volumes during startup.

For a complete description of SCSIProbe's features and use, read the text file SCSIProbe.ReadMe, included in the SCSIProbe 3.5 folder.

TattleTale

TattleTale is a program created by John Mancino that provides information about your Macintosh and its system-related software.

The TattleTale information can be viewed onscreen by category, printed, written to a text file, saved in a special Bug Report format, or saved in database-readable format. It can tell you about your Mac's CPU (central processing unit) type, attached drives, monitor type, general system attributes, and much more. Figure 4 shows TattleTale's view of the System-related information.

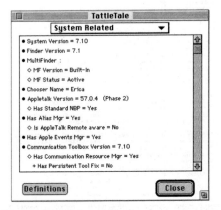

Figure 4 TattleTale's System Related window.

Installing TattleTale

TattleTale is stored on the disk in compressed form; you will have to decompress the TattleTale files before using them. Double-click on the file TattleTale.sea, then click on the continue button. A dialog box appears asking you where you want to install the application. Choose your destination disk or folder and click on the Save button. When TattleTale is installed, double-click on the TattleTale Appl 1.5.4 icon and the TattleTale window will appear with your Mac's information.

Under System 7, you also can place this file in the Apple Menu Items folder in the System folder, so that TattleTale is accessible from the Apple (🍎) menu.

System Errors DA

System Errors DA is a desk accessory created by Bill Steinberg. It is a list of the System error messages that can be returned by your Macintosh when there is an error. Figure 5 shows the System Errors DA window.

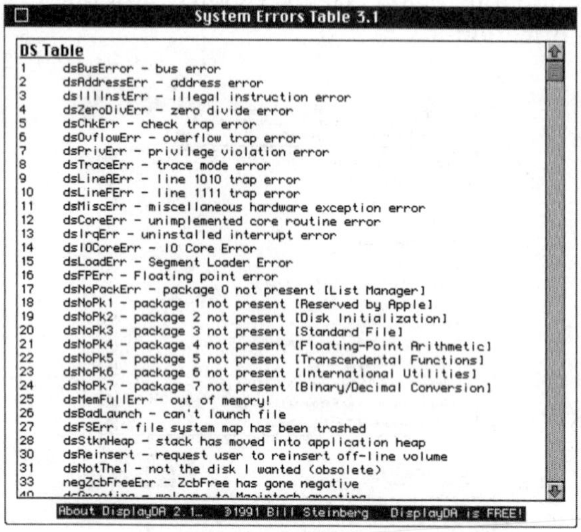

Figure 5 System Errors DA window.

Although many of the error descriptions are cryptic, you can use the error codes to help you identify a problem when a dialog box gives you a system error number.

For more help troubleshooting System errors, see Appendix B, "System Errors."

Installing System Errors DA

Under System 6, use the Font/DA Mover to install the desk accessory in the System file. (The Font/DA Mover comes with System 6 system software.) Double-click on the desk accessory (or the Font/DA Mover) to launch the Font/DA Mover. You will see a dialog box with two windows. One window should display your open System file. (If it doesn't, click the Open button beneath one of the windows. Use the Open File dialog box to select and open your System file.) Click the Open button beneath the other window; using the Open File dialog box, open the SysErrTableDA suitcase. Click on the System Errors DA name and click the Copy button (located between the two windows) to copy it over to the System file.

Under System 7, double-click on the SysErrTableDA suitcase. Drag the System Errors application icon onto your hard disk to copy it to the hard disk. You can double-click on the System Errors icon; it works like any other application. You can also drag the System Errors DA onto your System folder. The Finder will install the file in the Apple Menu Items folder, and then it will be accessible from the Apple (⌘) menu.

System Picker

System Picker is a utility application which allows you to choose the System folder that will be the active System folder upon restart. When System Picker is first opened it looks on all hard disks (including the Portable's RAM disk) to create a list of System folders. This list of System folders is contained in the pop-up menu that appears in the System Picker window (see figure 6). To restart the Macintosh from another System folder, choose the System folder you want to use from the pop-up menu, then click the Restart button. (The selected System folder becomes the "blessed" folder.)

Figure 6   System Picker window.

To make searching faster, System Picker saves the current list of folders when quitting, then retrieves this list the next time System Picker is opened. How deep System Picker looks in the folders is determined by the search depth number set by selecting a number from the Search Depth submenu under the Options menu.

Installing System Picker

Open the System Picker folder and drag the System Picker application to the disk (or folder) to which you want to copy it. Double-click on System Picker, and it will launch and immediately start searching disks for viable System folders.